Brendon McCullum

DECLARED

Brendon McCullum

DECLARED

with Greg McGee

mower

A catalogue record for this book is available from the National Library of New Zealand

ISBN 978-1-927262-62-7

A Mower Book
Published in 2016 by Upstart Press Ltd
B3, 72 Apollo Drive, Rosedale
Auckland, New Zealand

Designed by www.CVDgraphics.nz
Printed by Everbest Printing Co. Ltd., China
Front and back cover photos: Getty

To Lis, Riley, Maya and Evie

Thanks for being my inspiration. I can't wrap it in a few simple words what you guys mean to me.

Lis, you have seen my faults and accepted them. You have loved me when I didn't love myself. You encouraged me to keep going when selfishly you must have wanted me to quit. You have been the reason, I feel, that after 14 years of international cricket I walk away a far better person than I ever felt I could be. I thank you.

We will never get back some of those lost memories of you kids growing up so fast while I was away chasing my dreams. But I hope in some small way you are all proud of the person you have allowed me to become.

I look forward to spending the rest of our lives together, forging the next chapter as a family.

I owe you guys everything, but you all already know that because you know me better than I know myself!

Thank you
Lots of love
Brendon

Contents

Writer's Note

After the rout in Cape Town in Brendon's first test as captain in early 2013, the media became an important litmus test in determining whether the Black Caps were attaining their twin goals of changing the way they conducted themselves as New Zealanders on and off the field, and, more particularly, changing the way they were perceived by New Zealanders. That second aspiration — how they were perceived by Kiwis — was always going to be mediated in large part by cricket writers, so it's not surprising they figure prominently in this book.

Sir David Hare in his autobiography *The Blue Touch Paper* describes journalism as 'dangerously easy to do badly'. Given that, hats off to almost all the cricket writers quoted in this book, for their eloquence and fairness — and to the rest for providing grist to the mill. There's too many to name here, but I'm grateful for the context and objectivity they — or most of them — have provided, particularly Dylan Cleaver, whose book *Brendon McCullum: Inside Twenty20*, about the T20 part of Brendon's career, was a very useful resource.

Thanks also to Heath Mills for his article 'Getting Started', published in *Between Wickets*, which described the baptism of fire for the New Zealand Cricket Players Association back in the dark days of 2002, and to Lis McCullum for her unceasing attention to detail as the drafts rolled in.

* * *

Getting to know Brendon was a treat. Very different in personality and temperament from my only other biographical subject, Richie McCaw, he nevertheless shares at least a couple of attributes with Richie. The obvious one is indefatigable courage, but the other one might be a surprise to someone who doesn't know them. Their smiles. When either of them walks into a room and smiles, the room lights up.

However, Brendon's natural effervescence was all but gone when I met him in Adelaide, a few days before the historic pink ball test. He looked absolutely buggered, worn down not just by the kinds of pitches that forced the retirement of Mitchell Johnson, but also by the Cairns shadow which had hung over him for years. The Cairns trial in London, the build-up to giving evidence, the white heat of the media lights, had drained him.

That night over a bottle or two of red wine in a Vietnamese restaurant just down the street from his hotel, he kept telling Lis and me that he believed he still had a couple of fights left in him. He said it more than once, as if trying to convince himself.

I watched the first day of the pink ball test, flew home, then watched luck make a punch-bag of him and his team, as Nigel Llong cocked up a decision that had an enormous bearing on the result. Brendon came home with a 2–0 series loss that deserved to be an honourable draw.

Being home didn't help his luck in the two return tests. Nor did blowing out his back again. By the time he got to the last test in Christchurch, he was on a regime of anti-inflams, painkillers and steroid injections just to keep him upright. At dinner at Garth Gallaway's home, he couldn't sit in the chair for more than five minutes, had to keep getting up, prostrating himself over the table to try to stretch the sciatic nerve off the bulging discs. By that time, his mantra was down to one more fight, one more fight in me.

I had my doubts as I turned up at Hagley Oval for the first day of his final test. I thought it might be a bridge too far, that the flame might already be extinguished. When he came out of the dressing room way too early and walked through an Australian guard of honour to the crease, most of his friends and family in the McCullum marquee would have been fearing the worst. The ball was hooping all over the place, to the extent that Kane Williamson, recently ranked #1 test batsman in the world, had made something like seven runs off 66 balls.

I wouldn't have been alone in that marquee in feeling a glum acceptance that Brendon would shortly be retracing his steps through a politely clapping, gleeful bunch of Aussies. All the old tropes came to mind: fairytales don't happen; sport is cruel. The crowd held its breath and expected the worst.

But Brendon was right. One more fight. To hit the fastest test century ever was something. To do it under those circumstances on that pitch was something else. One of the men whose record he obliterated, the mighty Viv Richards, had hit his runs for a dominant West Indies in a second innings blast with a declaration in sight.

Putting aside for the moment the cool savvy he showed that day in changing his guard, and the amazing hand–eye that allowed him to see and hit a wildly swinging ball, what stays with me from having seen him staggered and almost felled by the accumulated punches he'd taken over the past couple of months, and from the debilitating effects of the back injury that had damn near crippled him, what stays with me and will always stay with me, is the sheer guts of what he did that day. That when the crunch came, he stepped towards it one last time.

Greg McGee
July, 2016

It's no time for cameo sound bites. How affected was he by alleged match-fixing approaches? How did he find the strength to drag New Zealand out of the mire after the Ross Taylor captaincy saga and the Cape Town 45? How did he come up with the captaincy innovations and build the *joie de vivre* which made New Zealand one of cricket's most popular touring teams?

President John F Kennedy once said 'to whom much is given, much shall be required'.

Please, Brendon, unleash any shackles of stoicism and lay it all out there.

— Andrew Alderson, *New Zealand Herald*, on the announcement that Brendon was to give the 2016 MCC Spirit of Cricket Lecture at Lord's

1
A Pie, a Pint and a Punt

> I just love his confidence. The world was there to be taken and that was the way he saw it. He saw every day as an opportunity to do something special . . . It wasn't always successful . . . Cricket is an awful game because you fail so regularly compared to your successes. Even the greats do it. To have that attitude is fantastic.
>
> — Craig Cumming, quoted in the *New Zealand Herald*

I'm not into memorabilia; I don't keep scrapbooks. I love sharing memories over a beer or wine, reliving old glories and embarrassments, stories and characters, but stuff that other people might find precious, I've just given away. My friends know that about me. When I scored 302 at the Basin Reserve against India in 2014, a good friend grabbed the bat off me, made me sign it for my son Riley and told me he'd keep it safe, because he knew that otherwise it would sit in my garage and I'd end up giving it away on a whim to whoever showed an interest.

Maybe one day the sight of that abused piece of willow will help rekindle memories of an extraordinary couple of days. Maybe one day I'll thank my friend for his foresight, or maybe Riley will. But I doubt that I'll need it to conjure up memories of those or any other days of the life I've spent playing cricket, because cricket has been my life, pretty much.

I was the kid in South Dunedin who lived for Saturday mornings, when I'd pull back the curtains and hope it wasn't raining. The bedroom I shared with my older brother Nathan faced south-east, so once I'd drawn back the curtains, then the net curtains, I could see over the top of the fence, the curving pylons at Forbury Park Raceway that held the lights for the night trots, and above them the sky over St Kilda beach. I was often disappointed. 'Scottish mist', the locals call it. I grew up not taking summer for granted. A day of sunshine was precious, because a day of sunshine was a day of cricket.

Since I was four years old, until very recently, summer meant cricket. Thirty years of opening the curtains and hoping for sunshine. In Dunedin, if you were a cricketer, you had to be an optimist. I love that cartoon in which a psychologist half fills a glass of wine and asks the patient whether it's half full or half empty. And the patient grabs the glass and drains it — problem solved!

My father Stuart played for the Albion club and Otago. He lived for cricket too, played for the love of the game. Everyone did then, because there was no other reason. You couldn't get rich playing cricket. Otago paid an allowance which, according to lore, paid for a pie, a pint and a punt. Stu loved all three.

Saturdays, Mum would pack the chilly bin and we'd play our own cricket in the morning, mostly at Logan Park down by the University Oval, then go to the old man's cricket in the afternoon, Mum lugging the chilly bin and deck chairs from ground to ground. We'd be away from 7.30 in the morning till 9.30 at night, dressed in our whites the whole day.

From the age of four or five, I began to know my town by its cricket grounds, as Mum and me and Nathan traipsed after Stu. The Albion home pitch was Culling Park, a few blocks away in St Kilda. But every other weekend, we'd go west, over the big hill to Bishopscourt in Kaikorai Valley, or to the North East Valley ground at the bottom of the motorway, or south, way south, over Flagstaff to Brooklands in Taieri. To the east, not far from home, was the coldest ground on earth, Ocean Grove, sitting up on the cliffs behind Tomahawk, looking out over the sandhills of St Kilda to a sea which, Mum said, went all the way to Chile. Of course it did, where else would those freezing winds be coming from?

Mum would set out the blanket and the deck chairs, and Nathan and I would go and play with the other cricket kids on whatever grassy margin we could find. That would be our day. Go and play, come back for a sandwich or a ham and cheese roll out of the chilly bin, watch a bit of Dad, go and play, come back for more food. Until close of play, when Mum would pack up and go home, leaving us to play on in the twilight. Dad would be having a beer in the clubhouse and occasionally he'd bring out a packet of chips and some fizzy drinks to keep us going while he had another pint. Paradise.

My appetite for cricket was huge. I was part of the eternal arguments between kids the world over about who got to bat first, but I was keen to field too. I loved to keep wicket. Always, even when I wasn't much taller than the makeshift stumps, that was me, crouched down, trying to get the bowler to lure the batsman out of his crease so I could swoop in and stump him.

I had an almost suicidal urge to be close to the action: when I was about eight, I must have been fielding at very silly mid-off because I got clocked above the eye with the bat as the guy was completing a cover drive. I remember waking up on the grass, with Dad and some of his mates looking down anxiously at me. I can't have been too bad, as we didn't go home any earlier.

Apart from the occasional bumps and bruises, the cricket was idyllic. The rest of my life, a bit patchier. Nathan and I were protected from the worst of the economic hard-scrabble of my parents. Dad always had a job, but his career aspirations revolved around cricket. Some people have told me he could have played for New Zealand. But he'd never let his ego get in the way of his joy in the game, the camaraderie. He was a team man, must have been: he was twelfth man for Otago almost as often as he played for them, more than 70 times, so clearly he liked being around that environment with the guys even when he didn't make the team.

Stu could bat. One of Dad's contemporaries told me recently that he'd fancied himself as a tyro fast bowler, until he bowled to Stu, who hooked and pulled him for a boundary off every ball.

Stu was a sales rep and was on the road a lot. Between that and cricket he was away six months of the year, and the burden of bringing us up mostly fell on Mum. She had RSI in her forearms and couldn't work, so there was just Dad's income. Somehow, between them, even when they weren't happy with each other, which was quite a lot of the time, they made sure we had most things. Mum was emotional, but not in an 'I love you' kind of way. She was just there for us, but particularly for Nathan. She had to be.

Nathan, aka Mattress, had it tough when we were young. He had really bad asthma so he was on a nebuliser the whole time. They said he would never play sport, because he also had Perthes disease, which affects the head of the thigh bones, and he spent the years between about four and six with his hips in plaster, so he got around with a sort of waddle. On top of that, he seemed to be allergic to almost everything. Not surprisingly, he needed a lot of Mum's attention. And that'd sometimes really piss me off, because when we got into those brotherly fights — when he said the sky was green and I was certain it was red — Mum would always side with him. The sky was always bloody green because 'he's been really sick'. So I may not have been the most understanding younger brother, but I kept telling him, 'Keep your pecker up, Mattress, you'll be all right, mate.' And sure enough, he was, though it was a hell of a battle for him. Still waddles, though.

Our home was in Waterloo Street, down on the South Dunedin flats, between the hills and the sea. Ordinary little house, corrugated iron roof, weatherboard walls. It had a postage-stamp backyard, a perfect rectangle, just big enough for a short run-up and a swing of the bat. You had to play straight, whereas out on the street, you had a big leg and off side. Waterloo was a backstreet, so there was never much traffic.

It was a great neighbourhood to grow up in. Everything was three minutes away. In one direction, Forbury Park was between us and the wild dunes of St Kilda beach. When the night trots were on, the glow of the big lights from the park would look like a spaceship. A couple of blocks south was St Clair Primary, where we could sit on the roof of a shed by the cricket pitch and watch the horses come up the home straight. And a couple of blocks north, King's High School.

When I got to King's as a third former, I was knee-high to a grasshopper but John Cushen, the geography teacher and deputy principal and former fast bowler for Otago, saw something in me and selected me for the 1st XI. I was so young that he had to ask Stu and Mum's permission. Stu was never going to say no, so I got used to playing with older kids, and socialising with them. Maybe, as a result of those early years, I've always had good friends who are older than me, and my socialising habits were pretty precocious too. The potential problems, from my parents' and teachers' points of view, definitely came from some of the off-field activities.

After every game, for instance, the 1st XI boys would go and have a few beers at someone's house, usually a seventh former, so I would get invited. Stu and the old lady would give me three beers to take along and that was all I was allowed.

I started batting at 11 in the order as a third former, and worked my way up to four, but I was never really a batting star, even when I became captain of the 1st XI in the sixth form. Wicketkeeping was my passion but being captain meant I could take the gloves off and have a bowl too, medium pacer.

I played age-group for Otago and met the boys from the poncey schools up the hill, Otago Boys' and John McGlashan. Most of their top players got coaching from Dunedin cricket guru Billy Ibadulla.

Billy ran a cricketing school at an indoor facility in one corner of Kensington Oval, and some of the kids from up the hill would go to him several times a week. We couldn't afford him, but somehow Nathan and I got the occasional lesson from Billy. I'm still not sure how that happened, whether Billy said to Dad, 'What the hell, bring them in, Stu,' or whether Dad found some cash or pulled a favour.

It was an indication that I was taking my batting more seriously, but even with Billy's occasional help, I never scored a century in schoolboy cricket, and I didn't really think about having a future in the game, just immersed myself in the moments.

And it wasn't all cricket: my appetite for sport was huge, and in winter I would play for the soccer 1st XI on a Wednesday, then 1st XV rugby on a Saturday. The training for each team was on alternate days, so that was the week.

I loved competing, but it was being with the guys that I loved the most. I wasn't a great fan of spending time by myself; I wanted to be around mates, laughing and joking. Soccer and rugby gave me different groups of mates, because there wasn't that much crossover. I liked that — the rugby guys were kinda tough and rough and egotistical, whereas the soccer guys prided themselves on their skills and probably thought of themselves as a bit more educated.

I also had my old mates, like Thyson and Joe. Joe's father, Eion Willis, Big Willow, played hooker for Otago and used to run the tent village at the Southern club ground, Bathgate Park, before All Black tests at Carisbrook. From the age of about 13, we'd be able to sneak in there and have a few beers.

By the time I was 14 — Mattress was 15 — my parents thought it was safe to go away on a trip to Hong Kong and England for six weeks. Home alone! A woman, Patricia, would come in and cook us a meal a couple of times a week. Mattress had his learner's licence, so before Stu and the old lady left they got him a dispensation from the police so he could drive me to sport in the old lady's car. They also left us enough money to last the six weeks. Within the first three days, I persuaded Mattress to drive us down to Sammy's bar and we blew the lot on the pokies.

The last thing Stu said before he left was that his company car was not to be touched. One day I had to go up the hill to Corstorphine and Mattress didn't seem to be around, so I thought, bugger it, and grabbed the keys to Stu's company car. I'd never driven anything before, but it had an automatic gearbox and seemed pretty straightforward. So I'm doing well, stopped at the lights at a major intersection, when I see Mattress pull in behind me in Mum's car. He's frantically waving his hands at me, tooting his horn, flashing his lights, so I stick the company car into reverse, to back it up a bit, give him a bit of a fright. That worked: he looked like he was shitting himself. So the light turns green and I plant hoof. Unfortunately, it's still in reverse, and I ride up on the old lady's bonnet and damage both cars in the one manoeuvre.

I'm not sure how I got out of that one.

It won't be a surprise that I wasn't a top student, but I did my best and was pretty much a model student until the sixth form, when Thyson and I got suspended for holding parties. They were bloody good parties — we'd hire out halls, a band, a DJ, security, and sell tickets through different kids at different schools. We even put on the after party for the seventh-form formal, a big event on the Dunedin social calendar. We were going great guns until it all came undone at the first ever Highlanders night game, when Thys and I and a couple of others had rung in sick, taken the afternoon off, and were way past our best by the time a couple of teachers saw us at the game.

But we couldn't have been too bad, because Thys and I were co-head prefects the following year, as first-year seventh formers. I failed Bursary, but was captain of the 1st XI cricket team, captain of the 1st XV rugby team and also played for the soccer 1st XI.

By that time, I was getting around a bit, having played age-group cricket for Dunedin Metro, Town and Country, up in Oamaru at King George Park against North Otago, and Central at Alexandra, and South Otago down at Balclutha, and then in the South Island regional tournaments for Otago in Nelson and Ashburton. I was about 16 when I first made the New Zealand Development team, not as a batsman but as a keeper, and it was as a keeper that I went to the Under-19 World Cup in Sri Lanka in 2000. The following year, I was actually captain of the Under 19s that played South Africa here in the Youth Test Series, and I got three tons in three tests. That was the first time I realised that, hey, maybe I can actually bat.

After that, I did my big OE — I left home and travelled all the way to North East Valley, which was about as far as you could get from Waterloo Street without leaving Dunedin. I was 18 and shared a scungy flat with some mates. For some reason, I wasn't getting on with the old man. It wasn't that bad, maybe just a rebellious stage I was going through. Mattress was still happy at home, but I wanted to get out and do my own thing.

I thought initially that I'd left school, having hit the heights at King's the year before, but my first job, stacking shelves at the Foodstuffs warehouse, was a bit of a reality check and I lasted a week. I looked back at the pleasures of school and thought to myself: 'You know what? I reckon I'm not quite done with that.'

King's hadn't named the head boy by the time I got back, and they asked me if I wanted to be co-head boy again with another good mate, Luke, but I didn't really want the responsibility. I was happy to go from captain of the 1st XV to vice-captain too, just stepping away from any real responsibility — very good decisions, as it turned out, because it was a big year socially in that squalid flat.

I was doing a catering course at school, but really didn't get to class much. Most of my sporting downtime that year was devoted to Flatting 101 and, funnily enough, there seemed to be hundreds of kids, mates and students from the uni who seemed to be taking exactly the same course!

Mum and Dad weren't so happy with my shifting out, but I think they knew I always had that streak, that once I got something in my head and wanted to go and do something, I needed the freedom to do it.

The drinking age had just been lowered to 18, so I was finally legal. That flat was the coldest dump I've been in in my life and I reckon the four of us took up smoking partly to keep warm. That's an addiction that's stayed with me ever since. I've tried to kick it, but never quite succeeded.

Another thing that kept me warm was rugby. Despite a feeling that I was on a bit of a downward trend because of my extracurricular activities, I got selected for the South Island Secondary Schools side. I was playing first-five and Dan Carter was on the bench — talk about a late developer!

Dan replaced me in the second half of the first game. The second and third games he started at wing and I started at first-five. That game, against Northern A or B, was my last game of rugby. I got Man of the Match, but all I can remember is getting sidestepped in the last minute on a wet track by Ben Atiga, who ran on to score under the posts to win the game.

They spoke to me about the New Zealand Secondary Schools side, but I was too old for that team — they were going to a world cup where the age limit was different. Maybe if I'd been eligible for that team, things would have turned out differently.

So I carried on living the life at the flat, trying everything. I think someone spoke to me about the Highlanders Colts or development squad, but by that time the New Zealand Cricket Academy was put in front of me, and that was a four-month commitment over the following winter. I had to make a decision one way or the other. If I went to the Academy I could no longer play rugby, and if I went to rugby it probably wouldn't have been a great look for the Academy, and I would have missed out on the professional development stuff as well.

That was really different for me, looking at sport, whether cricket or rugby, as a profession, because I really had no idea, I just played the game. I would go out and throw the ball around, buy into a team and have a bloody good time. So being introduced to the possibility of a professional career was quite a pivotal moment.

In retrospect, I probably should have gone somewhere else for my OE. Left town, buggered off overseas, instead of making all my mistakes in front of people I knew. Some of them still look sideways at me from that time, thinking I'm that rebellious 18-year-old. I should have gone away, got that out of my system and come back with my reputation intact as the model student they used to know.

One thing that stayed the same, no matter what I did, was the sport. It was the biggest, most constant and stable part of my life. I loved every minute of every game, whether it was cricket or rugby or soccer. I just played, caught up in the moment where none of the other stuff mattered. It wasn't about the results — you hoped you had a good day, but it didn't really matter. I just looked forward to playing. Playing was enough.

I guess I've inherited that love of playing cricket from Stu, along with his love of being around the environment, the boys, the camaraderie. I've got to be careful of the pies, and I'm also fond of a pint — and wine that he could never have afforded — not to mention the punt.

I'm privileged to be able to earn a brilliant living from cricket, where he couldn't. But that level of professionalism also makes the game and everything around it so much more complicated than when he played. There've been some hard lessons along the way and I suppose it was inevitable that the kid I was lost his innocence and made mistakes. But I also learnt that if I lost that kid inside me, his simple joy in being out there, his sense of fun and sheer delight in playing the game, his love of being able to have a crack, the feeling of sun on his back, the smell of grass . . . if I lost that kid inside me, I was lost too.

2
Flat Track Bully

> The bowling attack that this West Indies team has brought to the country is laughable . . . Should New Zealand beat the West Indies, should Brendon McCullum continue to score runs on the sort of meek tracks where he can hit through the ball, then slap the man on the back, say thank-you for everything and move on.
>
> McCullum is a cheeky chappie, he can be most engaging, but he can no longer put his back into test cricket.
>
> — Mark Reason, *Dominion Post*

Some of the significant turning points in your career, in your life, you see coming. This one blind-sides me.

It's 4 December 2013, the day after I'd scored a century in the first test of a home series against the West Indies at the University Oval in my home town of Dunedin. It has been a long time, three years, since my last test ton. I'm not a great man for stats, but it's easier to ignore the numbers when they're stacking up in your favour. I'd scored a double ton against India in late 2010, but in recent times, as I was being reminded fairly constantly by the media, I'd scored 2, 8, 20 and 1 against England over there, followed by a hardly inspiring 21, 22 and 11 against lowly Bangladesh. And this was after I'd made the decision to abandon the wicketkeeping gloves and live or die as a specialist batsman.

It isn't just my batting under the gun. That run of low scores arcs back into 2012, when I took over as New Zealand captain in circumstances that caused a lot of anguish. According to more than one report, I have former captain Ross Taylor's blood on my hands.

The ton against the Windies may not have been the flashest innings in the world against the best bowlers, but given my personal travails, it's bloody significant and I'm hopeful that it'll give me some respite from the incessant pressure I've been under for what seems like an age.

Close of play, outside the dressing room, I kissed my wife Ellissa and hugged my children Maya and Riley. I was just exhausted. Sky Sport wanted an interview but mentally I was cooked, and I had to say no.

I sat in the corner of the changing room under the old grandstand, as the beers were brought in to celebrate. It was actually Ross who spoke for the team, about how I'd been under a bit of pressure and to see me come through and get a ton and perform and be able to put the detractors back in their box was a really gutsy thing for us as a group. I'd shared a big partnership with Ross, almost 200 runs, so that moment in the dressing room felt like the two of us had turned a corner too.

I went back to the hotel and to Lis and the kids and slept well, thinking, 'Okay, I can wake up tomorrow and I can actually have a bit of a win in the column. I can have a day where I'm not going to cop shit, everything will be sweet for at least a day.'

The ton is doubly satisfying because I've worked so hard for it. I'd come back from Bangladesh at a low ebb, after my back had blown out again. Two bulging discs were pushing on the spinal cord and giving me intense sciatic pain. I was on painkillers for that, then found out that I had arthritis in my back as well. I'd worried that the back might be a career ender this time, but good rehab had got me fit and strong and it seemed to be manageable.

I'd then spent weeks out at Lincoln, just about every day, with Craig McMillan. Craig wasn't the New Zealand batting coach at that time, just a mate who was happy to help me get ready. We spent hours and hours out there working on my defensive game, because I knew that I needed a better defence if I was going to cut it as a specialist batsman at test level. Stephen Fleming helped out as well.

I've always been one for not running past the principal's office. I like to work away behind the scenes, put in my hard yakker away from everyone else. People talk about how long and hard Kane Williamson works in the nets. It's true, but he doesn't pip me by much.

So I'd done the work and went into the Windies series really hopeful about how I'd perform: I felt like I was actually ready now to become a test batsman.

The week before the test I'd turned out for my old club Albion and that had lifted my spirits, even though I'd been cleaned out by a 17-year-old fast bowler on a rough track out at Brooklands on the Taieri Plain.

When we turned up it was raining and we ran the covers out in the downpour. When the rain held off we batted. We were using the regulation ball, the club version with the bigger seam, and it was doing a bit, particularly in the hands of this kid who was steaming in and really letting it go. He was all over me. I ended up getting about seven runs and then I chopped one on. That was the only downside — otherwise, that afternoon was magic.

Upstairs in the pavilion at halftime, we all had a pie or a savoury and a laugh together. Then we bowled and won the game. Afterwards both teams sat around out on the field in the late afternoon sun and had a beer. Just that: out in front of the Brooklands Oval pavilion, lazing on the grass with a beer in hand, shooting the breeze. I remember thinking that was really cool. It reminded me of the innocence and purity of my joy in the game as a kid.

I was fortunate that experience was so fresh in me. I was soon going to need it to keep me in the game.

That night after the Windies ton, when I slept the sleep of the exhausted, I thought I'd at least get a little bit of breathing space, had maybe broken free of the constant criticism. Across the previous couple of years, I'd spent so much time and energy thinking about how we were going to turn the team around and what was required to do so. I got on that treadmill, where everything I thought about was tuned to that. I probably neglected to think that one of the most important aspects of turning a team around is leading from the front. So to be able to make a ton when the team needed it, and help put us in a commanding position in the first test of the series, felt so good.

I'd been leading without performance. Now I'd got one on the board, maybe that would enable us to take another step up, win a test, the first under my captaincy, put us in the frame to win a series, safe in the knowledge that the captain could actually play.

Next morning, after breakfast I'm sitting downstairs in the foyer of the Southern Cross and David White, CEO of New Zealand Cricket, comes over to congratulate me on the ton. While Whitey's speaking to me, Chris Cairns walks past, suave in his Sky commentator's dark suit. He looks at me, puts his hand on my shoulder and says, 'I'm really proud of you', and keeps on walking.

I look at White. 'You've gotta be joking.'

White just shakes his head disbelievingly.

I know that allegations have been made about Cairns' role in match fixing. Almost two years before, in March 2012, he'd won a high-profile libel case in London against Lalit Modi, the mover and shaker who set up the Indian Premier League. Despite the trial win, the mud seems to be sticking to Cairns, with rumours that the ICC Anti-Corruption and Security Unit, the ACSU, has been talking to New Zealand players about Cairns' and others' involvement in match fixing.

I know they're more than rumours: I'm one of the players who has spoken about Cairns to the ACSU. None of that has been made public — yet — but rumour is running rampant, with journos circling like rabid dogs. I'm pretty sure White knows what I've said to the ACSU. Clearly Cairns has no idea. Or does he?

I'm worried about Cairns' reaction when he finds out I've testified against him. I originally talked to the ACSU back in February 2011. I was hoping that might be the end of it, but the ACSU came back just the previous week and asked me to expand on my original statement.

Between making those two statements, I'd been a bit stunned as I watched the progress of that defamation action in London. Cairns was suing because Modi had tweeted that Cairns had been involved in match fixing.

Modi's tweet about Cairns might have been seen by only around 15 people, if Cairns himself hadn't drawn everyone's attention to it.

Lis and I had sat there utterly gobsmacked as we watched Cairns take on Modi. Still, it was none of my business and I'd kept my head down, until the ACSU came calling again.

It's a strange feeling, testifying against a former teammate, and I'm not quite sure why the ACSU have come back to me. Where's this all heading? Whatever, I've done what I need to do under the rules that govern me as a professional cricketer and the rest is up to the ICC. I'm hoping they keep my name out of it for as long as possible — Cairns seems to be ready to wield the long handle against anyone who opposes him, and I've got enough problems without that.

But as Cairns walks out of the foyer of the Southern Cross, I keep turning his words over in my head, looking for some hidden meaning or irony. Was he just playing me?

A bit thrown by Cairns, I let White go and dive into the nearest newspaper. Some players maintain they don't read what's being said about them. I find that hard to believe. I read everything I can. I want to know what people are saying and what fans are reading, to keep my finger on the pulse, particularly in these volatile times. A big part of what the Black Caps are trying to change is how we're viewed by our countrymen, and the media are naturally a major element of that.

I wish I hadn't picked up that paper, though. The headline kicks me right in the guts: 'McCullum Has No Business Leading New Zealand'.

It gets worse from there. It's Mark Reason, whom I've never met as far as I'm aware, writing for the *Sunday Star-Times*. Mark seems to write from an elevated position, looking down on the rest of us — or maybe just me:

> *[McCullum] . . . can no longer put his back into test cricket. His average on overseas tours as captain, against South Africa, England and Bangladesh, is 15. This is unlikely to get better because he has irreversible technical deficiencies. He is a hitter, and when McCullum can biff through the line on New Zealand's lifeless pitches, he is a champion. But against some pace, swing and seam, he is second rate.*

So, a flat track bully, that's me. Not good enough to play test cricket, let alone captain a test side.

I've had to live with a lot of that. For what seems like a long time, I've tried to regard it as water off a duck's back. But my feathers are wearing thin. The drip, drip, drip is getting through. Mark Reason is particularly nasty. It seems like every second Sunday, he's describing me as a fraud, or intimating that Ross was dropped from the captaincy due to 'unconscious prejudice' relating to his ethnicity, or because I conspired against him behind the scenes, or whatever.

It's not what I want to read after scoring a ton, even on a 'lifeless' New Zealand pitch. I wonder if Reason has ever talked to batsmen from overseas, from the subcontinent for instance, about our 'lifeless' pitches?

More seriously, he purports to have other reasons for wanting a change. One of which is that I'm a shareholder, with my mate Stephen Fleming, in a company called Quality NZ, which sells high-end New Zealand goods to India (among other places). The principal shareholder is former test swing bowler Geoff Allott, who's now on the Board of Cricket New Zealand, but wasn't when he set up the company, or when I became a shareholder.

'Cricket is used to promote the brand,' writes Reason. 'It matters not that there has been no wrongdoing, the obvious conflicts of interest do not allow for objectivity on any side. Of course McCullum wants to play against India at any cost and continue his profile in the IPL. He effectively has a stake in Indian cricket.'

So, basically, I'm hanging on playing test cricket for New Zealand so that I can get on the tour to India and use my profile to market goods for a company I hold some shares in.

'It is unacceptable,' he continues, 'and just one more compelling reason why McCullum can no longer captain his country before the eyes of the world.' His suggestion is: 'Let him depart with the grace that was not afforded to Ross Taylor. And then let's move on . . . Time for a fresh start. Time for the future. Time for some decency.'

Some *decency*, mate?

I should be able to dismiss these patronising gibes from Reason.

It isn't so different in kind or degree from what I've been getting for the past couple of years. It's the timing that makes it the straw that threatens to break this cheeky chappie's back.

I'm not a quitter. I buy into the whole deal of being a professional cricketer, with all the public accountability that entails, taking the brickbats on the chin. I've always tried to keep my eye on the big picture: I've always loved the game. But this morning, I've finally had a gutsful. The kid who used to pull open the curtains on Saturday morning, praying it wasn't raining, seems to have got lost along the way.

This Sunday morning, as I stare round the foyer at the Southern Cross, I wish it would pour, so I can pull the curtains on the game I used to love.

The rain does come. Three days later. It costs us my first test win in 10 tests as captain, in December 2013, a year to the day after I'd taken over from Ross.

He went on to score 217 not out, his maiden double ton: at that stage it looked like Rosco and I had set the game up together. We racked up 609 in our first innings, then bowled the Windies out for 213 in their first innings. At 396 ahead with three days to play, it's my call: enforce the follow-on, and put them back in, or bat ourselves, consolidate our lead, then declare.

If I enforce the follow-on, the risk is that our bowlers will be too tired to make inroads again. On the other hand, if we bat again, our bowlers will have time to recover, but the risk is that we'll run out of time at the end — it's Dunedin, there's always a good chance of rain.

There's certainly heavy weather brewing off the field. Hours after our conversation in the foyer of the Southern Cross, Chris Cairns suddenly takes 'gardening leave' from his position as part of the Sky commentary team and becomes the focus of the cameras as he exits University Oval. Someone in the know must have said something to Sky. Maybe New Zealand Cricket were worried about Cairns being in the same hotel as us, the contamination factor.

That doesn't help the rumours. Decent journalists like Dylan

Cleaver of the *New Zealand Herald* are zeroing in on the names of the New Zealand cricketers involved. My name isn't being mentioned yet, for which I'm grateful. But David White is forced to make a public statement before play starts on the third day. He confirms that New Zealand Cricket is aware that the ICC is investigating some former New Zealand cricketers, but he's not in a position to give any names. But somehow the journalists are putting names out there. Lou Vincent and Daryl Tuffey are mentioned. Lou immediately confirms that he is involved.

I try to keep my head down and focus on the cricket.

I make the call to enforce the follow-on. The West Indies' Darren Bravo makes 218, but when we finally dispose of them for 507 early on Day 5, we still have the winning of the game: the equation is 112 runs in two sessions.

The Windies have nothing to lose and open the bowling with a spinner. It works. Shane Shillingford has Peter Fulton, Hamish Rutherford and Aaron Redmond back in the dressing room in no time at all. I can feel the rats of doubt beginning to gnaw, so I try to impose myself, kill the rats, take the game away from the Windies.

I off-drive Shillingford for four, but shortly after get caught from a slog-sweep for nine. We're four wickets down for 44 runs and the Windies are beginning to believe that the light at the end of the tunnel is no longer a train, but a glorious victory against the odds.

Rosco and Corey Anderson steady the ship, and we're back in cruise control at 79 for four, half an hour before tea. We need just 33 runs from 33 overs when a curtain of rain closes the game down.

'Test Slipped Through Fingers' is one headline, with a photo of me out in the field with my head in my hands.

Afterwards I make all the right noises, say that sooner or later the wins will come. I have to defend my decision to enforce the follow-on without dissing the team. I do my best to put a brave face on it, and lament our bad luck with the weather.

The truth is, we shouldn't have needed any luck. The Windies' second innings wasn't about our tired bowlers; it was about shoddy fielding. Four catches were shelled, including Darren Bravo on 82.

McCullum Collection

Left: Me at six months and Nathan at 18 months . . . matching outfits have been a constant theme in our lives. Below: 27 years on — this time in our Black Caps kit — and about to bring New Zealand home in a Twenty20 match against the West Indies at Westpac Stadium in Wellington in 2009.

Photosport

McCullum Collection

Nathan and I with Mum and Dad, circa 1982.

Otago Daily Times/Stephen Jaquiery

South Dunedin Physics 101 — the harder you hit it, the further it goes. Albion v Green Island, Logan Park, Dunedin, 1987. Inset: Aggressive running between the wickets — especially with Nathan batting at the other end.

McCullum Collection

Dunedin senior club cricket, 1992. Short on numbers, Nathan and I stroll out with Dad (third from left) and his Albion teammates to help out with some fielding.

Otago Daily Times/Peter McIntosh

Getty

Above: Taking a high ball for King's High School against Otago Boys' High in a 1st XV match at Dunedin's Tahuna Park, September 2000.

Left: Hitting out for the Otago Volts against the Northern Knights in a State Max tournament at Albany, November 2001.

Photosport

On debut for New Zealand against Australia in a VB Series match in Sydney, 2002. I was run out for five.

Getty

A hug from Flem after taking my first catch in test cricket, against South Africa at Hamilton in March 2004. It was a memorable debut as I scored 57 in our first innings.

Getty

Dan Vettori congratulates me after my maiden test century, against Bangladesh in Dhaka, October 2004.

Getty

The retro look for my Twenty20 international debut, against Australia at Eden Park in February 2005. That's me on the far left.

Getty

On my way to a 20-ball 50 against Canada at Gros Islet, St Lucia, in the 2007 World Cup. It was, at the time, a New Zealand one-day record.

Photosport

It's not every day you take a catch to dismiss West Indies legend Brian Lara. We won this Super 8 World Cup match in Antigua by seven wickets.

Photosport

Leaving the field after scoring 80 against Bangladesh at Queenstown in December 2007. I got to 50 off 19 balls, breaking the record I'd set against Canada back in March.

Behind the brave face, I'm despondent that we've burnt our chance to put a win on the board.

Lis has been a sounding board for my ups and downs across the years, and there have been plenty of them, but what she hears when I get back to the hotel must concern her. I tell her I've had enough. After what we've been through, it must be tempting for her to agree with me, but she just hears me out.

I can't walk out on the team mid-series, so I pack my bag with a heavy heart and head off to Wellington for the second test.

Lis waves me goodbye from Dunedin. When she gets back to Christchurch she gives a heads-up to the people closest to me: Garth Gallaway, my solicitor, friend, mentor, and Stephen Fleming, my former captain, friend and advisor, and our close friend, Mitch MacDonald.

Shortly after I reach Wellington, Mitch turns up, 'just happened to be in town'. I have a calming beer with him.

I tell him some of what he already knows: that since I'd taken over the captaincy of New Zealand from Ross two years ago, despite the best of intentions and working harder at my cricket than I've ever done before, everything has somehow turned to custard. And no matter how I try, I just can't seem to be able to get past it. I tell him I've reached the end of whatever it is that's been sustaining me.

Mitch is a sympathetic listener and, in the end, gives me the message I'm to hear from Garth and Flem over the next couple of days: give up. Walk away, if that's what you really want to do.

There's no doubt giving up the Black Caps would make my life easier. The IPL has taken money out of the equation. That's what the Mark Reasons of this world don't get. It's purely about playing test cricket as New Zealand captain. Do I have the desire for it any more, the stomach for all the crap that seems to go with it?

I've got a theory that in New Zealand sport the longer you've been around the bigger the target you become. I think once we lost Fleming and Astle and McMillan and those guys, I became the next target because I've been around longest.

Fair enough, I thought at the time. I'd had a pretty good run with the media and the public in the early days, and, to be honest, since I'd become a senior member of the team my performances probably haven't been where they should have been. But the level of personal abuse I've copped since taking over as captain from Ross is on a whole different plane from anything else I've seen in New Zealand sport.

Mitch and Garth and Flem must have put their heads together. Psychologically, their message is pretty astute. It takes all the pressure off and makes me really look at that option.

When Lis arrives from Christchurch, she suggests I find a quiet place on my own and write down a list of the pros and cons. She's conflicted: on the one hand, she'd love to have me home more, but knows I've got to be really sure in my own mind that it's the right decision, made at the right time and for the right reasons.

So I sit in a café in Wellington and write down the pros and cons on the back of a napkin. What if I walk away?

3
Musical Chairs

> Brendon hasn't had the best season. Not that he has been playing badly either, but we want to get the best out of him and feel that not having the burden of vice-captaincy should help that.
>
> — Dan Vettori

The captaincy scrap between Ross and me was seeded four years before, in October 2009, when coach Andy Moles was sacked. Andy was a nice guy and might have been a good coach for a better team, but we weren't that team and needed more than he could give.

I'd been vice-captain to Dan Vettori for a couple of years by then, since he took over from Stephen Fleming, but when Moles was sacked, Dan and fellow selectors Mark Greatbatch and Glenn Turner decided to strip me of the vice-captaincy too.

The timing of the announcement wasn't great for me, coming just days after Moles had been sacked. Running up to that, there'd been rumours about player dissatisfaction with Moles, mutiny in the camp, player power running rampant, and my demotion looked like I'd been the ringleader and was being punished.

Not true. I did have problems with Andy's input to the team, felt that we needed a new direction, and as usual I wasn't backwards in coming forward with my thoughts to other players, but I wasn't alone, and I never made approaches to New Zealand Cricket about Moles or was present at secret meetings.

The problem with Andy was epitomised by the ICC World Twenty20 tournament earlier that year. We'd had a great build-up, using an aggressive game plan that catered to the explosive batting power we had and the smart, resourceful bowlers. But we'd got beaten up by Australia in a warm-up match and we suddenly lost our nerve, threw out our plans and reverted to timid type.

I'd felt at the time that we needed a coach who had more confidence in us, who could have kept us on track. Before the advent of specialist bowling and batting coaches within the team environment, we'd get that sort of technical help when we needed it from wherever: what we needed from our team coach was a game plan that we could all buy into, that best suited our talents, and the confidence to execute it. That's what John Bracewell, the previous coach, had given us. As off the wall as some of his ideas were, Braces had the ability to instil confidence in individuals and integrate their talents into a coherent game plan. We didn't get that from Andy Moles when we needed it.

I should have seen my sacking as vice-captain coming.

On the tour to Sri Lanka in August of 2009, I was still notionally vice-captain, but excluded from all the discussions that mattered, no longer invited to management meetings and told I was no longer a tour selector. Suddenly, no one wanted my input into how things were run.

I admit that I was pissed off that no one, coach, captain or manager, had raised any issues with me. I reacted badly. That wasn't a great tour for me. I decided I'd go out and bat the way I believed we should be playing and bugger the team plan. I'm not proud of that; it wasn't my finest moment.

Whatever, I could live with the decision: you don't necessarily need a vice-captain in a team — having a viable leadership group is more important, so that there's always a couple of players who are capable of stepping up if needed. So I bought the rationale behind not having a vice-captain, even though I wasn't that happy about the timing and the way the reasons for the decision were presented publicly.

'We have talked about it,' said captain Dan Vettori, 'and he is comfortable about what we are trying to do to improve his game.'

When it was pointed out to Dan that I had previously talked of my desire to lead New Zealand, and of that aspiration being a motivating factor keeping me in the game, Dan said that losing the vice-captaincy didn't change anything, that I was still a senior player in the side and would be the captain if he got injured. 'We rely on Brendon heavily, wicketkeeping and opening the batting, so it's just to ease his load.'

Right, so it was all for my benefit — and there were those close to me, like Flem, who thought it would be good for my game.

Until then, I'd thought Dan and I had worked well together, though results had been pretty scratchy. He was a lead-from-the-front guy and his performances were outstanding, but he'd had to take on way too much as a captain because of Moles' weakness. That was also partly a product of his personality. If he was in the job, he was going to do it to the best of his ability, and if that meant he risked running himself into the ground, then so be it. He had an enormous weight on his shoulders because he was such a better player than everyone around him. As his workload increased, he began pushing people away a bit, and I had a sense that some people weren't reaching the best of their own abilities because they relied on Dan to take care of it.

As an on-field strategist, he was quite conservative and methodical in his thinking. I thought we worked nicely together because of the difference in our approaches — I would generally chip in with the more aggressive options, and he would always give my suggestions a fair hearing.

It helped that I admired him as a man and valued him as a friend, and it doesn't surprise me that now he is doing well as a coach, because he was that kind of captain. But, back then, I believe Dan felt he had to go along with the other members of the selection panel, Greatbatch and Turner, whether or not he trusted them or liked them.

After the ditching of Andy Moles and my relegation from the vice-captaincy, we went to Dubai for an ODI series and Twenty20 series against Pakistan, where Dan was temporary coach, so his workload went up another notch. It might have been a streamlined leadership team, but it wasn't a particularly functional one. Our manager at that time was Dave Currie, who I found egotistical and not always helpful in the team environment, so that loaded even more onto Dan.

However, I accepted my demotion from vice-captain with good

grace, knuckled down and got on with it. And Flem's advice about the demotion being good for my game looked like being on the button, as I played well in that series.

But if there was one constant at New Zealand Cricket at that time, it was that nothing would stay the same for long.

About five weeks after demoting me with the rationale that we didn't need a vice-captain, they named Ross vice-captain.

I was still coming to terms with that when Mark Greatbatch was appointed coach, in January 2010.

When I looked at it objectively, I could see there was a consistency to what Greatbatch and Glenn Turner were doing. They seemed to share a point of view, a mentality if you like, about the type of game we should be playing, a view that gelled with what we'd done historically.

My playing philosophy wasn't fully developed at that stage, but my exposure to Twenty20, particularly the IPL which had kicked off in 2008, was beginning to influence the way I looked at test cricket. Even back then, I thought that there were some aspects of the T20 approach which, if applied to test cricket, might enable the New Zealand team to better exploit its talents and limitations.

I'm not one to sit on my hands when I think I've got something to offer, so Dan and Greatbatch and Turner wouldn't have had to be mind-readers to know in which direction I thought the team should go.

All of which made it understandable that they wanted to put me to one side. The team can't be getting confused messages about strategy, so once I'd been removed as vice-captain I put my head down and didn't entertain any thought of the captaincy. The people in the positions of power at the time had a different direction and a different affiliation with certain members of the team, and that was fine. I copped it pretty sweet and tried to move on.

What lingered was annoyance over the way the whole thing had been managed. I felt they owed me an explanation. Particularly Glenn Turner, who'd been my coach when I first began playing for Otago. Rightly or wrongly, I sensed Greatbatch's hand behind the changes, and I can't deny that affected my relationship with him from then on.

A pity, because he'd coached me in the NZ Under 19s and had been brilliant.

Greatbatch's 10 months in charge during 2010 made a promising, if predictable, beginning. We swept Bangladesh in the T20 and three ODIs, and in the solitary test at Hamilton, where both Martin Guptill and I made 180 plus to set up the win.

Australia toured in late summer. We split the T20s, narrowly lost the Chappell–Hadlee Trophy 2–3 in the ODIs, then got cleaned out in both tests.

Losing to Oz is one thing, but losing four out of five ODIs in Bangladesh later that year — the other one was washed out — was quite another.

That winter, I made the decision to give up keeping at test level.

It wasn't just my back. I had a disease in my left knee, osteonecrosis of the lateral femoral condyle. It means there's dead bone which doesn't renew itself, sitting on the outside, just underneath my patella.

Between the back and the knee, keeping wasn't fun any more; in fact, it was an absolute grind just to get out of bed in the morning. Keeping had been my first skill, ahead of batting, and I'd always worked very hard to be able to keep operating at my best. I'd always be the first one on the training ground, doing my keeping drills, getting myself into the zone so that I could feel on top of it. But my back and knee gradually curtailed the amount of specific keeping-related drills I could do, and I reluctantly realised that if I couldn't do the hard work behind the scenes, it was only a matter of time before that would show out on the field, and I wouldn't be able to operate at the level I wanted to. I didn't come to that realisation easily, but once I did, there really was no choice: rather than doing it half-arsed, I'd rather shut that door. I knew that once shut, at test level, I could never go back to it, so it was a big decision that caused me some anguish at the time.

Greatbatch made a public pronouncement of the obvious, that I was now to be selected for the test team solely on my ability to score runs. No shit!

I was only too aware of that. There was a tour to India coming up, and I doubted that I had the mental capacity to be a frontline batsman. Particularly since the only spot in the Black Caps batting line-up that looked like being available was opener. Of course, I said I was up for it, but deep down I was desperate to find some personal improvement, get a mental edge that might help me transition from keeper/batsman to top-order batsman.

With what seemed like perfect timing, Kerry Schwalger walked into my life.

An acquaintance told me about this guy who was 'a genius', who had worked with the Yankees in New York, et cetera. So he arranged a meeting with Kerry, who pressed all my buttons, mostly the ones that started with the word 'insecure'.

Kerry was a different look — big mushroom of fancy hair on top of a face that looked as if it'd seen a bit of work. He talked about his Victoria's Secrets girlfriends in New York and his Baywatch girlfriend in LA, which didn't really endear him to Lis — 'Come and stay with me in the Big Apple, we'll have fun!' When I first met him he was wearing a flash suit and a red and blue tie. I've since learnt that red and blue is the ultimate selling tool. In fact, I think he told me that!

Although he was originally from Christchurch, he'd talk up a storm in an accent which was sort of mid-Pacific, a bit American, a bit Kiwi. The American part was understandable, given he'd spent so much time working with A-Rod and the Yankees, he said. He was eloquent, fast-talking, used big words, a Kiwi who apparently had a house in Santa Monica, had a house in New York, had a house in . . . He said he was earning $35,000 a month in passive income from a hair product. That alone should have alerted the boy from South Dunedin! He actually told me that when he sells his products he just targets people's emotions and that's how he gets his products across the line. Certainly worked with me.

But what he offered me wasn't just all talk. It would have been much easier to see through him if it had been. He believed that your unconscious mind and reflexes were your best ally at the crease, and that you had to get your conscious mind out of the way, quieten your mind, and let your reflexes take over — remove your thought processes, because they were stymying your ability to access your skills.

He told me if you can't quieten your mind then just hum a song to yourself. So as the guy is coming into bowl, just hum a song. I tried it and I was like, how good is this? Then I told Tim Southee about it, because he couldn't stop thinking about all kinds of things as the bowler ran in. He got 150 in the first game he played after that, rang me up — 'Mate, it works!'

I told Kerry I'd often be a bit rigid and get hard hands when I was facing spin. He said try wiggling your toes as the bowler is coming in — in your shoe, just wiggle your toes, and that will take away your thought process, and you'll be able to just play the ball on its merits. That seemed to work too.

Then he'd do what he called contrast drills.

One was where you would bat normally for six balls and then you would have someone throw six balls quick-fire at you, so you didn't have time to reset or think; it was all about your natural flow. So you are just like bang, whack it, bang, whack it. Amazingly I would hit just about every ball in the middle. But when Kerry slowed it down to where I had time to think about it, I'd struggle to time it. It was actually a really good drill.

Another one was Bounce, Hit. So again, think about nothing else other than when the ball bounces — say 'bounce' when it does, and when you hit it, say 'hit'. He said Federer uses this all the time. I was like, that makes sense — bounce hit, bounce hit, bounce hit, so you don't think it; all you are doing is getting the timing. He said, you can be at the non-striker's end and then you can just say that to yourself — bounce hit, bounce hit. So when Kane, say, is at the other end and he is facing the ball, when it bounces say to yourself 'bounce' and when he hits it you say to yourself, 'hit'. That will get your natural timing going.

Back then Matt Henry was one of the guys. We had a net out at QEII Park, before the quake. Kerry would have four bowlers running in, and he'd bring the wicket forward so the pitch halved in length and you had half the time to react. He'd organise the bowlers so that they were constantly releasing balls at you, full tit. I'd hit one, and look up just in time to see the next one releasing. You had no time to think about anything. When the bowlers went back to the full pitch, I seemed to have all the time in the world. It was a brilliant drill.

My self-doubt about whether I had the game to be able to succeed solely as a batsman receded. I've got one crack at this, I thought, so bugger it, I'm going to spend the money on making it work. So I signed Kerry up on a monthly retainer to be my mental conditioning coach, which included neuro-imaging strategies.

Kerry told us he was working with other people in Christchurch, like netball coach Marg Foster and cricketer Hamish Bennett and a golfer out at Clearwater and even Wayne Smith. But I'm pretty sure I'm the only one who ended up actually paying him money.

Kerry's input seemed to work when we toured India in November.

In my first innings as a specialist batsman, opening, I put my head down and made 65, batting for almost four hours, staying out there with Ross long enough to give Jesse Ryder and Kane a stable base to put on tons and get us almost abreast of the Indians' first innings total. In their second innings, Chris Martin bowled brilliantly, five for 63, but lacked supporting firepower, and ran out of gas on a lifeless pitch. A worthy draw, given India at that stage were the number one-ranked test nation, and we were number eight.

We emulated that draw in the second test at Hyderabad. The Indians took a first innings lead of 122, and we were under the pump to salvage something. My innings of 225, the third-highest second innings in test matches in India, enabled us to hang on for a draw.

In the third test at Nagpur, on a fizzing pitch, the Indians showed the true gulf between the teams, winning easily by an innings and 198 runs.

The worst of it was that after batting so well as an opener in the first two tests, I had to come in at number eight at Nagpur, because of my bloody back. I was jumping in the air at the warm-up, right before the toss. I could feel my disc go in the air, knew I was in trouble, didn't want to land. When I did land I fell down and couldn't move. I'm lying there in absolute agony, with Dan hovering over me. 'Can you play? Can you play?' I can't actually move, but I say, 'Yeah, sure I can play.' So he goes over and loses the toss and we bat first. I'm supposed to be opening and I can't even sit upright.

I was so angry. I'd given up keeping so I could preserve my back and it'd blown out again. I came in way down the order full of painkillers and anti-inflams, barely able to walk. I hung around and somehow made about 40. Second innings I opened but I may as well have stayed in the dressing room. I missed the ODIs, nursed my back and wondered, not for the first time, what my future held.

Even though we lost that series, and came away with some credit, it hadn't exactly been a stellar year, and Mark Greatbatch must have been feeling the pressure, despite a bizarre attempt to avoid it.

He seemed to be in a peculiar position of his own making, a kind of Clayton's Head Coach. He didn't really want to be known as Head Coach, because of the pressure and responsibility, so he was officially the Batting Coach. That role might have suited him, but as de facto Head Coach, since we didn't have any other, he was out of his depth. He lasted 10 months, and I confess that by then I was pretty keen to see him go.

In December 2010, John Wright was appointed Head Coach, while Greatbatch was kicked upstairs to Convenor of Selectors. Glenn Turner was booted off that panel to make way for him, and former Aussie coach John Buchanan was appointed Director of Cricket, in charge of the high performance programme.

An impartial observer might have wondered what the hell was going on, whether the game New Zealand Cricket was playing was musical chairs or rearranging the deck chairs on a certain doomed vessel.

Interestingly, or perhaps bizarrely, Wright had been offered the job of Batting Coach previous to Greatbatch being appointed Batting Coach, which was effectively Head Coach. Wright had turned down the Batting Coach position because he wanted to be Head Coach. So, for the last 10 months, we'd had a Head Coach who wanted to be called a Batting Coach, instead of a Batting Coach who wanted to be

Head Coach. Now, with John Wright, we at least had a Head Coach who wanted to be Head Coach. That had to be an improvement, you'd have thought.

We didn't have to wait long to find out.

4
Wright and Wrong

'He's up and down like a yo-yo,' said one well-placed source, who spoke on condition of anonymity. 'He's all over the place. It's about sound decision making and we have seen at the crease you don't get that too often with Brendon. Personally, I don't think he's captaincy material.'

— Michael Brown, *New Zealand Herald*

John Wright began his tenure as New Zealand coach in late 2010 with a huge coffer of public goodwill. He was a revered opening bat for New Zealand and Derbyshire, a former New Zealand captain, and known far and wide in cricketing circles as one of the good guys. Articulate, well connected, Shake was a man who enjoyed a beer or glass of wine and a laugh. And, most important, he'd come home with a pedigree as a coach, after binding the disparate personalities of the Indians into a team which got to the finals of the World Cup. When he came back to New Zealand, as far as the cricketing public was concerned, it was a matter of when, not if, he took over the reins of our team.

I doubt that even the man he ousted, Mark Greatbatch, had any negative feelings about Wrighty taking over. They always seemed to get on well, and when they were playing Wrighty was always the senior pro, so Greatbatch probably felt like the rest of the New Zealand fans, that the prodigal son had assumed his rightful position.

Wrighty would have been well aware that the playing and talent pool he had to draw on here was very different to that in India. That was immediately confirmed by the series against Pakistan in late 2010, early 2011.

In the first innings of the first test at Hamilton, Gup, Kane and I all made fifties, but none of us kicked on and we were all out for 275. Pakistan replied with 367 and we crumpled to 110 in our second innings, my measly 35 being top score.

We managed a draw in our second test, which gave the series to Pakistan, but on this tour the tests were the entrée to a main course of ODIs, in preparation for the imminent ICC World Cup in India, Sri Lanka and Bangladesh.

It wasn't the best warm-up. We won the first ODI, the second was washed out, then we lost three in a row — and the series — before a consolation win in the last. I found runs hard to come by in any of them.

That was overshadowed by the news that Dan was going to retire as captain after the World Cup. I definitely harboured ambitions in that direction, which made my relationship with Wright pretty important.

John Wright was obviously a very intelligent man and, from the first, I felt that he'd come to the job with a plan. He had some really good messages, talked a lot about basics, knowing where your off stump was, for instance, and being able to bat time and create partnerships. But I thought his strategies for test match cricket were better than the ideas he brought to our ODI game.

He was very conservative in the style of play he wanted us to implement: get to 35 overs two or three wickets down and launch from there. I was batting in those first 35 overs, so he was asking everyone to play very conservatively up to that point and then put all our eggs in the last 15-over basket. I thought as a strategy it was archaic, and that might have been the beginning of our differences.

He was great company in social situations, and I really enjoyed sitting down and having a beer with him and talking. At the end of the evening, he would say, 'Love ya Baz, love ya.' Then next morning he would walk past me at breakfast in a shitty mood. They were either huge mood swings, or . . . I began to feel that he didn't trust me, and some of the senior players felt the same way. When we had a beer together, his good nature would win out and he'd relax, but when he was back in harness as Head Coach, he'd revert to his suspicions about us — or me, particularly.

In fact, I desperately wanted to commit to Wrighty because I enjoyed him, but when I began feeling that he didn't trust me, that made it difficult. I developed a suspicion that rather than try to get more out of his senior players, he'd decided to get rid of us and was waiting for his opportunity.

So that was the way it rolled with Wrighty. We'd have some bloody good times together, a few beers, talk some rubbish and smoke the occasional durry together, even have a game of golf every now and then. Absolutely loved his company. And then I'd feel like everything had changed, that he was trying to get rid of me. I found his behaviour strange and confusing.

There could have been something going on behind the scenes with John Buchanan, who had coached Australia against Wright's India. Here were these two who had been in control of the two titans of the game, trying to find a power base in one of the minnows. Maybe Buchanan thought that as Director of Cricket and being responsible for high performance, his philosophy and systems should be implemented by the Head Coach. If they were clashing behind the scenes, Wrighty may have thought Buchanan was getting support from some of us, but as far as I'm aware, none of us was holding a candle for Buchanan and, in fact, I had no idea that anything was going on until much later.

The ICC World Cup was hosted jointly by India, Sri Lanka and Bangladesh in early 2011.

Before our first match against Kenya at Chennai, the Black Caps attended a presentation given by John Rhodes, a representative of the ICC anti-corruption unit, the ACSU. It was made clear to us that if we were approached about match fixing and didn't report it to the ACSU, we would be as guilty as the person who'd approached us.

That was the first time it'd been made clear to me exactly what our reporting obligations as professional cricketers were. Before that, my impression was the rules were pretty sketchy as to your reporting obligations and, particularly, the penalties if you didn't report. I hadn't tried to keep it a secret — I'd had casual conversations about Cairns with my captain, Dan, with my agent at the time and with others whose opinion I trusted, like Kyle Mills and Stephen Fleming. Clearly that was no longer good enough, and I'd be in the gun if I didn't take it through official channels, so I talked to Dan and we told John Rhodes we had something we needed to share with the ACSU.

Dan and I went to his room at the hotel and went through the details of Cairns' meeting with me in Kolkata three years before, in 2008. It was all pretty casual, and I realised later, pretty bloody slipshod on Rhodes' part — he didn't even have a tape recorder, just sat there and took notes, telling us that he'd just get it down on paper and 'it'll probably go down the bottom of the file and never ever be seen again, but at least you know that you have done the right thing'.

Yeah, right. At the time, I thought it was done and dusted and got on with the cricket.

We qualified last in Group A, after Pakistan, Sri Lanka and Australia, beating the likes of Kenya, Zimbabwe and Canada. We did have a significant win against Pakistan, anchored by a big ton by Rosco, but our victory over South Africa in the quarter-finals was quite rightly described as a stunning upset. Jesse Ryder scored a weighty 83 and Jake Oram got Man of the Match with four for 35 and a magnificent boundary catch to dismiss Jacques Kallis.

Normal service resumed in the semi-final when we lost badly to Sri Lanka, after only posting 217. After the match, Dan lamented that the 'top order came up short' and it had been tough to recover from that. In fact, we'd been four down for 161 after 39 overs, hardly disastrous, in fact right on Wrighty's template. We were still promising at six for 204 after 45 overs, but when we lost four wickets for just 13 runs, our fate was pretty much sealed.

That was Dan's last act as captain. He formally stepped down when we got back to New Zealand, and precipitated the next chapter in the captaincy saga, which turned out to be one of the major regrets of my career.

After we got home from the World Cup, I got a call from the then CEO of New Zealand Cricket, Justin Vaughan, and I met him at a café in Latimer Square. He'd talked to me in India at the World Cup about my captaincy potential, and now he told me that NZC wanted me to put my name forward for the captaincy and that they were going to ask both me and Ross Taylor, as candidates, to present our cases. I took Justin at face value and was naive enough to believe that if the chief executive was urging me to put my hat into the ring I must have a realistic chance.

I was told the selection panel would comprise Justin, Head Coach John Wright, Convenor of Selectors Mark Greatbatch, and Director of Cricket John Buchanan.

I had a feeling that Wrighty might be difficult to persuade of my merits. Greatbatch, through the Wairarapa connection, had become very close to Ross, so I thought he'd probably also be a lost cause for me. I had no idea where Buchanan sat, but he was steeped in Aussie cricket culture and might be a sympathetic ear and open to a new approach. On balance, with Justin Vaughan there, I felt that I might need a lot of luck for things to go my way, but I was in with a chance.

On the morning of the presentation, I arrived at Lincoln University prepped up and ready to go, only to discover that Justin Vaughan was no longer on the panel. That threw me, but the die was cast and I laid out my PowerPoint presentation in front of Greatbatch, Wright and Buchanan.

I talked about how I wanted to take the team forward, that we needed to completely change how we played the game and that meant we had to ruthlessly cull some players in and around the playing group because they were dragging too much negative baggage; they weren't the right characters to embrace the changes I wanted to make. I named names. Some of them were my best mates. I wasn't advocating shutting the door on them forever, I was saying that the team needed to take a new direction and we needed players who hadn't been beaten up so many times that when it became touch and go in a game they would go into their shells, try to avoid losing rather than take a punt on winning. I wanted people who were prepared to have a crack, not fall prey to 'here we go again' thoughts.

When I'd finished, I fielded some pretty weak questions from the panel. I got the feeling they didn't have any idea which direction they wanted to go or how they were going to take the team forward, and maybe even felt threatened by the fact that I had come up with a plan. Buchanan had said very little. Then and later, he was hard to read, difficult to have a conversation with. I got the feeling that far from being a new broom, he was still just wanting to get his feet under the desk, trying to align himself with what he thought was the status quo.

I left Lincoln thinking I'd done everything I could, delivered a solid, well-prepped presentation. But I was also thinking that before we got players who were prepared to have a crack, we might need a panel who didn't think having a crack was pie in the sky. I rang Lis on the way home, said I can't do any more than that. If they want to head in a different direction, that's fine.

I was told I would be rung over the weekend.

It was Sunday night before I heard from John Buchanan. 'We're going in a different direction,' he said.

I got off the phone, told Lis, went outside, had a beer and let things settle. It hurt at the time, because I felt as if I'd been coaxed into believing I had a chance, whereas in truth they were just trying to put some public process around a decision that had already been made. I felt they'd used this public process to make it appear that both our merits had been fully appraised and that Ross had been the better applicant — all fair and above board, so I could have no argument with the decision.

Within days of the public announcement of Ross's captaincy, Greatbatch was a guest at Ross's wedding. That would have been a long, awkward day for Greatbatch had his panel appointed me captain!

As time passed, I felt more and more embarrassed about the way it had been done — so publicly. I felt that I'd been set up. It wasn't good for cricket, it wasn't good for Ross, it wasn't good for me, it wasn't good for our relationship, or any team with the two of us in it.

I'd captained Rosco in the New Zealand Under 19s and we'd had a lot of fun together as youngsters and had a good relationship. We weren't best mates, but we had a healthy respect for each other. I think the public selection process put a lot of pressure on our relationship that didn't need to be there. I started looking at Ross in a different light and that feeling was probably mutual.

Now, after everything that has transpired, I can look back and say that missing out on the captaincy at that time was the best thing that could have happened to me. I'd fallen victim to the seductive idea that someone thought enough of me to captain the team, rather than doing some rigorous self-analysis as to whether I was ready for it. And the fact that I hadn't been astute enough to work out that applying for the captaincy wasn't the right thing to do — and worse, I'd willingly engaged in that process — proved I wasn't ready for it.

But neither was Ross. He'd made the same mistake. He was younger than me and, I believe, no more ready for the captaincy than I was. And he was just as compromised by New Zealand Cricket's decision to have a public selection process.

What happened next made us both a lot wiser — and certainly older — but it gouged a rift between us that will probably never heal.

5
False Dawn

> . . . with Ross's captaincy it is early days, but the boost of confidence he'll get from [beating Australia] and the players he will now have belief in will carry a long way.
>
> — Stephen Fleming

I was nudging 30 years old when Ross took over the captaincy in June 2011. I'd had my share of injuries. Bulging spinal discs and my bad knee had made it impossible to keep wicket in any form of the game. The end of my test career was looming and I wanted to feel like I was a part of something special before I finished. I remember resetting my goals and saying this is what I want to do in the game during this time.

I did that with Stephen Fleming, mainly, just realigned where I wanted to go. The first thing I had to accept was that the captaincy would now never come. So what did I want to do, how long did I want to keep playing? I needed to recalibrate exactly what I wanted to get out of the last few years of my career.

Flem had my stats, how many test hundreds I'd scored and my average and so on, and we talked about the upcoming series, and what I might aspire to do. Flem was trying to get my head back in the game after my disappointments, but I'm not really motivated by individual stuff and, to begin with, it all felt a little soulless.

I also leaned heavily on my mental skills coach, Kerry Schwalger, who was unfailingly positive and a great one for boosting the ego.

I settled down and I was comfortable enough playing under Ross. If there were any sour grapes, they weren't directed at Ross, more at myself for falling victim to the process.

The wheel seemed to turn again when Wrighty told me that I was vice-captain, that if Ross left the field, I would take over. That put me in a delicate position, given the way the selection process had been played out so publicly. Players would come to me to get to Ross, but I had to be conscious of being respectful and giving Ross space. I didn't want to be seen to be trying to manage, or telling Ross how he should captain.

We were both walking on eggshells as a result of that public process. Everyone seemed to expect me to react, to be pissed off, to be trying to undercut him and maybe Ross did too, and that affected his ability to lean on his vice-captain.

That spring we toured Zimbabwe, played just the one test, a thriller which we won by the skin of our teeth. I opened and didn't make much in either innings, but Martin Guptill set us up with a ton for a substantial first innings lead. Which we blew by crumbling in our second innings, held together by a second successive 76 by Ross. We were almost run down on the fifth day by an admirably aggressive Brendan Taylor century.

I made better contributions in the one-day series prior to the test, where we won the first two, but then fizzled to a loss and a draw in the last two.

You couldn't fault Ross for leading from the front. His contributions with the bat were exactly what you'd expect from one of the best batsmen in the world. In many respects, the team seemed to carry on as before — Dan was still there, taking big wickets (five for 70 in their first innings) and making valuable runs down the order.

The acid really went on when we toured Australia at the end of the year. We were cleaned out in the first test at the Gabba. Ross won the toss and decided to bat and we were five down for 96 after 26 overs. I scored best among our top five with a paltry 34, and we were only saved from complete embarrassment by Dean Brownlie and Dan, who almost nailed a century in another huge rearguard action.

Australia put 427 on the board, courtesy of a big ton from Michael Clarke and support from Ricky Ponting and Brad Haddin, then put us to the sword in our second turn at bat. Their new quick, James Pattinson, had our top five back in the pavilion after the first hour of Day 4. Five for 28 became 150 all out.

To be beaten by nine wickets seems like a rout, and it is, but we'd played okay, except for that hour on Day 4, where the test was won and lost. Looking forward to Hobart, we felt that if we could just hang in there for longer, we might be able to put some pressure on them.

We did exactly that — turned it around and squared the series with a famous win at Hobart, our first test win in Oz since 1985 and our first test victory over them anywhere since 1993.

You need some luck in this game, and we had a bit. It seems sacrilegious to say we got lucky because Dan was injured and couldn't play, but that gave an opening for Trent Boult to debut, and we then had four seamers on a track where the ball went everywhere, and as a result we were able to attack relentlessly.

You could take a look at that scoreboard and wonder where the improvement was. We were put in to bat on a green track and made 150 again, with James Pattinson again ascendant, and Dean Brownlie the only one to get past 20. Shades of Brisbane. But this time the Aussies couldn't hack the pitch either, or the fire and accuracy of Doug Bracewell and Trent Boult, falling over for 136. Game on.

We didn't bat that much better in the second innings, but Ross and Kane had a good partnership and we got to 226, which turned out to be enough. Just.

Oz were sitting pretty when Doug Bracewell bowled a spell of swinging pace which was as good as anything I've seen, taking out Ponting, Clarke and Hussey on 159 before lunch, then helping clean out their last five for 60 runs in the afternoon. David Warner batted right through and was left stranded on 123 when Doug bowled Nathan Lyon at the other end. We'd won by seven runs.

It was an extraordinary result. When Warner and Ponting were at the wicket together, Australia had only 82 to get, with eight wickets in hand. I'm still rubbing my eyes at that one.

It was a very happy dressing room. I remember saying to Ross and Wrighty as we were leaving that there were guys who had played for

New Zealand for decades and never beaten Australia, and here we've done it under you guys, a new coach and a new captain. I told them they had a wonderful opportunity ahead of them and I meant it.

There was a lot of optimism on the back of that win, and it's important to remember what a huge fund of goodwill there was towards Ross's captaincy, even from someone who was supposedly at the centre of the 'conspiracy' to get rid of him.

Stephen Fleming, who'd never beaten the Aussies in 14 years as captain, declared the result could be the galvanising moment that Ross needed, to build a winning era: 'It's not the finished product by any means, and certainly with Ross's captaincy it is early days, but the boost of confidence he'll get from that and the players he will now have belief in will carry a long way.' Flem noted it would be a tough summer with South Africa touring for a full series, 'and it is not going to get any easier. Hopefully they can keep improving and this test will certainly help the confidence levels, and we're a much better team at home than away.'

When I looked at it objectively, I wasn't so sure. Doug Bracewell, supported by Trent Boult and Chris Martin, played out of his skin on the kind of green, low-bounce pitch that we were more accustomed to than the Aussies. So the conditions favoured us and we were always going to win some games like that because we had started to develop more talented players.

It was already clear that Ross as captain was going to be great at some things and not so good at others. He was always going to lead from the front, but tactically there was a bit missing. No one was too worried about it; it was just something we accepted. Flem himself had talked about how long it had taken him to learn the role, to grow into the captaincy. It was early days for Ross and we all felt there was every chance that he would grow and prosper in the role.

In January of 2012 we skittled Zimbabwe at Napier in the only test, where Ross pulled a calf muscle, and we swept the ODIs under my captaincy, as a prelude to South Africa's tour of New Zealand in March.

Being captain exacerbated my differences with Wrighty. We clashed over strategy. It was the old story, really, that, particularly in the ODIs, I thought his approach was outdated. But it wasn't just that.

By then, Wrighty had settled into the job, and had revealed a lack of structure: he had an idea of how he wanted the game to be played, certainly, but not a detailed day-to-day plan which provided the guys with the resources and information and opportunities to achieve that. He could do great team talks, seemingly off the cuff, with one-liners to help us keep some perspective, like 'There's more than a billion people in China and not one of them gives a rat's arse about us.'

Our manager, Mike Sandle, had been appointed at the same time Wrighty had become coach, and I may have been imagining things but I sensed some growing frustration on Mike's part. He was super organised, or wanted to be, but trying to get detailed information from Wrighty and Ross about what they wanted and when was a bit like trying to herd cats.

Predictably, beating Zimbabwe proved no indication of form when South Africa arrived.

That tour didn't start well. We lost two out of three T20 appetisers, then got cleaned out in all three ODIs. I top scored in all three, but if your best from the top order is around 50, it's not going to be enough against a batting line-up with the likes of AB de Villiers and Hashim Amla. There just aren't that many levers you can pull as captain or coach if you have no runs to play with.

The first test at Dunedin was drawn when rain washed out the last day, with New Zealand needing 264 runs and South Africa eight wickets. Ross and I were unbeaten at the end of Day 4 with an 82-run partnership and we felt we were definitely in with a crack, despite having to get a total which would have been our highest successful run chase ever. The pitch was getting ever lower and slower, blunting the likes of Steyn and Morkel, Tahir wasn't getting a lot of spin, and by the end of the day, after we'd hit 40 off 31 balls, we'd forced Graeme Smith to string out the boundary riders.

We took some encouragement from that, even though, particularly in their second innings, the South African batsmen seemed untroubled by our attack.

The second test in Hamilton tempered our enthusiasm about our ability to really compete. We got done by nine wickets and there wasn't a lot to be pleased about in our 185 first innings total. Although we restricted South Africa to 253, we then collapsed again, this time for 168, and South Africa cruised home with nine wickets to spare.

What stays with me from that match was Kane Williamson's attitude as he and I walked out to face the South Africans in the second innings. We were obviously really up against it, with Steyn and Morkel and Philander running rampant, and Kane turns to me with a happy grin and says, 'This is amazing.'

'What is?'

'Playing these guys. Just tells you you've got to keep doing it, doesn't it?'

Under the pump, against the most fearsome fast bowling in cricket, and he was loving it! No wonder he's so good. And in the following test, he proved it.

Even though we got a draw in the third test at Wellington, the gulf between the number two- and number eight-ranked test teams was clearer than the one-nil test series result indicated. South Africa declared twice, for 474 in the first innings and 189 for three in the second. They were in total control after we'd only managed 275 in our first. Ross took a hit on his arm and retired hurt in that first innings, so I took over the captaincy.

We were never in with a show, particularly without our number one batsman, and only eked a draw through Kane's coming-of-age ton in our second innings. As South Africa closed in for the kill, Kane negated everything that Steyn and Morkel and Philander were able to hurl at him in the final sessions, helped by some gritty resistance from Doug Bracewell, and finished on 102 not out, a truly great innings under that pressure.

We still had an extraordinarily full year in front of us, with tours to the West Indies in June through to August, then on to India, to the T20

World Champs in Sri Lanka, followed by a two-test series against the same hosts.

It's years like that which really stretch the fibre of the guys, on and off the field. You spend so much time in one another's company and, conversely, so little time with wives, children, sweethearts, family. The team becomes your family, effectively, and you're all interdependent in ways that have a big effect on performance.

On that sort of long haul, the team has to bind round a larger sense of purpose, and that's to do with the kind of cricket you're trying to play, yes, but in some ways the easier part of captaincy is on the field. It is the other stuff, like speaking to guys about their families and making sure everything is okay off the field, making sure they're mentally in the right space, how they deal with the media, the long time away from home. The fact that this guy's girlfriend might be going to a twenty-first birthday party tonight and he's a really jealous man. Like how he deals with playing the game the next day when all he has thought about all night is that his girlfriend has been out. Or an older guy who has sick kids and his default is always about his kids. Partners, children, parents, family, might weigh heavily at one time or other. Someone might be heartbroken, someone might be homesick.

Captaincy is about knowing all that, who needs support when. And then to be able to somehow get them all in the same space, sitting on their seat on the bus and heading in the right direction the next day.

If that binding off-field stuff isn't happening, and there's a lack of on-field direction as well, the cracks become canyons and swallow the team.

6
Warning Signs

> . . . the result means the teams swap positions on the ICC Test rankings table, with West Indies moving to seventh and New Zealand falling to eighth.
>
> — ESPN Cricinfo

In May 2012, a month before we embarked on the first of those tours, to the West Indies, John Wright announced he wasn't going to extend his coaching contract beyond August, meaning the Windies tour would be his last.

Wrighty made it clear that the biggest reason for not continuing was his differences with Director of Cricket John Buchanan: differences, specifically, over planning systems, values and beliefs. Which pretty much covers the spectrum, I guess. Given that, it's difficult to imagine any meeting of the minds between the coach of New Zealand and the director of cricket, and when it was made public I did wonder how long this conflict had been going on.

I'd also heard through the Indian grapevine that Wrighty had been offered a lucrative contract to coach in the IPL. I did wonder how he was going to manage that in concert with his New Zealand duties.

In the end, not only did he avoid any criticism for abandoning New Zealand, he turned it into a PR triumph against Buchanan, an Aussie about whom New Zealand cricket fans already had their doubts.

For what seemed like the umpteenth time, the coaching role was once again up for grabs.

Before I left for the Windies, I got a call from Matthew Mott, who told me he was going to apply for the job and asked me to be his referee. Matthew was an Australian who had put together an impressive coaching career around the world. He'd coached me at New South Wales and at Kolkata and I'd got on brilliantly with him. I thought he'd be an outstanding candidate for Head Coach of the Black Caps because he was quite an innovative, brashly confident Australian, with a profound understanding of the game and great people skills, and I thought that was exactly what we needed. I agreed to be his referee.

Mott had some previous experience with New Zealand Cricket. He had been the outstanding candidate once before, when Andy Moles had been appointed. He'd come over and scouted the place, decided he'd live in Christchurch, close by Sumner, so he could surf. I understood he'd actually been offered the job back then, but had turned it down at the last minute, letting Andy Moles in.

Then Mike Hesson, who'd just returned from coaching Kenya, told me he was also applying. Mike had coached me at Otago and was a family friend — in fact, Lis and I had stayed at his place for three or four months back in 2002, when I came back to New Zealand after a short period in Oz. When I moved to Christchurch and played for Canterbury, he stayed in touch, and eventually lured me back to play for Otago, where he'd set up a brilliant playing environment.

I knew Mike's playing philosophy worked at provincial level with a team which was, on paper, far from the most talented in the competition. He'd instilled belief, and he'd put a squad of players together who loved their cricket, wanted to play, and were always up for a scrap. Sounds basic, and it was, but surprisingly, those elements aren't always present in professional cricketers. With the Otago guys, cricket wasn't the be-all and end-all of their lives, but on the field cricket was the be-all and end-all of their day.

That Otago team became real over-achievers: we won domestic ODI and Twenty20 titles and went to the Champions League in India. We didn't get the same success in the four-day game: our positivity and energy in the field couldn't overcome our lack of depth and skills.

I could imagine that Mike's approach with Otago would work

for New Zealand, which shared some of the same strengths and weaknesses compared to the other international teams. So I told him he should go for it, he'd be a great candidate, but I also told him I couldn't be his advocate in any way, because I was already a referee for Matthew Mott.

Meanwhile, there'd been another change at the top of New Zealand Cricket — David White was the new CEO, and he headed the coaching selection panel, along with John Buchanan and Stephen Fleming.

I didn't appear before them, but went off to the Windies and didn't think much more about it, until on tour I was phoned by a woman from NZC who wanted to talk to me in my capacity as referee for Matthew Mott. I did my thing, highly recommended Matthew for the role. Hesson wasn't discussed. I finished my little rave, put the phone down and thought no more about it, as I tried to concentrate on a tour that was rapidly turning into a disaster.

I was late on the Windies scene, through no fault of my own. Wrighty had persuaded me to take a break from the T20s and ODIs and just come over for the tests. I was reluctant to take a break, because missing opportunities to play for the Black Caps in any format didn't sit easily with me, and I also suspected Wrighty's motives in not wanting me there. But there wasn't much I could do, he was adamant, so I bought into the idea of a rest and read about the team getting off to a bad start, cleaned out in both T20s.

Next minute, manager Mike Sandle rings me from the West Indies on behalf of Wrighty. He tells me that Ross has been injured in the T20s, and is likely to miss all five of the upcoming ODIs. Can I come over and captain the side in his absence? By that time, I'd got my head around not being there, but I wasn't going to turn down an opportunity to lead the Black Caps.

By the time I've flown three-quarters of the way round the world to get there, Kane has captained the Black Caps to losses in the first two ODIs. The last three are all at Basseterre in St Kitts. I go straight from the airport to the nets and, watched by John Wright, somehow hit the ball like a dream, only to be told by Wrighty that I look a bit tired and they'll keep Kane in place as captain 'for the sake of continuity' and hold me over to the next game. So I've made a 'mercy' dash across the bloody globe to end up next day sitting on the sideline carrying the drinks. At least we won the game, our only victory in five ODIs.

Three days later, for the fourth ODI, Ross had made a quicker than anticipated recovery, and captained the side to losses in the last two games.

After Mike Sandle's assurances on the phone on behalf of Wrighty about coming over and captaining the ODI side, I could make some educated guesses at what had transpired behind the scenes: either Ross was highly resistant to my captaining the team and leant on Wrighty to change his mind, or it was just an organisational cock-up by Wrighty. The rest of the tour suggested the latter, because much of it was a shambles.

Wright spraying the team and me in particular after the ODI clean-out didn't go down well. I hadn't scored many in the fourth ODI, but only Kane had scored more in the fifth. And Wright's behaviour was increasingly bizarre. Having a beer with you in the evening, he's sweetness and light, then next morning he's the bear with the sore head. One morning he told Tim Southee, 'I know what you're doing, I know what you lot are up to!'

You wonder what he was telling Ross. If Wrighty was suspicious that the senior players were against him, that would surely have seeped into Ross's perspective too.

I could sense Mike Sandle's frustration — he was a very organised, empathetic man. Most days, Mike set up his laptop in the lobby of whatever hotel we were staying in, and used the lobby as his office. So players passed him going in and out of the hotel, stopped to chat, catch up, and if they needed to talk to him about something, they knew where he was. If they needed a more private audience with him, it was easy enough to ask him if they could have a word. As a result of this relaxed interaction, Mike had a handle on what was going on with everyone. He made sure he was always available, so you didn't have to make an appointment and go to his room to actually see him.

As notional vice-captain — that's the way I was feeling by then, very notional — I tried to make a point of being in the lobby bar for a beer before dinner. The players knew that, and they also knew they didn't have to drink; they could have a glass of water. It was about being together in a casual way, giving everyone the opportunity to connect. I had little rules, like always seeking out the dirty dirties — the players who didn't make the playing XI — on the first evening of a test for a beer, because they're the ones who'll be looking homeward and questioning why the hell they're there.

Ross was the exact opposite to Mike Sandle, and was seldom in the lobby. He spent an enormous amount of time in his room. If you wanted to talk to him, you had to knock on his door.

I don't think he consciously stayed in his room. I doubt if he even thought about the fact that the players needed to see him, that they might like to see their captain outside the dressing room and field of play, or that they might need more from him. I don't think Ross had any idea what his leadership style was going to be, and he showed no awareness of how he was going to build a team or what his plans for the team were, the kind of culture he wanted to create.

The young players tended to just accept it as the norm, because they knew no different, but the rest of us knew there had to be a better way. There was still hope that Ross would grow into it, particularly when important news from home filtered through as we were girding our loins to try to salvage something from the two tests.

On 20 July, a few days before the beginning of the first test, we heard that Mike Hesson had been appointed the new coach. So much for my Matthew Mott recommendation!

I was disappointed for Matthew, but felt that New Zealand Cricket had probably got it right, that Hesson would bring skills and structure that would support Ross much better than Wrighty's approach.

We followed up our T20 and ODI disappointments with worse: we got done for dinner in both tests by a Windies team that was hardly formidable.

We lost the first test by nine wickets, after which Ross made a speech about guys with starts (like, presumably, Guptill who got 97 in our first innings and me, who got 84 in our second) needing to convert to hundreds. Fair enough, but it was the failure of the middle order batting that cost us the test — we'd collapsed from two for 223 in our first innings to all out for 351, then from two for 195 in our second to all out for 272.

I didn't agree with what he'd said, but it was good to hear Ross say something. He seemed to have two gears in the presence of the team: silence and shouting.

I suppose you could call the second test an improvement, when we were beaten by only six wickets, after innings totals of 260 and 154.

By that time, the team was on the edge of imploding. Players had got to the point where they just didn't care any more. It became about self-preservation. The captain and coach were completely uninspiring and it was like, if you are going to play cricket for New Zealand and you've got this hopeless situation, you may as well find some mates in the group and have a good time with them. And then when you are on the field just play for yourself — just try to get a performance so they can't drop you.

I was starting to get incredibly frustrated. And wondering: what is the point? Everyone talks about how you've got one window to represent your country and it's meant to be the greatest time of your life et cetera, but it was effin' horrible. I had a young family and was missing out on so much at home, for what? The cricket was uninspiring, nothing about it was fun. Maybe the younger guys were okay, because it was all new and they knew nothing else. And every now and then we'd win, because we had more talented players, so that if the stars aligned we might fluke something, as — it had now become clear — we had in Hobart.

I'd abandoned all thought of ever becoming captain of the Black Caps: the real question was whether I wanted to play for them, whether I wanted to be in that environment at all.

That Windies tour wasn't a great end to Wrighty's tenure. From the promise against Oz in Hobart, we seemed to have gone backwards at a rate of knots.

I'm not sure whether the fact that we knew Wrighty was going had any bearing on results. Maybe it threw more pressure on Ross, but the series confirmed my feeling that Ross needed to step up more as captain, that it wasn't enough to try to lead from the front by scoring a truckload of runs, then disappear into your room.

I'm not sure what effect the news of Hesson's appointment had on Ross over there. Ross knew Hesson was a mate of mine, but I doubt that people were in his ear at that stage about a possible conspiracy by Mike and me against him. Maybe he went into his shell a little more; it was very hard to tell.

Ross had been a good vice-captain. He'd always come up with something a little different, but it was never orchestrated. It was never two or three or four steps in front of the game. It was always 'What about this?' Some suggestion that was a reflex to what was happening in the moment. Often really helpful. He had a good gut feel about where the game was at. But we needed more from a captain. We needed to be at least a couple of plays ahead of the game. We needed to make moves in advance, to try to set up certain outcomes. We needed a longer view, a plan which anticipated the game a bit more, and a captain who could articulate it. But, with Ross, we tended to be doing this one minute, then next morning we'd be doing something different.

Partly as a result of his frustrations with us and ours with him, we were becoming a very emotional group on the field. Some of our behaviour was pretty erratic. Ross would brood, then shout. Tim Southee and some of the other bowlers got into spraying the batsmen and there'd be cheers and jeers when we got guys out. I don't blame Ross for this, but it was symbolic of our set-up.

We went home to lick our wounds and ready ourselves for the Indian tour under the new coach. It was just a matter of weeks away, not much time for Mike Hesson to make his mark.

I knew what Mike would bring to the coaching role, all the systems and preparation and planning that Wrighty lacked. Wrighty's coaching style simply exposed Ross's weaknesses, and I was hopeful that if Mike wrapped his systems around Ross, Ross's weaknesses would be compensated for and he'd have a far better chance of succeeding as captain. Maybe Ross and Hess would be the perfect match.

It had to work. I believed that Ross, with the power base behind him in New Zealand Cricket and in the wider cricket community and the media, would never be sacked. He was impregnable. If results didn't improve, Hesson would go, not Ross. Which meant that Mike Hesson was the last throw of the dice: if Hess couldn't help Ross, we were stuffed, and I'd be gone too.

7
The Coup that Wasn't

> New Zealand were once a dangerous side when cornered, but there is no fight in their game any more.
>
> — Andrew Fernando, ESPN Cricinfo

New coach, new attitude, fresh start, high hopes . . . But when we got to India in late August 2012, just a couple of weeks after getting home from the West Indies, the new coach seemed to make no difference at all — the first test against India felt like a continuation of the last test against the Windies.

India batted first, scored 438, and didn't need a second innings, as we capitulated for 159 and 164, losing a total of 18 wickets to spin. India won by a massive innings and 115 runs with a day to spare, even though much of the third day and part of the fourth was washed out. I was out there with Kane trying to at least make the Indians bat again, when I got sawn off by an lbw after an audible inside edge. I was pissed off and showed it. We lost nine wickets for 66 runs.

My response to a bad decision was an indication of how the team were travelling, and I was later fined for dissent by the match referee.

We made a better fist of the second test, only losing by five wickets, after Ross delivered a ton in the first innings to take us to a respectable 365 and then we actually got a first innings lead, albeit only 12 runs, by dint of Tim Southee's career-best seven for 64. But 248 wasn't quite enough in our second turn at bat. We had them five down with still a hundred to get, but Kohli and Dhoni were good enough to take it away from us.

So that was four tests in a row we'd lost, but at least in this one we'd shown some fight, and, as new coach Mike Hesson was at pains to point out, some positives.

'To get a first-innings lead against a quality Indian side showed that we'd made some improvements there . . . In the end, we set them a challenging total that gave our bowlers a real chance. Sure we would have wanted more [runs]. We still have to keep that positive mindset.'

He also talked about the dressing room.

'The players are extremely hard on themselves, individually and collectively. Some talk about the inadequacies in other players to try and help them. We've got a good leadership group that's learning to lead. We're trying to get the guys to evolve so they can challenge each other and start to ask tough questions.'

But asking questions is difficult if the captain doesn't talk.

I know Mike Hesson came to the Black Caps in good faith, wanting to make his relationship with Ross work. He was very clear with me that he wanted to help Ross become a good captain and he wanted Ross to remain captain of the New Zealand cricket team, and was prepared to work with me and the other senior players to make that happen.

I wish I could say the same of Ross, that he had good faith towards Hess at the beginning. It seemed to me that right from the start, Ross was suspicious of Hess's motives. So instead of taking Hess on his merits, Ross seemed already closed to him.

I knew there had been a bit of talk behind the scenes after Hesson's appointment, and that some were seeing a conspiracy. It wasn't a very complicated scenario they were pushing: that my mate Stephen Fleming had influenced the selection board to give the coaching job to my other mate Mike Hesson, whose ultimate goal was to replace Ross as captain with me.

One problem with that narrative was that I had recommended Matthew Mott to the selection panel, but details like that tend to spoil a good conspiracy theory, and as events unfolded, it was clear that logic would play an ever-diminishing role.

I don't know what Ross's support group were saying to him, but I know what they should have been telling him: Get close to this guy

Hesson, because he's got the structure you need to build the team around you.

Hesson could have been a huge advantage to Ross, bringing him the kind of complementary strengths that Wrighty hadn't been able to provide. Hess was not the kind of coach who thumped the table and told everyone, 'This is the way forward. It's my way or the highway.' That's not the way he operated. He wanted to empower a captain and a leadership group to create a vision of how they wanted to play the game, then he would facilitate that dream, if you like. Put in the hard yards around them, do all the planning and micro-managing that made sure the team had the best chance of executing that vision.

The senior players wanted to buy into that, I wanted to buy into that — I knew my career was getting towards the end, and I desperately wanted to be part of something special with the Black Caps before I gave it away.

So, time and again on what became a long grind of a tour, with changes of format and players around the core group coming and going, Mike set up a lot of meetings as a group, trying to provide the perfect forum for Ross. Wrighty had never done that for him — the only opportunities Ross got to talk to the team would be during emotional moments in games, when he'd start yelling and shouting. At these meetings, Mike would canvass everyone's thoughts, and then try to hand it back to Ross to synthesise what was out there, tell us the way he wanted to go forward, put his stamp on it. All Ross had to say was, 'Thanks lads, that's awesome and this is the direction we're going based on your thoughts. I'm the skipper, this is what we're doing and I need you all to buy into it.'

Ross would say nothing. Not a word. What the hell was he thinking? I had no idea.

Ross is a reasonably trusting guy in most circumstances, so someone must have been telling him to watch his back. Whatever, he put the shutters up against Hesson. A quiet guy at the best of times, going further into his shell didn't help — he'd surface with angry outbursts, instead of a coherent plan.

Again, as in the Windies, I got the feeling that Ross had been told by his outside support group that captaincy was about scoring runs and leading from the front, and that he was safe as captain as long as he kept doing that. I felt that that was always his focus, just on him getting runs. Which, to his credit, he continued to do. But if you're captain, you've still got to lead, give direction, whether or not you're making runs. If the captain isn't talking to or about the group, helping to bind them in a common purpose and a plan, the players start looking around for someone or something to fill that vacuum.

The newer players who hadn't been long in the environment just accepted the status quo and tried to get on with it, but the more senior players needed more, to help them feel that they were still developing skills, to help them feel they could deliver to a team strategy. They needed a plan, and an outlet to discuss it. They wanted to be able to get to Ross, to be able to ask him, 'What do you want us to do?'

For whatever reason, they didn't feel they could approach him directly. Maybe it was because to get to him they had to seek him out, go to his room, knock on his door, possibly disturb him. As on the Windies tour, he spent an awful lot of time in his room.

So the senior players would come to me to get me to talk to Ross, to ask him for more direction.

That placed me in a predicament. I didn't want to be their messenger because I didn't want Ross feeling as if he was being ganged up on, that people were telling tales behind his back. If anything, Mike Hesson's appointment worsened that situation for me.

I got caught in the middle of the situation of a captain who wouldn't talk to his coach or his team. I was keeping my powder dry in the team environment, trying to be the supportive vice-captain, but behind the scenes I became increasingly frustrated as I watched the Black Caps spiral downwards.

After the two tests against India, we played them in a couple of T20s, in preparation for the T20 Worlds hosted by Sri Lanka.

The first T20 against India was rained off without a ball being bowled, then we won the second by one run after I managed 91 off 55 balls — which seemed like our first win in any format in a long time.

We moved on to Sri Lanka for the T20 Worlds, where we were in Group D with Pakistan and Bangladesh. We managed to beat Bangladesh and advance to the Super 8s, where we finished last in Group 1, after losing to England, Sri Lanka and the West Indies.

When the rest of the teams headed off home, we stayed on in Sri Lanka for a full tour. Sri Lanka is a beautiful place — I've since been best man at my best mate's wedding there, and loved it. But it's a tough place if your team is struggling and you're not having much fun as a group. We were in an artificial environment, where security was tight and we weren't allowed to go anywhere or do anything. And it rained. A lot.

As we staggered on through that miserably wet tour, one T20, five ODIs and two tests, the rain matched our mood. The T20 and first ODI were washed out without a ball being bowled, the next three ODIs were completed, but were badly rain affected and decided by Messrs Duckworth and Lewis, not in our favour, and in the final ODI, when we might have sneaked a win, the heavens opened yet again, and flushed us away. As one local scribe put it: Sri Lanka 3, Rain 2, NZ 0.

I had nowhere to go with my own concerns and frustrations. I couldn't take them to the coach because that'd confirm the conspiracy theories in the mind of the captain, and I couldn't take them to the captain because that would confirm his suspicions that I was disloyal and in league with the senior players.

When Gary Hermansson had been mental skills coach for the Black Caps years before, he'd suggested we develop a routine where we drop the bag marked *Personal* at the door of the dressing room, and pick up the bag marked *Cricket*. A simple but graphic way of compartmentalising, a way of parking everything that was going on in your personal life and making sure that the only thoughts and aspirations in the *Cricket* bag related directly to your performance between the boundary ropes.

Sweet, except that I was finding that harder and harder to do, as our tour went on and on, seeming like an extension of the previous tour to the Windies. In those circumstances, your world gradually compresses into the team and support staff, partly because security stops you from getting out on your own much. As it went on, there was more and more leakage between the *Personal* and *Cricket* bags because it was increasingly difficult to distinguish which was which.

There's the old cliché that in this situation the team becomes a kind of family, with all that that implies, the love and respect and common purpose, but also the tensions and conflicts, the rifts and sibling rivalries and all the relationship grist that's kept psychiatrists in work for centuries. It's a cliché because it's true. And our family, the Black Caps family, was an increasingly dysfunctional one.

And just like a family, there are feelings you can articulate to the family in a helpful way, and others that are pretty negative and shouldn't really be let loose in that environment. It's all very well talking about honesty in the team environment, and aspiring towards sharing the truth about how you're feeling, but that comes with considerable restraints: you can't be destructive, you can't just vent your spleen, give voice to all your inner frustrations and antagonisms. You just can't do that without creating a lot of collateral. So you either bottle it up or release it somewhere else.

I'm not sure how others coped with that situation — I was the recipient of a lot of splenetic stuff from the senior players — but I at least had the advantage of a guy outside the team environment, a guy who seemed reasonably informed and objective, and who I was paying $1500 a month to listen to me, and then hopefully give the kind of advice I needed to get back on the field with a clear head.

I'd originally employed the eccentric Kerry Schwalger to be my mental conditioning coach, which included neuro-imaging strategies — that's what our contract said. And to begin with, that's the role he performed as I grappled with giving up wicketkeeping and becoming a specialist batsman. But over the past year, that side of it, the mental skills side, had languished, partly because I'd been back in Christchurch so rarely. Kerry had still done his best to keep me focused and believing in myself — mostly through over-the-top emails about my supernatural abilities, featuring a lot of exclamation marks.

To be honest, some of it might have been laughable, but I still lapped it up.

But as the team and my hopes and aspirations to be part of something special with the Black Caps got sucked into a black hole, I began using Kerry in a different way. From whatever hotel we were in, I'd simply vent my spleen by email at the end of another frustrating day, tell him exactly how pissed off and bitter I was at what I saw happening around me, getting rid of all the stuff I couldn't take into the team environment, trying to clear my head and my spleen of all the crap, so I could go out and play the next day without all this shitty fug holding me back.

I thought it was safe to say whatever I liked to him, my most private thoughts, because everything between us was completely confidential, and it was therapeutic for me to have that release valve.

Kerry saw his job as fighting my corner, and that's more or less what I'd asked him to do. But as time went on, some of his responses became bizarre. Instead of absorbing my frustrations and trying to move me on, he began giving it back to me in spades — there'd be long, intense raves in which he'd impersonate me, using words that I'd never use and a sustained level of invective that'd make your hair curl. It was outrageous and a bit disquieting to read 'myself' saying these things, but around the raves there'd still be some rational advice that was sometimes helpful.

We had two tests to get through before we were out of our misery. John Buchanan flew in before the first test, but people were coming in and out all the time, and I didn't attach any special significance to that, although the team was clearly on the ropes. It was mid-October, and the core of the team had been on the road since mid-August, following a brief respite at home after touring the Windies, for the best part of two months. We were frayed at the edges and the dynamic between coach and captain was by now toxic.

I knew Mike Hesson was very frustrated. He sensed we were struggling as a team. On a couple of occasions, he said to me that he'd really like to hear his captain talk in team meetings and sign off on definitive plans. There wasn't much I could do about that, because Ross must have decided I was part of the conspiracy against him and he wasn't talking to me either.

I got the sense before the first test in Sri Lanka that Hess was giving it one last try. He called a meeting to get everyone's thoughts on the table, but you could see that it was very much geared around Ross. He told Ross that everyone could put their thoughts out there, and we could talk them through, then Ross would decide which direction he wanted the team to go in.

At that round table all the players, certainly the senior players like Millsy, stood up and said their bob's worth. But Ross said very little and seemed disengaged from it all, and we left that meeting, once again, no closer to having a direction.

Maybe it was at this point that Hesson lost faith in Ross. I'm not sure; Hesson wasn't confiding in me, but he's not that hard to read. He's not overtly emotional, just gets a very serious look on his face and starts fiddling with his glasses. I could see that he was fed up with Ross. We were at the stage where something had to give.

A lot of the whispers round the place were that it was Hess who would go, that the media and public were behind Ross, not Hess. That was fair enough, and I didn't know any different. But it didn't take a genius to look around the dressing room and figure out that if by some chance Ross was the one who got the boot, there was only one other realistic captaincy option. Me.

Quite a few players came up to me after that meeting and expressed their disappointment. That's putting it mildly. What they said was variations of 'Would someone just make an effin' decision!'

I was very conscious that I had to be respectful and supportive of Ross while he was still captain, try to assist him and not get too far in front of myself and start to plot and plan. But it was difficult to keep myself from asking 'Is there a better way?' when you feel like a passenger in a slow-motion plane crash.

In an effort to clear my head enough to play, I continued venting in emails to Kerry that I hated what Ross was doing to the Black Caps, and that his captaincy surely had to be on the skids. But by mid-

October, when we got to Galle in the south-west of Sri Lanka, for the first test, even venting to Kerry wasn't working any more. Morale, mine and the team's, was at rock bottom.

Maybe it was predictable that we'd get utterly cleaned out in the first test against Sri Lanka at Galle. The fight we'd shown in that second test against India at Bangalore had evaporated into the clammy Sri Lankan atmosphere, along with any sense of team spirit.

After being more or less on even terms at the end of the first innings, we were all out for 118 in the second, and Sri Lanka cantered home without losing a wicket. A humiliating 10-wicket capitulation.

That test match was so frustrating that I started to run back to the hotel from the ground every day after stumps just to clear my head. Guys began joining me through the week and talking to me, asking me: 'What is going on with this team, what is happening?' The whole time I was sort of stuck between a rock and a hard place. I wanted to agree with them, because that was how I felt too, but I couldn't be disloyal to Ross in front of the team.

The atmosphere in the changing room after that loss at Galle was awful, and I picked up on a fair bit of animosity towards Ross. The team was finally imploding. I decided things had gone far enough and asked Ross to come into the dunnies out the back with me.

I said to him, 'This is your effin' team, mate. You need to grab it by the scruff of the neck and I will help you along the way, otherwise we're going to lose our way completely.'

Ross was standing leaning against the window. He had this expression on his face, again difficult to read. Again, he said nothing. I was unaware of what, if anything, had happened behind the scenes at that point and was genuine about trying to reach out and motivate him, because it was obvious to everyone that the shit was coming to a head, that it was about to blow.

To me it was one last try: we both knew that I'd be next in line. From my point of view, I wanted a clear conscience — I'd offer him my support if he was prepared to step up, but if he didn't, or couldn't, it wasn't on my head.

Later, it transpired that the horse had already bolted.

Ross had apparently been told four days before the beginning of the test in Galle by Mike Hesson, Mike Sandle and assistant coach Bob Carter that as soon as we were home they were going to recommend to New Zealand Cricket that he be relieved of the captaincy. There's some debate as to exactly what was said, whether Ross was going to be sacked as captain in all forms of the game, or just from T20 and ODIs, but whatever the case, Ross understood he was going to be sacked from everything.

There's also been conjecture about when I was told, whether I'd been told by Hesson that Ross was a goner. Hess is way too smart to have told me first. When I talked to Ross in the dunnies at Galle, I knew nothing and was acting in good faith.

I wish we had been told what was going on before that first test. It would have broken the tension, the compression, the sense that something had to give. All that angst, trying to work it off by running back to the hotel after a full day in the field in the Sri Lankan heat. I guess I can understand why we weren't told: Ross would have been in an untenable position, a lame duck captain. And, of course, whatever decision had been made by Hess and whoever else in Sri Lanka would have to be ratified by NZC. But if we'd known, there would have been a sense of relief for everyone. But on we stumbled to the second test.

Not surprisingly, in hindsight, Ross became even more withdrawn. We suspected that something had changed, but weren't sure what. Martin Guptill might have been told by Ross: they were very tight, sharing an agent (Leanne McGoldrick) and mentor (Martin Crowe), and it would have been strange if Ross hadn't talked to them about such a dramatic turn of events.

The rest of us might have still been labouring along in the blind, feeling the incredible tension and not knowing what exactly was going on, but for Ross maybe there was an element of relief as well as the disappointment. The pressure was off him as captain. He could just concentrate on his batting and that certainly worked. In a Man of the Match performance, he and Kane scored big tons to set up our first innings total of 412, then Tim Southee and Trent Boult took nine wickets between them, skittling the Sri Lankans for 244. Ross then held our second innings together with 74, and Tim and Trent did the job again for one of our best wins.

Another fluke, like Hobart? Or an indication of what we might be capable of on a regular basis if we could deliver on our potential? Who knew.

And so we flew home.

I ended up sitting next to Hess on the plane, and he talked to me about moving forward with the New Zealand team and about how we needed to make changes here and there and to the style of play. He told me that he'd had a conversation with Ross about the captaincy, but that decision would have to be made by the Board of New Zealand Cricket. He then asked me, if the Board ratified the decision to replace Ross as captain, and it offered the captaincy to me, would I be interested?

I told him I would have to think about it, I would have to speak to Lis, and to others around me, like Garth and Flem. When I spoke to Flem about it, he said, 'Why would you do it? Don't do it. You don't need it.'

Subsequently, there was a lot of debate about who'd said what to whom at which meeting over there, whether Hesson had told Ross before Galle that he was recommending Ross was to be relieved of the captaincy for all forms of the game, or just for ODIs and T20s. Some have speculated that Hess then had a change of heart after Ross's match-winning performance at Colombo and changed his recommendation so that Ross could stay as test captain.

I have no idea, I wasn't at the meetings, nor was I privy to anything that was said in them. Had I been asked, my take on it would have been that if you are going to make a move like that — ditching the captain — go for broke, make a definitive move.

What I do know is that on my old man's birthday, 6 December, David White rang me and offered me the One Day and T20 captaincy.

I said, 'Okay, I'll get back to you.'

So I put the phone down, and Lis and I talked about it.

Later that day, Whitey advised me that Ross had turned down the test role, so New Zealand Cricket were now offering me the test captaincy too.

I looked at Lis and said, 'What do you think?'

It was 18 months since I'd tried to reset my goals with Flem, and I was now on the wrong side of 30. I'd spent a lot of that 18 months on the road, and much of the journey had been stressful and unsatisfying, watching the team I loved gradually implode. It would have been easier to say no and walk away, but when I sat down and discussed it with Lis, I found I still had that desire to do something special before I gave it away.

And that's what it came down to: take the job or retire. I was carrying too much baggage now to hang around if someone else was captaining the side. Ross was always going to carry on, and the new captain could do without having me there too.

So it was decided: one last shot.

On 7 December 2012, NZC announced that I had been appointed New Zealand's captain in all three formats after Ross Taylor declined an offer to stay on as leader of the test side.

It was done.

I felt sorry for Ross, particularly for the way it had played out since the public selection process back in June 2011.

I felt I'd supported him to the best of my abilities, but he simply wasn't ready. I hadn't been ready to become captain back then either, but observing Ross in action for that 18 months, watching it all unravel at close quarters, had made me ready: I had a much clearer vision of what the role required.

Looking back now, I might have been ready for the captaincy, but there was no way I could have prepared myself for some of the collateral that came with it.

8
The Invisible Tablecloth

> McCullum had Taylor's blood on his hands and at stumps on day one against South Africa, he had blood all over him.
>
> — Jarrod Kimber, ESPN Cricinfo

Less than a month after I'd been appointed captain, we were in Cape Town, in January 2013, about to play South Africa.

Before the beginning of a test series we always have a captain's meeting and a cap presentation — you hand your cap back after each test and you get re-presented with it the night before the next match. Ken Rutherford was the guest and he spoke to us about what the cap meant to him and about playing in South Africa. Then the captain speaks. It's an opportunity to lay down a template about how we're going to play.

I spoke about us being a small nation, but dynamic, that we had our challenges but we could overcome them by being strategically smart and by getting total buy-in from the group. If we did that, we could give ourselves every chance against the bigger nations. I talked a bit about the specific strategy we were going to employ, then acknowledged that there was probably a lot of anxiety and apprehension within the group about how big a task we had in front of us — and I was talking for myself as much as anyone else in the room — but if any of us were in any doubt as to what to do over the course of the next five days, to always take a step forward, never a step back.

With that in mind, I'd decided to open the batting when Peter Fulton got injured in the warm-up game. I was supposed to bat at number four because Ross had opted out of the tour, but in line with my philosophy of making a strong statement, I said I'd step up and open.

Next morning, I got up and did my research on what choice I should make if we won the toss. What the stats from past games were telling me, what the weather and pitch looked like.

It was a cracking day, but the wicket at Newlands looked a little green. I'd read about 'the tablecloth on Table Mountain'. If there was no tablecloth — no cloud cover — you bat all day, but if there is a tablecloth, put them in. I stared at the mountain looming over the city and saw not even a hint of cloud. So when I went out onto the pitch to toss the coin with Graeme Smith, I'd decided that if we won the toss, I'd take the aggressive option and bat. Make a strong statement.

I won the toss. We batted. And were bowled out by lunch for 45 runs. My first innings as captain.

It wasn't much consolation that 45 wasn't a record low score for New Zealand. We'd made 26 back in 1955, and 42 in 1946. Those scores were separated on the stats table by four scores in the thirties by South Africa. But not this day. By stumps they were 200 for not many.

I sat in the changing room at the end of that day and thought, 'What do I do?'

We didn't muck around there too long, because we didn't want to over-analyse it.

When we got back to the hotel, I went for a run with Bob Carter and we talked about what had gone wrong during the day. We agreed that shit can happen sometimes, that even if you take the right options, it sometimes doesn't work out, and however we analyse it, we had some bloody hard work in front of us trying to retrieve the situation we were in.

I went back up to my room and had a shower and then I heard a knock on the door. It was Mike Hesson. He grabbed a beer out of the fridge, sat down and started talking. Five minutes later another knock on the door. Bob Carter. Five minutes later another knock on the door. Mike Sandle.

There was nothing scheduled about that meeting, but it was perfect timing. The four of us sat there with a beer in our hands, and we asked some questions of ourselves. What do we do? Where to from here?

Before we could answer those questions, there were some others. Where are we as a team? What are our performance levels? How are we viewed? How do we want to see this team viewed and where do we want to see our performance levels?

The first thing we agreed was our team had no soul. People didn't know what to expect when they turned up to watch us play, they had no idea how we were going to play. And that when we lose, we lose bad.

There was no whiteboard or discussion about how we were going to move this team forward. It was more just 'What do you reckon, Bob?' Everyone just threw it in there:

'Jesus Christ, why do we always carry on?'

'Why are we so soft when we lose a couple of early ones?'

'It seems like we lose a couple and then next thing we're fielding.'

'We'll win three sessions in a row, we'll have them on the ropes and then we'll lose one session, but we'll lose it so badly that we lose the game.'

'How come we've always got arrogant people in the group? We've always got prima donnas within our set-up. Why can't we just have those good hard bastards that New Zealand is founded on? Those number eight wire-type humble Kiwis?' and so on.

We looked at the environment the players were coming into. It had changed a little from what it used to be, where some of the senior players acted like wankers, egotistical and unwelcoming, like some kind of boarding school hierarchy where the seventh formers lorded it over the third formers, bagging them whenever they felt like it. Some of that had flowed on into the current team, even though the worst culprits had moved on. The environment still wasn't what it should be, particularly for young impressionable players coming in. Some of the older guys were great, and others were basically good guys but they were strutting around as though they were world beaters, yet we had done nothing.

Except, we all agreed, lose touch with our fellow New Zealanders.

That was the key to what we discussed: how could we build a soul which reflected who we were as a group of men, and as Kiwis, a soul which flowed from us and was authentic and true for us?

We talked about the different elements of that soul. We had to release the shackles of worrying about winning and losing and instead enjoy playing with our mates and having a crack on the field in our own way. If we did that, we'd have a better chance of winning anyway, we reckoned. We'd never be the All Blacks, but maybe that was an advantage because the expectations on us weren't the same. Win or lose, we had to enjoy being out there.

Part of that was getting rid of the sledging, not because of any highfalutin moral stance, but because it just didn't sit comfortably with us. Instead of sledging the opposition, it'd sit more comfortably with us as Kiwis if we actually dropped our guard with our opponents, got to know them a bit, shared some time with them, learnt about them, respected them.

It wasn't about projecting an image of being nice guys, or being righteous, it was about trying to be authentic about how we acted around the game, how we played the game and carried ourselves. We had these guys coming into the Black Caps at 20, just like I did, and perhaps spending 10 years or more of their lives in that environment, like I was doing, and it was really important that we all got the maximum satisfaction from that time together and were able to mature as people together in the right way, rather than waste so much time, like I did, trying to be something we aren't.

These were the kinds of things that we bounced around that night. And we didn't definitively write down *This is what we need to do to move forward*, but we kind of knew after that meeting that it was going to be hard for the next wee while, but we now had an idea of how we wanted the team to be viewed and how we wanted to play the game.

Which meant that now we had to have a hard look at the personnel we needed to play that way.

First, we had the rest of that test to get through. We lost by lots, but at least our second innings went somewhat better than the first. I got a 50 and Dean Brownlie scored a really good 100, which gave us 275 and a little bit of credibility.

Counteracting that was the sight of one of our senior players backing away to leg when their fast bowlers let go. If we were embarrassed by the scoreline, the sight of one of my good mates, Jeetan Patel, being so obviously intimidated by their quicks was even worse. He wasn't alone in looking a bit shy of the pacemen. We were a laughing stock: we looked scared.

Okay, they were bowling fast, genuinely quick and intimidating. But if you're going to play this game and you're going to represent New Zealand you have to stand there and fight it. What happened in that test was really damaging back home and with everyone who saw it.

We resolved that we wanted to be seen by New Zealand as not taking a backwards step, not running away from the challenge but stepping forward to meet it. We had to have that attitude, and then if we happen to lose, we lose, so be it.

In the days leading up to the next test, we discussed this and the players were told to man up. It wasn't expressed in those terms exactly, more that if you want to play for New Zealand, you have to show a bit of courage in these situations, regardless of how scared you are. Everyone is fearful facing genuine fast bowling, but you've got to be able to deal with it.

For all the talk, much the same thing happened in the second test — in fact we lost by more, an innings and 193 runs. Amla, du Plessis and Elgar all made centuries in their first innings of 528 for eight declared, and then we capitulated for 121 and 211, with BJ Watling making 63 in both innings, supported by a half century by Dean Brownlie in the second.

It was pretty obvious that we were missing Ross, our premier batsman, whose absence also fuelled the fires of the conspiracy theorists back home. It would have been great if Ross had been able to come out and say, 'Look, I lost my job but I'm committed to scoring runs and performing for New Zealand and being a part of this team.'

But the people surrounding him at that time were never going to let him do that. Martin Crowe told the media he'd burnt his New Zealand blazer because of his disgust at the way Ross had been treated.

If Ross had had different people around him he might have been able to get a bit more perspective on what happened. He wasn't the first captain to lose his position due to the team performance and he won't be the last. If you looked at it objectively, his decision not to come on the South African tour was quite bizarre, and really only explicable in terms of people fuelling his emotions behind the scenes. If anything, that probably made him feel worse, more hard done by. But the brutal truth is that no one is New Zealand captain as of right: you either do your job or you get dropped.

After the results on that South African tour, I was only too aware of that, and was grateful to have Ross back in the fold for the England tour of New Zealand in March. Looking back, that South African experience was a real turning point. After that, we thought, bugger it, if we're going to do this, let's do it properly, no pussy-footing around.

Changes were made before we took on the Poms. Jeetan was the obvious casualty, for Bruce Martin, which was a shame because in every other respect Jeets was a great team man. He just couldn't overcome that fear.

Peter Fulton came back from injury to open, with debutant Hamish Rutherford, who had scored a lot of runs in domestic cricket and gave us a right/left opening combination. Guppy simply hadn't scored enough test runs, and Ross came back for Daniel Flynn. Flynn was a great team man and hard as nails, but was a victim of being constantly shifted up and down the order. We decided to go with six batsmen — me at six — and the keeper at seven, so all-rounder James Franklin was another casualty.

We were always going to go better at home in familiar conditions, where the guys have their support networks around them. Even given that, the results during that series were encouraging.

We bowled England for 167 in the first innings at Dunedin, with Bruce Martin taking four wickets in his debut, supported by Neil Wagner. Then we amassed 460 in our turn to bat, with Hamish scoring a huge ton on his debut, with good support from the top and middle order — a half century from Peter Fulton and my own 74. We couldn't quite crack them in the second innings, with openers Cook and Compton both getting centuries, and Trott and nightwatchman

Steve Finn sticking around for fifties.

It was an honourable draw, where we really gave it a crack, even though we'd lost a day to rain. Afterwards I was proud of the way our bowlers had stuck to the task, particularly Neil Wagner who bowled 43 overs in their second innings and took another three wickets to go with four from the first.

The big thing I took away from that test was our ability to give it everything and keep fighting, so that we were a red-hot crack right up until the last few overs, where we had them six down and just needed another wicket or two to get into their tail.

A different sort of tail did us in the second test in Wellington — the tail end of Cyclone Sandra, which washed out the last day. This time England might have felt more frustrated, as they enforced the follow-on with a big first innings lead, but couldn't crack us second time around when Kane and Ross dug in. Which left everything to play for in the final test at Auckland.

In our first innings Peter Fulton got a big ton, supported by a 90-odd from Kane, and we got out to 443 then bowled them for 204, with Trent Boult (6/68) and Tim Southee (3/44) showing they were coming of age as a genuinely world-class fast bowling duo. We were able to declare at 241 for six in our second innings, with Peter Fulton getting another ton and 69 from me, and were 480 runs ahead, and in a position to apply the foot to England's throat in their second innings.

On the last day, I had to leave the field after straining a hammie chasing the ball to the boundary in the first session, and was limping for the rest of the day. I've been criticised for chasing so hard, but it's part of the statement we need to make about our commitment: if I won't give it 100 per cent, how can I expect anyone else to?

We had them seven down with four overs to go and needed a breakthrough fast. I threw the dice and gave Kane the ball. He got Stuart Broad with his third ball. Broad had stuck around for 77 balls, so that was a big wicket. Then Kane got Jimmy Anderson with his fifth ball, also caught at first slip. Nine down, one wicket to get in three overs.

Monty Panesar came out and got an inside edge past the stumps. We put England under severe pressure, but Monty held on. At the other end, Matt Prior really saved the day for them, with a fine ton, but, again, he was so lucky. When he was only on 20, the ball lobbed from his gloves right onto the stumps, but somehow the bails stayed on.

Again, as in Dunedin, I was stoked with the team effort. We tried to the last ball, really attacked them. At one stage we had nine men around the batsman. We may not have quite got there in the end, but there was a picture from that test that I'd never seen before in a New Zealand team, and that I — and no doubt every cricket lover in New Zealand — wanted to see again: the opposition nine wickets down and desperately hanging on against a New Zealand team that was throwing the kitchen sink at them.

The first part of the performance equation seemed to be in place: we'd at least become more difficult to beat.

Ross's return had helped. He'd not scored many runs, but had held on with Kane in Wellington to force the draw, and had added class and stability to our middle order. I was relieved to see him back, but can't pretend there weren't problems reintegrating him into the team after what had gone on.

That was a delicate process, because he clearly didn't trust me or Hess. We tried to acknowledge that and make concessions, without being seen to be pandering to him. Mike Hesson probably struggled with that more than me: where to draw the line on how much rope Ross was allowed.

Everyone else would chase the ball to the boundary as hard as they possibly could; Ross would jog after it. Everyone would clap and support one another when there was a wicket; Ross would stand like a statue in slips with his arms crossed. But the crowd, to begin with, would cheer every time Ross touched the ball. There are team photos from that time, in the changing room after the game. Everyone else has got their whites and their black cap on and Ross has taken his off, and he's fully changed with a baseball cap on.

I felt at the time there wasn't a lot I could do about any of that, except push on and try to make him feel as comfortable as possible in the environment.

I think Ross at that time was trying hard to overcome the advice he'd been given by his hard-core backers. I understood he was getting help from Gilbert Enoka, whom I had worked with too, and trusted. So I tried to go with that, bent over backwards to make him feel part of everything, but I can't deny there was an element in me that wanted to ask him, 'What makes you so special?' and say to him, 'Come on mate, just get on with it f' chrissake.'

But I never did. Instead, I tried to take comfort from the fact that the mass of the group was heading in the right direction.

We still had some growing up to do, but we were starting to move on from the era which had dominated New Zealand cricket's attitude for a long period of time — and I'm including myself here — the constant sledging and bat throwing, ripping out changing rooms, half-arsed training, scruffily dressed, the general untidiness about how we went about things.

We'd asked ourselves how New Zealand expected us to act and behave and how the country wanted to see their team perform and play. I wanted us to be accessible and engaging and humble, so if they saw us down the street they felt they could have a yarn with us. And I wanted to see us treat each other and anyone in the team environment with that same generosity of spirit. All that, coupled with a determination not to be easy beats: if we were going to be beaten, it wouldn't come easily. We knew we couldn't win every game, but we wanted to make it a lot tougher for opposition teams to win.

That drawn home series against England, the number one-ranked test nation in the world at the time, was a big step forward for me, for Mike Hesson and for the team. That last session at Eden Park, when we had nine men around the bat, made a big impression. We still hadn't shown enough to have the public or the media 100 per cent behind us, and we accepted that as a work in progress, like the team itself.

What wasn't acceptable were the vicious personal attacks coming from an unlikely source.

9
Hardly Cricket

> Despite a formidable record as a wicketkeeper-batsman across all formats, McCullum has often been branded a pretender who talked more than he walked. His failures or frankness were kindling for talkback-radio bonfires. Hosts threw in a lit match and stood well back. The shredding of his reputation sometimes morphed into its own sport, despite longevity. He has played a New Zealand-record 87 consecutive Tests and the fourth-most ODIs.
>
> — Andrew Alderson, ESPN Cricinfo

The English say April is the cruellest month, and anyone who's tried, like me, to play county cricket in an English spring will understand why. Since 2008, though, April has meant India for me, the IPL. So shortly after that dramatic finish to the test against England at Eden Park, I left for India and the Kolkata Knight Riders. Any satisfaction I took away about how the Black Caps had progressed through that test series didn't last long.

I guess you have to forgive a bit of journalistic hyperbole: they have to make a living too. Even the journalists acknowledge that I've copped my share of criticism, as the quote above demonstrates. So when I read quotes about, for instance, having Ross Taylor's blood on my hands, it might piss me off, but they're reporting a perception and there's not a lot I can do except shrug and move on.

But that April of 2013 in India, I realised that there were others smelling that same blood, and these guys weren't journalists trying to hype a story to sell some copy — although the group allegedly included some journos — but a nebulous group of high-profile New

Zealand cricket 'supporters' who attacked me personally while trying to take the moral high ground.

John Parker, a former test cricketer for New Zealand and, for one test, interim captain of the Black Caps, published a document called 'The Taylor Affair'. By published, I mean that he sent it to media outlets and then did an interview about it on Radio Sport.

In the introduction to the document he claimed to be speaking for many others:

'The following document has been contributed to by former Test captains, coaches, players, cricketing governance people and others who have been part of or close to the inner operations of the New Zealand Black Caps over the recent past.'

Parker's reason for not naming any of these people:

'They do not wish to be named as it is the facts that matter and an accurate history of what has happened, not the names of the people involved as there is a risk they would become the focus rather than the process.'

Journalists and media people such as Ian Smith, Mark Geenty and Bryan Waddle were among the names on an email list of supposed supporters, along with big names in New Zealand cricket, such as Jeremy Coney, Glenn Turner, and my old sparring partners John Wright and Mark Greatbatch.

One advantage of being in Kolkata when this broke was that I was able to confront John Wright about his involvement with Parker. He denied being part of it, said that he'd just been sent emails. Bryan Waddle said much the same thing to me in England later — promised me that he wasn't part of it, didn't agree with any of it, and had been very supportive of me throughout. I also asked Ross whether he knew Parker. Ross said he may have met him once in passing in a hotel lobby. All of which made me wonder where Parker got his material from, because that was a pretty consistent response.

When 'The Taylor Affair' broke cover, most of the 20 names supplied by Parker headed for the hills. The *New Zealand Herald* tried to contact every one of the names on Parker's email list and reported that 'almost to a person they either did not return calls, did not want to be named, claimed to be part of the email chain but didn't have input into the report, or had unsuccessfully requested to be removed from future correspondence'.

Whether or not they'd asked for it, they'd all had access to an email put together by Parker which detailed all my business interests, listed all the directors, in an attempt to highlight a conflict of interest between me and New Zealand Cricket.

Mark Greatbatch and Ian Smith were the only ones who publicly admitted an association with or sympathy for the published document, and John Parker was the only one who admitted authorship, so he was the one who had to take responsibility for the statements made there.

That introduction was followed by 77 points or clauses, which often sprouted sub-clauses, much of it in mangled bush-lawyer legalese.

Clause 1, with three sub-clauses, took almost the length of the first page to say that Mike Hesson had little credibility as a coach. Being identified as a high achiever by the New Zealand Academy coaching system counted for nought in terms of coaching credibility, apparently, nor did the fact that he had coached Otago and Kenya, because he never reached first-class level as a player.

That kind of logic circuit-breaker is spread throughout the document, but no matter how illogical most of the document was, I was aware that it tapped into a view that had some credence with people who had supported Ross, people like Martin Crowe who said that he'd burned his New Zealand blazer when Ross was deposed. It gave public currency to the view that I had been part of a conspiracy, through personal links to Stephen Fleming and Mike Hesson particularly, to undermine Ross's captaincy.

According to Parker, from the moment Hesson was appointed, by my 'Manager', Flem, Hesson's agenda was to get rid of Ross. I was in on this conspiracy from the start, as were 'the older players' in the team, which he named as my brother Nathan, Kyle Mills, Jake Oram and Dan Vettori.

You'd have thought that Parker might have used his many contacts at the top level for a bit of rigorous enquiry. Surely it wouldn't have been that difficult to find out that my recommendation to the coaching selection panel, which included Greatbatch, had been Matthew Mott, for whom I'd been a referee, not Mike Hesson.

You'd also have thought that Mark Greatbatch, who was one of the few who came out publicly in support of Parker, would have told Parker that when I applied unsuccessfully for the captaincy, I had told the panel, including Greatbatch, that I was holding no brief for any senior players who couldn't adapt to the different strategy I wanted to pursue.

You'd have thought that Parker would know that another of the so-called conspirators, Dan Vettori, had been instrumental in removing me as vice-captain back in 2009 and installing Ross to that position five weeks later.

It seems, though, that once you start seeing a conspiracy, all roads lead to the same flawed conclusion. By clause 10, the conspiracy extended to the players' union:

'10. This group of players is close to the NZCPA or the professional collective/union and just happen to be high up on the list of NZ Cricket's contracted players.'

Parker doesn't mention that the highest-ranked player, number one, was none other than Ross Taylor.

By clause 11, Parker has really hit his stride:

> *11. This group of players are all ageing and not performing as they perhaps once did. Oram is well past his used by date, McCullum is mostly injured and appears to want to play on his terms, at least while Taylor is Captain. Nathan McCullum is Brendon's brother and Vettori is eternally injured after a wonderful playing career.*

In among the in-depth research indicating I was related to Nathan, there was stuff that looked like schoolboy insults, and which were just as credible for anyone who checked. It's peculiar, for instance, that I can be 'mostly injured' while also holding the record for the most consecutive tests from debut for any nation, a record that some experts predict will never be beaten. John Wright could also have confirmed that I only missed the first three ODIs on the Windies tour of 2012 because he, the coach, insisted I take a break. Previous to that, the only games I'd missed were for the births of my children.

Parker's piece goes on to allege a power struggle between Ross and Hesson which pre-dated the Sri Lankan tour, a power struggle that put Ross and the younger players on one side of a divide and Hesson and me and the older players on the other.

I've no idea where Parker was dredging his information from, but you'd have to think that if he'd actually shown this material to all the people, such as Greatbatch and John Wright, whom he said shared his views, they would have been able to correct at least some of it, particularly my views on the need for change in respect to some of the senior players.

Pages follow of mostly speculative stuff about who said what to whom and when, over Ross's sacking, and whether he was sacked as captain for all forms of the game or just T20s and ODIs, and whether a review was carried out and by whom and who was spoken to and when, and who was lying to whom. All perhaps of some interest to cricket administration train spotters, but not to me: I wasn't in the rooms, and I've no idea what did or didn't transpire.

But in among it was a clause which was of consequence to me:

'23. McCullum knew all along of Hesson's movements according to certain players.'

None of the 'certain players' were named, and none came forward, but it was a clear allegation that I knew of and was involved in the decision to replace Ross as captain. Apparently, not only did I know in advance of his being sacked, but I lied to the New Zealand public that I hadn't known:

'76. McCullum came out in the media the week of 21st of January [2013] saying he knew nothing of Hesson's plan to make him captain.'

By 21 January 2013, of course, I'd been captain of the Black Caps for over a month. The period Parker was referring to was before Ross was sacked. That had happened, apparently, just before the test in Galle, back in Sri Lanka in mid-October 2012. Parker was saying I had known in advance that was going to happen, and had lied about not knowing.

These are just the worst allegations in a theme of my dishonesty and pursuit of self-interest which permeated the document, and which supported the general tenor of the piece that I had connived with Fleming and Hesson to get rid of Ross:

> 52. *Therefore there appears no clear performance logic to this change of leadership, unless it is driven from one or more of three places*
> a. *Hesson's closeness to the McCullums and Fleming*
> b. *The NZC Board who only approximately 18 months ago supported Taylor*
> c. *The senior group of players who understand that they have more chance of retaining their central contracts if McCullum is captain.*

Parker went on to make the case for more cricketers on the Board, rather than corporate business types:

> 59. *It highlights the issue of governance in sport and the supposed need for Corporate people as they know about making sport into business. If that is their need why are so many sports in financial trouble and in what state is their corporate world in?*

If nothing else, that clause is an argument for a basic literacy test for any former cricketers who want to be involved in governance!

Here's another doozy:

> 64. *The senior players appear to be unknowing of the position they have placed themselves in as if they play better for the new Captain have they not been trying for the former one therefore what sort of people have we been paying huge amounts of money? I fear the result is they are not skilled enough to be in charge of this possible conclusion.*

By the time I got to that one, I feared John Parker wasn't skilled enough — or well informed enough — to be in charge of his own possible conclusion, which he eventually got to, but which unfortunately was no better articulated:

> *Was Hesson acting with the Board's consent (or just White's) or was he just very naive and therefore should have been spoken to very firmly but apparently not, even though this has spiralled out of control we were told no heads will roll even before things were concluded!*

Parker's prose may have been spiralling out of control, but the essential allegations contained in this document were that I had prior knowledge of Ross's removal as captain, and also that I'd put my own interests ahead of those of the team.

On 4 April, John Parker went on Radio Sport and confirmed that the document had its 'facts as near to perfect as we can' and that it was 'as accurate as we can get', building on statements in the document itself that 'it is the facts that matter' and that it is 'an accurate history of what has happened'.

My lawyer and friend, Garth Gallaway, agreed that Parker's statements amounted to a serious attack on my honesty and integrity, not to mention my commitment to team ethos as a professional cricketer. Through him, Parker's lawyer was contacted and Parker was asked for an apology and retraction.

In response, Parker delayed and attempted to straddle the moral high ground, maintaining that the focus of 'The Taylor Affair' was on the governance of New Zealand Cricket, and that his references to the events surrounding Ross's removal as captain were simply made to highlight major issues at head office and a lack of cricket experience on the NZC Board. It was the radio host's fault for 'taking sentences in isolation' and 'comments out of context'.

I didn't buy that, and Parker seemed hard to locate, 'undertaking further travel', and having 'no access to a computer'.

After much agonising, Garth went public on the Friday, saying that if Parker refused to apologise, I would sue him. It created something of a storm but we had had enough and wanted Parker to know what was around the corner. It was a huge call to go public and commit us to this course, and Garth barely slept all weekend. Predictably, Mark Reason, in the *Sunday Star-Times*, described my threat to sue a former New Zealand player as a disgrace. It didn't seem to matter what nonsense Parker was peddling.

When he did surface from Outer Mongolia or wherever, Parker seemed ready to go to court, telling his supporters that 'backers were in place'. Two days later, 23 April, he capitulated, and signed a 'Resolution by John Parker and Brendon McCullum'.

They key parts of that for me were Parker's admission that I was not involved in the decision to remove Ross, nor was I dishonest with the New Zealand public when I said I'd not been involved in that decision, and that he'd not meant to discredit me in respect of his allegations that I'd put my own interests ahead of the team's. Parker sincerely apologised for any harm to my reputation which may have been caused.

New Zealand is such a small place, and New Zealand Cricket even tinier, that relationships and friendships and business links and other potential conflicts of interest are inevitable and even pervasive in the administration of the game. Where the conflicts of interest are overt, there are protocols in place to overcome the problem, but if everyone involved in NZC administration and selection panels over the years had to declare an interest and get out of the room every time a name they knew well was being discussed, or with whom they had some connection outside cricket, there'd be no one left in the room to make the decision.

As a result, there has to be a degree of good faith involved in administering the game, and a degree of goodwill from those outside the administration, an acceptance that people in positions of power are doing their best for the larger interests of the game, not pursuing personal agendas.

I didn't really speak to Mike Hesson about Parker, because I was in India, but he must have been going through hell. Everyone just assumed that Hess and I were great mates. Hess did me a favour when we came back from Australia and he and Kate put Lis and me up, and I've known Hess for a long time, but we are such different people. We get on well and we have great respect for each other, especially within the cricketing world — I admire his coaching ability and his understanding of the game and of people. I also think he's a really good guy, and I'm happy to have a game of golf with him and a beer and go out to dinner and suchlike. We aren't best mates, we don't live in each other's pockets, and we're not, as people like Parker would have it, as thick as thieves.

So I don't really know what Hess was going through, but I imagine he was frustrated and upset about what had unfolded, because it looked at the time as if it was the kind of stain that he may not ever have been able to overcome in his coaching career, no matter how well it went.

The irony was, that even as 'The Taylor Affair' was circulating around the cricketing traps, I think Hess and Ross were actually mediating to resolve their issues, and began to get on reasonably well. It was good to see Ross extending a bit of goodwill there and working to get over his hump — with Hess at least.

There'd been no such goodwill from John Parker and the people he said were supporting him in 'The Taylor Affair', and the whole damn thing had been draining on me and my friends and family, and, in the end, a wasteful diversion of time and energy. All I could do was accept his apology in good faith and try to move on — and trust that he would too.

Photosport

Congratulating Jesse Ryder on trapping Owais Shah in front during the first of our two Twenty20 internationals against England at Eden Park, February 2008. Jesse was on debut and I was leading New Zealand for the first time. At right is twelfth man Paul Hitchcock.

Photosport

Surreal innings for the Kolkata Knight Riders in the IPL opener in 2008. I finished 158 not out and was so buggered I couldn't keep wicket when the Royal Challengers came to bat.

Photosport

Photosport

We lost the second test against England at Old Trafford in 2008, but I was pretty happy with this catch to dismiss Monty Panesar.

Getty

A memorable test for me against Pakistan in Napier at the end of 2009. I picked up nine dismissals — a New Zealand record — including this catch off Tim Southee to get rid of Umar Akmal in the second innings. Ross Taylor looks pretty happy with the result.

Getty

Helmet raised after scoring a Twenty20 international century — the first by a New Zealander — against Australia at AMI Stadium in Christchurch in February 2010. Inset: Aussie quick Shaun Tait doesn't seem too impressed with my innings.

Moments from my double century in the second test against India in Hyderabad, November 2010.

Getty

Photosport

Getty

Getty

Facing the media after New Zealand was dismissed for 45 on the first day of the first test against South Africa at Newlands in January 2013. Not the way I'd hoped to begin my career as test captain.

10
Madness

> McCullum . . . had two scores in the twenties, one below that and, for nearly three years, he has been without a hundred in Tests. The last one came in November 2010 when he scored a double-hundred in India.
>
> — Mohammad Isam, ESPN Cricinfo

Several of the clauses in 'The Taylor Affair' highlighted my lack of success as a batsman and a captain since I'd taken over from Ross, in marked contrast to the man himself.

We'd won four tests out of 11 in the time Ross had been captain, and he'd batted very well, averaging, as Parker pointed out, eight runs per innings more than he'd scored before he was made captain. My captaincy record was not impressive: we'd won zero tests out of five, although my batting average in those five tests was a healthy 47 — well above my average prior to being appointed captain. But that was about to change for the worse.

While it was some relief to be out of New Zealand when 'The Taylor Affair' broke, there was no relief from the need to score runs. I was playing for the Kolkata Knight Riders and the low, slow, turning home wicket didn't suit my style at all, so I wasn't much more than steady at best.

I was looking forward to a big improvement as we embarked on the 2013 tour of England. Unfortunately, those damning stats were about to get even worse.

The England series that winter was hugely disappointing: the improvements in fight and savvy that we'd shown against the same team during the summer at home weren't sustained — in fact we went backwards.

The first test at Lord's was crushing. In a low-scoring match, we'd been level pegging at the end of the first innings, scoring 207 in reply to England's 232, thanks mainly to an assertive 66 from Ross. Tim Southee had taken four for 58, then did even better in their second innings, with six for 50, leaving us to make 239 for the win. We never looked like it, surrendering abjectly for 68 all out.

Another hour of madness, like those in Brisbane and Cape Town. We lost both openers inside seven overs, and in a matter of minutes, as one scribe put it, 'all the momentum gained during the drawn series at home seemed from the distant past, as New Zealand plunged into the same abyss as during the 45 all out in Cape Town last year'.

We'd competed well session by session through the match, until that extended hour. Sometimes I'd even felt that we were dictating terms. When we started the final innings we thought 230-odd would be achievable, but to do that we needed a decent start, and six down for 29 runs was just disastrous. I was the sixth wicket. I'd tried to be assertive, slapped the first ball to the point boundary, repeated the dose a few balls later, then walked down the wicket, missed it, and was given out leg before.

Once again, I tried to put a brave face on it, saying that we'd put distance between our last collapse and this one, but in fact Cape Town was still pretty fresh, and Brisbane, and the details of distress, the chaos of the dressing room during a collapse like that, with batsmen struggling to get their pads on in time for the next fall of wicket, isn't easily forgotten. And maybe each of those experiences leaves you more vulnerable to the next one. It's hard to keep that 'here we go again' voice out of your head when the wickets start falling in clumps.

I wanted us to become a calm batting unit, one that doesn't need to be hyped up, and one that doesn't easily panic. Given the mayhem out on the pitch, I thought we'd stayed reasonably cool and calm in the dressing room, but we weren't able to carry that out onto the field.

I wasn't as concerned by that collapse as some of the others, because there'd been a really unusual element that helped take us down, one that I hadn't really come across before. Lights. We actually got too many wickets too quickly on that last morning. Courtesy mainly of Tim, we took their last three or four wickets for next to no runs while it was still overcast and the lights were on, and the ball was seaming sideways. Which meant we had to go out and bat in the same conditions, and we were six down by lunch. After lunch, the cloud lifted, the lights weren't needed and the ball stopped seaming, but by then it was too late for us; the damage had been done.

Despite our best intentions, the second test at Headingley wasn't much better. I had to keep wicket because BJ Watling was injured. About 50 overs in, I blew my back out and was next to useless for the rest of the game. But we'd lost that game before we started by badly misreading the pitch. We played four seamers and no spinner and lost by over 200 runs after the English spinner, Graeme Swann, took 10 wickets. Our batting totals, 174 and 220, simply weren't enough to give our bowlers a chance, particularly with no spinner. And my contribution looked pretty sick: 31 runs in the series.

We did better in the ODIs, winning two out of three, with Marty Guptill winning Man of the Series and Ross batting well too — in contrast, again, with me. Apart from a 40 not out to support Marty's incredible 189 in the second match, my return at the crease was negligible.

That series served as a warm-up for the ICC Champions Trophy, hosted by England and Wales. We began promisingly, just getting home by one wicket against Sri Lanka in Cardiff. Then we got rained out against Australia at Edgbaston and got beaten by England when the match was reduced by the weather to 24 overs. That was a match we had to win to get into the semi-finals, so we left England with not a lot to show for our two months of cricket.

In two turns at bat during the Champions Trophy, I'd scored eight and 18, not the kind of statement I'd wanted to make to the critics back home, who, despite Parker's contrite apology, were still there, waiting for an opportunity. I'd wanted to turn the team around, come back home strong and successful, a leader who was performing well in a winning team. Instead, we'd stumbled, taken a step backwards.

We didn't have long to regroup. In October, we were off to Bangladesh, not the easiest place to tour.

In the first test at Chittagong, we batted first and tons from Kane and BJ took us to 469, but Bangladesh headed us on the first innings with 501 in reply. Our second innings of 287 was most notable for a hat-trick to spinner Sohag Gazi, not necessarily what you want it to be remembered for. He got me too, and fluked Kane when a full-blooded pull lodged in a close fielder's thigh. The test meandered to a draw on Day 5.

The second test was also drawn. After Neil Wagner took five for 64, Corey Anderson got his maiden ton, supported by Kane and Ross, to give us a 155-run first innings lead. We had them three for 269 at the end of Day 4, only 114 ahead. We had seven wickets to get but will never know if we might have been in with a chance because Day 5 was washed out completely.

So, both tests drawn, tests we were expected to win. I tried to concentrate on the positives. Our bowlers had done really well in conditions they weren't used to. Neil Wagner, on his first trip to the subcontinent, had taken seven wickets, and we finally seemed to have a leg-spinner with bounce and turn and control in Ish Sodhi, who ended up with six wickets in the series at an average of 44.16.

Our batting line-up, with two exceptions, had also done well in both tests, putting up 400-plus totals, and there'd been no dramatic collapses — we'd lost wickets in the second innings at Chittagong because we tried to force the pace and get a result. The two exceptions to the batting successes were Hamish Rutherford and one Brendon McCullum.

I'd got into the twenties twice. That was it. My last ton, the double century in India, was nearly three years ago, November 2010, as I was being constantly reminded as my run drought continued. As much as I delighted in the performances of the other guys, particularly Kane, who was really delivering on his potential, I wished I was contributing more, and hoping that runs might come in the three ODIs that followed.

Some hope. My scores were 0 and 14 in the first two ODIs. With the series lost, I came home early, missing the final match and the short tour of Sri Lanka that followed.

My departure was variously reported:

'McCullum was understood to have exited fraught with exhaustion.'

And: 'Brendon McCullum, the New Zealand captain, is returning home immediately after being ruled out of the final two matches of the Bangladesh tour with "significant" pain from a long-standing back problem.'

Also: 'Following an MRI scan in Dhaka, Paul Close, the New Zealand physio, said: "Brendon's back needs careful management — it's flared up and is giving him significant pain. The best course of action is getting him home for rehabilitation as soon as possible."'

There was an element of truth in all of it. My back was a day-to-day proposition and, one way or another, I was pretty depleted and deflated. But the real reason for returning home was that Ross and I had been given dispensation to miss Sri Lanka, so that we could prepare for the home summer, with test series against the West Indies and India in prospect.

Coming home was a blessing, because I desperately needed to recharge and find a way to score some runs. It had been a year since Ross's last test in charge, the win in Colombo against Sri Lanka. In that year, under my captaincy, we'd played nine tests and won none. The three draws against England at home had merit, but around them, against South Africa and England away, we'd been humiliated. My personal stats were abysmal. I knew that if I couldn't turn both around quickly, I'd be next for the chop — both in terms of the captaincy and holding my place in the batting line-up. And deservedly so.

11
Home and Heart

> McCullum has Roman numerals stencilled on his right shoulder and bicep that refer, among other things, to his playing number (42) and the birthdates of his children. It's a public display of the importance of family and one of the strong themes that emerge when talking to people who know him well.
>
> — Michael Brown, *New Zealand Herald*

Ellissa and I met on my first tour with the Black Caps, to Australia on 8 February 2002. I was twelfth man in a Tri Series ODI game at the SCG, between New Zealand and South Africa. The changing rooms were in the members' stand, and as I went back and forth doing my duties, I couldn't help noticing a certain blonde with a lovely smile sitting a couple of rows back.

Lis says our getting together was Fate, and maybe it was, but Fate was certainly helped by the number of times I ran back and forth in front of her on all sorts of errands, some of which weren't strictly necessary. I think I waved to her and at the end of the game, with a bit of Dutch courage on board, she did something she would never normally do, came over and said hello. Fate.

She had a business degree and was working in the head office of Westfield Shopping Centres doing insurance, and had come to the game with a group of insurance brokers. Two days later, I left for home with the team, we kept in touch, and a month later she came to New Zealand for a couple of weeks, her first visit to this country.

I'd been talking myself up a bit, as you do at 20, but the reality was I was flatting in South Dunedin with a couple of mates and it wasn't terribly salubrious, in fact not much of a step up from the flat in North East Valley where I'd done my OE. I'd also been talking up my first car, a 1975 Falcon ute. I was so proud of it. On our first date, we made it round the corner from the flat, all of about 70 metres, before the Falcon gave up the ghost. It had cost me $3000 and was going to cost $2000 to fix, so that wasn't going to happen: I had to borrow a car for the rest of Lis's holiday.

In that couple of weeks, we went to two weddings and the New Zealand Cricket Awards, so it was a fairly concentrated introduction to my circle. That I would invite her to those sorts of occasions as a new girlfriend said a lot about how quickly we got close.

It was while Lis was there that I got a call one morning from Sir Richard Hadlee to tell me I was dropped from the Black Caps ODI squad. It wasn't entirely unexpected: I'd had the problem with my knee that season, couldn't keep wicket, and couldn't justify my selection as a specialist batsman.

That was April. Lis went back to Sydney, and at the end of May I decided to go and stay with her for six weeks. That became six months: I had no reason to go home and plenty of reason to stay. I don't think I've ever thanked Sir Richard for that!

Lis was from Lismore, inland from Byron Bay, where she'd watched a lot of cricket with her father and brother. She'd been to university there and then left for Sydney as soon as she graduated. Luckily for me, she'd not been in Sydney long enough to make a lot of friends before I appeared on the scene.

There were other attractions to keep me in Sydney.

Steve Rixon, who had previously coached New Zealand, was now coaching New South Wales. He took me under his wing so that I could train with him every day. Steve had kept wicket for Australia and, as my knee got stronger, he was the one who really taught me how to keep. My training partner was the NSW keeper, Brad Haddin.

Brad and I worked together every day, virtually, and got on really well. He was a bit brasher than me, more secure in his keeping, or maybe that was just a product of being part of Aussie cricketing culture. It was interesting years later watching him become the ugly

Australian on the field — I thought it was all piss and wind, but some people bit, and the harder they bit, the more he'd get his back up and go harder himself. I found that if you just laughed it off, he was likely to join in and relax a bit.

When we'd finished our individual skills sessions, Steve encouraged me to go and train with the NSW guys. So I would bat in the nets while guys such as Glenn McGrath and Brett Lee and his brother Shane, and Steve Waugh and Mark Waugh, Stuart McGill and Michael Slater were warming up. I wouldn't say I knew them, but I was around them, watching them train, trying to learn how they went about things.

These guys were the best of the best at the time and they knew it. They had a bit of swagger about them, an aura, a bit like the one around the All Blacks. I watched how they carried themselves, their confidence and their arrogance, and thought that was the way to do it.

From then on, for the next few years, I tried to carry myself like one of them, tried to play like an Australian. I developed a bit of swagger when I went out to bat, put on a show of being confident and hard-minded, and when it didn't work, I'd throw my bat around to show how much I cared about losing my wicket.

The culmination of that attitude came in 2006 at Lancaster Park when I ran out Muttiah Muralitharan. Sri Lanka were nine down in their second innings when Kumar Sangakkara got to a magnificent 100. The ball was still in the air, being returned to me as wicketkeeper when Muttiah left his ground to congratulate Kumar. When the ball hit my gloves, I whipped off the bails and appealed. Muttiah was given out and we went on to win the match.

Not surprisingly, the incident created controversy and bad feelings. The Sri Lankans were stunned. Their captain Mahela Jayawardene said at the time: 'Legally it was a run out, the ball was alive but we play in an age where we talk about the spirit of the game. Hopefully it won't happen again. It's not the way to play cricket.' Flem, as my skipper, tried to defend me, but Mahela was right. That was a mistake, which I now regret.

I wasted a few years trying to be brash and arrogant and hard-minded. It was a false attitude, not true to my character, and I wish I'd seen the light earlier about how to play and enjoy cricket by being true not just to the game's essence but also to my own.

The good thing about being around the NSW team was that I no longer saw them as gods. I also saw how hard they worked and watching them so closely helped me develop my skills and confidence.

Then I went up to Darwin for a little while, played cricket and shifted furniture — the perfect job for a shonky back! — but I saved up enough money to buy an engagement ring. This was August, just five months after that fateful encounter at the SCG. I hadn't even met Lis's family, but plucked up my courage and rang her father. My credentials weren't great, to be honest — 'Hi, Mr Arthur, I'm a recently dropped New Zealand cricketer with no money, no assets, and no immediately discernible future, d'you mind if I marry your daughter?' He turned out to be a man of few words but with a good sense of humour. 'Look after her, please,' he said.

I wanted to play for New Zealand again, so in October we sold Lis's furniture and stuff in Sydney, packed everything we had into three suitcases and moved back to Dunedin for Otago's pre-season, arriving just in time for the players' 'strike'.

We'd walked into a power struggle between New Zealand Cricket and the New Zealand Cricket Players Association, effectively the players' union. The Players Association wanted to review NZC's contracting system. The way the contracting was done was unfair to the bulk of the players — a few top players seemed to be profiting hugely from behind-the-scenes deals with New Zealand Cricket at the expense of all the others.

When I played that Tri Series for New Zealand, for instance, I'd get a match fee, and a bonus fee if we won the game, and then at the end of the tour or series each player would get a percentage bonus based on how he'd performed across all the matches. The rumour among the players was that this tour bonus was actually non-existent, in the sense that it had been allocated by NZC to a few of the star players before the tour even began. Certainly at the end of the Australian tour, I wasn't alone in getting a bonus of precisely zero.

The Players Association was intent on professionalising the game and making sure that the distribution of the available money among the players was based on merit, not on old-boy networks and favours done behind closed doors. This had become important because there was a lot of new money flooding into the game from the sale of broadcast rights and the commercial sponsorship of international teams and events, and an increasing number of people and commercial third parties were making a lot of money out of the sport or, as the Players Association put it, from the work of the players on the field.

There were more and more people in paid positions in cricket organisations — coaches, academy managers and administrators — who were telling players how committed they needed to be to get selected. These full-time employees knew they would be judged on their results, results which had to be achieved by part-time players who were having to fit training and playing cricket around actual paid work.

Heath Mills and Rob Nichol had signed up 128 players to the Players Association, including me, and, critically, the top six contracted Black Caps at that time, Stephen Fleming, Chris Cairns, Craig McMillan, Nathan Astle, and a couple of others. These guys were very much part of that privileged elite, but they were altruistic enough to appreciate the larger good that would come from the players being organised and having a collective say in their remuneration and working conditions.

I was committed to the union cause too, but the strike was hard on Lis and me. We had no money, and now neither of us had a job. We couldn't afford a flat, so we stayed with Mike Hesson and his wife, Kate. Mike was then Development Officer for Otago Cricket. At that stage they didn't have any children; they had us instead. They were extraordinarily kind to us. We had nothing and that's exactly what we paid them for food and board over the eight weeks we stayed with them, definitely outstaying our welcome. But there wasn't much we could do, as the strike dragged on.

New Zealand Cricket employed tactics which were straight out of the bosses' union-breaking textbook: play the lowest common denominator card to the public, stall negotiations, and while they're stalled, attempt to divide and conquer.

Technically it wasn't even a strike, because we weren't in an employment situation and weren't actually being paid, but *Strike!* was the word used by NZC as they went public with what were supposed to be confidential negotiations. 'Strike' and 'player power' were emotive words which got predictable responses from the public. The fledgling Players Association was quite often encouraged to eff off, and it was surprising how often some former players came out against the idea of players having representation. Glenn Turner, for instance, had actually sued New Zealand Cricket back in the day when his contract wasn't renewed. His bestie John Parker, Ervin McSweeney and others all bought into the evils of player power being peddled by NZC.

Other past players, such as David White — even though he had crossed over to the other side — were enormously supportive. White was at that stage Chief Executive for Auckland Rugby, but he'd played cricket for Northern Districts and a few games for the Black Caps. Dion Nash also played a major part in supporting Heath and Rob in their early endeavours.

Flem was the Black Caps captain at the time of the strike, and no doubt one of the star players who were best served by the skewed system, on something like $150,000 per annum, a huge amount in those times (only Cairns was on a higher salary). There was no IPL and bugger all other ways of augmenting your income, but he was resolute in standing up to New Zealand Cricket and trying to get a fair deal for all the players. He kept saying, 'I'm one of a hundred and twenty-eight.' I don't think NZC have ever forgotten that, or forgiven him.

These divisions and divides are rife in cricket in New Zealand, and they're mostly subterranean, out of the public gaze. But every so often, years later, you'll see someone stand up and offer a supposedly objective opinion on some issue of the day, which will actually be seeded back in these old battles. If you know the institutional history, it's often difficult to take these opinions at face value when they surface.

As part of New Zealand Cricket's divide-and-rule strategy, I got an offer from Otago Cricket — $1000 up front and then $1000 per game. The downside was that I would have to flip — desert the Players Association — to get the money. Given we had nothing, neither income nor assets, a grand seemed like a lot of money to us. But there was no way I was going to scab on my mates, so I turned it down, and on we went.

Other players got similar offers, as NZC tried to break the union by picking off prominent players. The big names got offered big money, and the support of those big names who were on interim contracts never wavered, at least until the end was in sight.

On Saturday, 9 November 2002, New Zealand Cricket made one last big effort to pick off the two most important players. They knew if they could flip Flem and Cairnsy, others would follow, so huge offers were made to both players by NZC. Flem turned the offer down.

On that Saturday, after the meeting between NZC and Flem and Cairns, the Players Association were advised that NZC had scheduled a press conference for Monday 11th. There was no agreement at that stage, nor much prospect of one, so there was a lot of speculation and anxiety by Heath and Rob and Players Association lawyer Andrew Scott-Howman about what exactly NZC was going to announce at that press conference in two days' time. Did they know something we didn't?

The negotiators pushed on regardless, and after an intense 36 hours, on the night of Sunday, 10 November, a Heads of Agreement between New Zealand Cricket and the Players Association was finally signed.

As part of that agreement, NZC tried to insist that Flem and Cairns both be present at the already scheduled press conference the next day. At first glance, this seemed like a face-saving attempt to imply that Flem and Cairns had helped broker the deal, to try to lessen the role of the Players Association. NZC's aim was to make it appear that they had sidelined Heath and Rob, and had resolved the matter through direct negotiation with the players.

Flem refused to take part in that press conference, repeating that it wasn't about him, he was just one of 128 players. Heath and the

Players Association Board and the senior players had a conference call on Sunday, where Cairns was specifically asked not to attend the press conference on Monday, but he ignored that request. His presence at the Monday press conference implied that he'd played a big part in brokering the agreement.

In any event, the 'strike' was over, and I was offered a Level 7 contract, which gave me a base income of something like $11,000 for the six-month season with Otago, augmented by match payments of around $500 for a one-dayer and $1000 for a four-dayer. And Lis and I were able to move out of the Hesson house, no doubt to their considerable relief, although they said nothing.

In retrospect, I reckon that a case can be made that the change in the Black Caps from the ego-driven culture that was a hangover from the 80s, to the team-first culture of today, was made possible by the platform established by Heath Mills and the Players Association. The lessons learned from putting egos and personal agendas to one side during that 'strike' back in 2002 informed a lot of the subsequent player-led improvements in New Zealand cricket, from equitable fees to the standard of practice and playing pitches, which lifted the domestic scene to a much higher level.

So Lis had her first summer in Dunedin. Someone once said that it wasn't the Dunedin winter that had driven them away, but the Dunedin summer. Lis was a bit shocked to be sitting inside in the middle of summer with a big jumper on in front of a heater while it poured down outside.

That wasn't the only reason we shifted to Christchurch the following season. The fact that I was a local son, born and bred in Dunedin, meant I was being taken for granted a bit. But the main thing was the opportunity to start a new life with Lis. In Dunedin I knew everyone, and who was related to who, and while it was great for me, it wasn't so great for Lis. We were getting married that September, so making a new home together in a new place seemed like the right thing to do.

It also helped my cricket. In Dunedin, I'd been the only Black

Cap, pretty much. In Christchurch I was surrounded by them, the famous names of New Zealand cricket, Chris Cairns, Nathan Astle, Craig McMillan, Shane Bond. It was great for my development to be training and playing with them, but there was also another benefit. When I got back into the New Zealand team and went away on tour, there were wives and girlfriends in Christchurch who were in the same boat as Lis.

To begin with, I was just part of the one-day team, so I wasn't away as much as some, but by 2004 I had made the test team and that meant long stretches away, at a time when Lis had our first baby, Riley. Luckily, the Bonds and McMillans and Astles all had babies at the same time — Lis and Tracey Bond were in the same antenatal class, and Tracey had a baby within two weeks of Riley — so there were several of us cricketing families going through separations of eight or nine weeks at a time.

New Zealand Cricket was reasonably accommodating to the idea of wives and families joining us on tour, but the problem was we had to pay for their flights and accommodation ourselves, and Lis and I just didn't have the money. It would have meant I was playing for nothing: our money would have been spent by the time the tour was over.

That wasn't the only reason it wasn't a good time for us. I was still very young and once I was away, I behaved like one of the boys, not like a married man with a child, a child I hardly ever saw. I thought I could have my cake and eat it, and I sometimes behaved like a prat while I was away. It was all a big jump from South Dunedin, and I got the speed wobbles.

Rampant egos plus testosterone plus booze plus bulletproof attitudes are a volatile mixture when you're a long way from home. There was a lot of clubbing and all the stupidity that went with it — the worst of it an incident outside the Tiger Tiger nightclub in Durban at the World Cup in 2003, where Cairnsy got king hit by this big bugger. Cairnsy went down, blood coming out of his mouth, and was obviously in trouble. When the guy turned on me, I tackled him into a shopfront, tried to pin him with my shoulder as he beat the shit out of me. Luckily, security arrived, but it was pretty hairy there for a while.

Meanwhile, Lis kept the home fires burning, and inevitably she and Riley became a little self-contained family unit, so that when I arrived home, they'd learnt to cope without me. What I'd learnt very quickly through living in hotels for months on end was that someone always picked wet towels off the floor, made your bed every day, washed your laundry, cooked your food and did your dishes. That worked really well when I got home!

In retrospect, it's difficult to see how we got through those times. For a few years it was hard yakker for Lis, especially with no family in New Zealand. After Riley, we made the decision not to have more children for a while, because it was too hard for Lis being stuck at home. More children meant more expense, particularly if we wanted to see each other on tour, and we had bugger all to come and go on.

We got through because of Lis. She was so strong and knew that I was doing what I needed to do, never put pressure on me to give it away, and somehow kept faith that I'd grow up one day. I was lucky too that Riley was a pretty calm sort of kid: if Dad was home, that was cool, and if he wasn't, that was just the way it was. Some of the other parents had kids crying and screaming as they backed down the driveway. I didn't have to deal with that until some years later, when we had the two girls, Maya and Evie. Now, going away and leaving them is quite traumatic, for them and for me.

It's funny listening to Lis talk about how the team dynamic of the time was reflected in how the wives and girlfriends behaved. Those were what I call the 'head prefect days', when senior members of the team expected automatic respect and deference from the younger members of the team, solely because they'd been around longer. Respect wasn't a matter of them earning it, it was a matter of us giving it, whether it was warranted or not.

That pecking order seemed to apply to the wives and girlfriends too — there was a definite separation between the senior and junior partners. That changed, because the personnel was always changing: players in and out of the team, and girlfriends coming and going.

Sometimes there'd be a lot of married guys with kids, then they'd move on and there'd be a much younger group. Lis would become friends with people, then they'd be gone from the environment. That was just the way of it.

In the early stages in Christchurch, there was a group of wives like Lis all at much the same stage with their families, so she was able to ring them and ask them what tour they were going on, and when, and synchronise travel plans. From the players' point of view, it was always great to see them, but their arrival tended to change the team dynamic a bit. They were, understandably, on holiday, and wanted to go places, do things. The players were working. Some coaches got a bit antsy when the women arrived, and it wasn't always a welcoming environment for them to come into.

My own first taste of the Black Caps test environment was pretty weird. It was the first test at Hamilton against South Africa in March 2004. By the fifth day, the pitch had developed craters which exposed the left-handers particularly. I'd battled at number seven in the first innings, done all right, scored a half century which helped us get past the follow-on and into the lead. But when it came to the second innings, trying to hang on for a draw on the last day, both Mark Richardson and Flem refused, for good reason, to bat on that pitch, so it was almost a case of calling for volunteers. I thought, 'Bugger it, I'll give it a go', so Michael Papps and I opened. I was still there on 19 off 72 balls, with Scott Styris, at stumps.

As a captain, Flem was big on culture, big on themes. So for the 99 tour of England, the catch-cry was BTB, Better Than Before, and he'd put together a video of past Black Cap heroes, which linked us to them. In South Africa it was The African Challenge, or, on another tour to England, it was about soaking up and embracing the history of the English grounds we were playing on. Flem was a big tweaker of his own game, and so new themes for each tour probably suited his psychological approach and certainly made it more interesting for us.

Looking back on it, the problem was there was no constant. The themes Flem chose gave us context and that really helped, but in some ways it was picking away at the edge. We never got to decide who we were, or what we aspired to be, or how we wanted to be viewed: we never developed an unchanging team identity, one that embraced certain values and certain ways of going about things which were consistent no matter where we were, no matter what conditions we had to adjust to. In that sense, as brilliant a leader of men and tactician as Flem was, the team didn't have a soul.

John Bracewell developed a consistent philosophy, which was to try to stay in the game longer, take the contest deeper, get to the fifth day of a test, and who knew what might happen. Braces thought the longer we could prolong the contest and stay in it, the better chance we would have of winning. The problem was it didn't work, because we didn't have the experience or skill-set to make it work. We played fewer tests than most of the other top-tier nations, and so were less experienced at those fifth-day situations. So when we managed to take it deep, we didn't necessarily have the personalities to be able to deal with that pressure, so we'd have a fourth-day meltdown or come a big gutser on the final day. In the end, the 'take it deep' philosophy just became a safer way of playing, of not losing too badly. It was war by attrition, basically, and we didn't have the resources and sustained firepower for it.

That's why in Cape Town we'd decided to always go for the aggressive option. It wasn't necessarily about trying to advance the game — that's been a bit misunderstood. It was actually more basic than that — ask yourself, what is the worst that can happen? The worst that can happen is that we are going to lose. We're losing anyway, so we might as well at least lose playing the way we want to play, enjoying the game. So if someone gets out trying to do that, taking the aggressive option, and, yes, trying to advance the game, let's not shit on them. Part of that philosophy was realising and accepting that you were going to have bad days trying to implement it.

What I didn't foresee back in January 2013, when we made these brave decisions in the aftermath of that first innings collapse, was quite how many bad days we were going to have — how many bad days I was going to have as captain, as a batsman.

And, when I came back early from Bangladesh with another blown-out back, tired to my marrow, and neither wins nor runs to show for it, I did begin to wonder how much grace I had from the powers that be as a captain to start winning, and how much grace I had as a top-order batsman to start scoring some runs.

All I could do was do what I could. So I rehabbed my back and spent most of my days out at Lincoln with Craig McMillan and sometimes Stephen Fleming, trying to develop my batting, and in particular a defence that would enable me to survive longer at the top level.

That, I'd thought, had paid dividends in the first test against the Windies at Dunedin. My first ton for yonks. The winning of my first test as captain so close I could almost touch it. Then a combination of drizzle and Cairns and a spiteful hack seemed to wash it all away.

So I dragged myself and my bags and my coffin to Wellington and tried to recalibrate what the hell I was doing and why.

12
Reset

'Carpe diem. Seize the day, boys. Make your lives extraordinary.'

— John Keating (played by Robin Williams), *Dead Poets Society*

So, a month after getting home, recharging, scoring the century I desperately needed against the Windies in Dunedin, I find myself sitting in a Wellington café, writing out pros and cons on a napkin, trying to figure out whether I still want to play cricket. Because that's the guts of it: if I step down as captain, that's the end of me as an international player. I don't want to hang around like an old ghost and have my presence inhibit the new captain. I'm in or I'm out.

It's one of those moments that are probably not unusual in mid-to-late career: find a new way of going forward (which might mean going back to the basics of why you wanted to do it in the first place) or . . . Get out.

The napkin isn't much use to me. I've never been one for writing stuff down. My thoughts shift away from my list of pros and cons to that afternoon the week before the Dunedin test, when I'd gone out to Taieri with my old club, Albion, and had such a cool time. It was like going back to childhood, the joy I used to have in just playing the game, the anticipation I used to feel on a Saturday morning, pulling open the curtains with a game of cricket in prospect. The innocence of the game, the fun of it.

I screw up the napkin and throw it away. It isn't about a list of pros and cons, it's about eliminating all the bullshit around me, the money stuff, the expectation, the performance pressure, the bad critics. It's about getting back to my childlike joy in just playing the game.

When I get right down to it, the joy of playing is really the only reason for being out in the middle. I'm not naive enough to think that the boiling cauldron of off-field criticism will suddenly disappear just because my attitude is 'pure', but I know that if I'm to stay in the game, it has to be because of the pleasure of playing. In that moment, I know that is the only reason to step across the boundary rope. All the other reasons are peripheral and ultimately distracting, maybe even undermining.

But I can get that feeling playing club cricket. Why keep playing for the Black Caps? I keep coming back to that moment in 2011 when I'd been deciding whether or not to put my name up for the captaincy: I'd done it because I wanted to be part of something special before I finished. Despite everything, that desire is still there, as strong as ever. I want to be part of something special with the Black Caps.

I think again of those young guys lying about on the grass at Taieri. They want to be where I am. While I'm in that position, I should cherish it.

When I leave that café, that's what I take with me, determined to hold these things close for whatever playing time I have left: I'm going to enjoy my cricket, play for that enjoyment, and I'm going to, even more, try to be part of something special.

That second test against the Windies in Wellington on 11–13 December is a first step back from the brink. We play close to the perfect test match, setting up a formidable first innings total, thanks to Ross's 129, supported by cameos from BJ (65) and Kane (45), Corey (38) and me (37), then Trent kneecaps them with swing and pace, taking six for 40.

We have a lead of nearly 250 and I have the same choice in front of me as I had last week in Dunedin: enforce the follow-on and put them back in, or bat ourselves, consolidate our lead, then declare. The risks are exactly the same as they were last week. If I enforce the follow-on, will our bowlers be too tired to make inroads again? But if we bat again, our bowlers will have time to recover, though we might run out of time. Wellington is no less susceptible to rain than Dunedin.

I'm getting conflicting advice — understandable after Dunedin —

but I'm prepared to gamble again — if in doubt, I've got to go with the attacking option. That's what we decided back in Cape Town, that's our credo.

I enforce the follow-on and have to give Trent a rest after just two overs. The Windies openers settle in and it looks like another great rearguard action, like Dunedin. I'm beginning to get nervous. Neil Wagner is struggling for his rhythm, as Edwards and Powell both cruise into their thirties and the Windies are 70 runs for none.

The test is won and lost after lunch. Tim puts in a magic spell, taking three for 24, and Neil Wagner finds his rhythm and menace big time, gets first test double centurion Darren Bravo for a duck, then works over Marlon Samuels superbly. Even though Samuels falls to Tim, Wags has set it up. This time our fielding complements the quality of our bowling and we hold everything — including a screamer by Trent to send back Denesh Ramdin. By this time, Trent is refreshed, and comes back to do his stuff — he takes another four wickets to make 10 for the match — and the game is ours.

Our first test win for more than a year, and my first as captain. The relief I feel is palpable. I've been talking up our progress for what seems like ages and, finally, there's a result to begin backing it up.

And for the first time as captain, we get to do the pledge in the changing room.

The pledge dates from Flem's time as captain, the video he put together for the '99 tour of England with the BTB (Better Than Before) theme. The video was in part a potted history of the teams that had gone before, which related back to a sequence from the film *Dead Poets Society*, where Robin Williams' character John Keating talks to his students about those who have gone before, the photos that line the wall, and that if the students listen carefully, they might almost hear the old fellas whispering, 'Seize the day!' Out of that came the pledge, the words of which are sacred to the Black Caps. The pledge kind of lost its way for a while, but it's something we've worked really hard on resurrecting in our culture. Respect for the past, a reminder of the values that keep the team tight. When Dan was captain and then Ross, launching the pledge was my job. This time, Ross starts it off, which is nice, and we finish it out on the pitch in the middle of the empty Basin Reserve, with a few curious journos and groundsmen straining to hear the words.

I stand out there, arms linked with my mates, reflecting on how close I came to not being here, not sharing this moment.

The third test in Hamilton a week later gives us a chance to win not just a test but a series. That doesn't look likely after I win the toss and put the Windies in on what looks like a green pitch. It's not. They post an imposing 367. Chanderpaul scores his twenty-ninth century, overtaking Allan Border on all-time runs, and is backed by a ton by wicketkeeper Denesh Ramdin. In reply, Ross holds our middle order together with another ton, supported by Kane with 58. The worry is the amount of spin Sunil Narine is getting. He takes six for 91 and we're all out for 349.

A draw would be enough to give us the series, and at this stage I'm thinking we might be lucky to get that, given that we have to bat last on a turning pitch against Narine. But Trent and Tim turn the match on its head, taking four for 23 and three for 12 respectively.

This time I get to watch the opposition lose the game in an hour of madness — I can imagine the turmoil in the Windies dressing room.

We begin our second innings needing 124 for the win. It's still nail-biting for us, given our history of low scores, but we get a start of 30 plus before Peter Fulton is done by Darren Sammy, then Hamish bats through, supporting another critical innings of 56 from Kane.

And we have another test in the bag, two in a row after a drought — and a series win, finally.

What's even more encouraging is that the elements of a genuinely competitive test team seem to be falling into place. In Tim Southee and Trent Boult we have two bowlers, left and right arm, who can swing the ball at pace. They have raw, natural ability and they're carrying no baggage, so they'll just get out there and try to take wickets. They trust me, know I'll back them to do that. It helps that they are so familiar with each other, such good mates.

When you put Tim and Trent together with Kane Williamson and Ross Taylor, who are both genuinely world-class batsmen, and BJ Watling, who has become one of the best wicketkeeper/batsmen in the world, it means that the Black Caps can tick off the three most pivotal elements in a good test team — the opening bowlers, number three and four batsmen, and the keeper.

Corey Anderson is beginning to look the goods as an all-rounder too, getting runs at six and chipping in with critical wickets as fourth seamer (he took three wickets in the first innings). Objectively, there are weaknesses still at opener, and I still need more runs to justify my place at number five, but . . . It feels like we are getting there.

Hess's influence is also telling. He's never been a forceful technical or tactical coach, but he's a great organiser. He gets to know the players as people and allows them to feel comfortable in the environment and to just go and play the game. He has brought a group of people together and given them the confidence to buy into the team cause.

He's also a bloody good selector. Peter Fulton's continued selection is an example. On pure stats, you could question his place at opener — and the media are constantly doing that. But Hess knows that Fults is a pivotal member of this team. He's a calm, experienced, committed presence in the team, and absolutely essential while we have so many players still in the learning phase of their international careers, too inexperienced to be part of any leadership group. Fults covers that weakness, while the younger ones learn, and while Ross works his way back into the fold.

Tactically, I think Hess works well in combination with me. He's quite conservative, and helps to balance my aggression. Normally, we end up sailing towards my point of view, but I tend to come back a little his way too.

Quite suddenly, or at least in a matter of weeks, my cricket world has gone from the depths of despair to real optimism. Christmas 2013 has finally arrived after a year from hell on all sorts of fronts, and I can look forward with some confidence to fronting up to the number one test team in the world early in the New Year and, maybe, finally, being part of something special.

13
Indian Summer

> The Basin's grass banks and wooden benches were crammed and heavy with expectation. Everything McCullum did was cheered. A leave, a block, a single. The applause when he reached the triple will stay forever with each individual present at the Basin that day. It never seemed to die down. It rose and fell, rose and fell, then rose again.
>
> — Abhishek Purohit, ESPN Cricinfo

On the morning of the first test against India in Auckland, in February 2014, it becomes clear when we get to Eden Park that for a couple of our team, performing on the field isn't assuming the kind of importance in their lives that it should.

News breaks that Jesse Ryder and Doug Bracewell were sprung in a central city bar at about 3 am. Neither are in the playing 11, but Jesse is cover for Ross, whose wife Victoria is close to delivering their second child, and who could be called away at any moment before the toss. Doug's there to cover any bowler who pulls up lame. Ironic is hardly the word, when Doug turns up from his nocturnal shenanigans with a broken foot.

This is just the latest, particularly for Jesse, who had another big night out after the last ODI just over a week ago. That too was a 3 am-er, even with Jimmy Neesham riding shotgun, captured on video trying to manoeuvre Jesse into a taxi.

Jesse, PR meister supreme, helps by making a suitably penitent, remorseful statement to the press:

'When contacted last night, Ryder slammed the latest reports on him saying "most of it's bollocks" but declined the opportunity to go into detail.'

I'm pissed off, had a gutsful of guys who don't want to play, don't want to or can't buy into what the rest of us are working so hard for. I don't want either of them anywhere near the team environment. Bugger them, we've got a test to play against the best team in the world.

We lose the toss and are asked to bat. I can only imagine what would have happened if Victoria Taylor had gone into labour that morning.

Once the test gets under way, it's easy to forget Jesse and Doug, because it turns out to be a thriller.

We post 503 in our first innings, with Kane, by now predictably, getting 113 and, less predictably, me getting a double ton, 224. Tim and Trent and Wags then pull off an amazing triple act against one of the most lionised batting line-ups in world cricket, Tim and Trent both taking three wickets for 38, with Wags taking four for 64. India are all out for 202, and we have a lead of over 300.

This time, I decide not to enforce the follow-on. When I cast my eye over the bowlers and senior players I get a sense that they need a rest before going out there again. I know we've got a bowling attack that can get the 20 wickets we need, even against this batting line-up, but they need to be fresh and primed.

They don't get nearly as much rest as I'd intended: we promptly collapse for 105, and inevitably thoughts turn to Headingley and Cape Town etc. But there's a crucial difference this time: we have 400 runs in the bank and we have a bowling attack which is developing into a world-class unit.

A couple of sessions later, with the Indians cruising along at 222 for two on a seemingly benign pitch, with all the moisture and swing gone from the atmosphere, it looks like I might have blown it, certainly to Martin Crowe, who criticises my decision and accuses me of handing the test to the Indians by not enforcing the follow-on.

But even then, at 220 for two, I have no regrets and still feel that, yes, we need something special, but we aren't that far away. I'm trying to work out the ebbs and flows of the game, when to push, when to pull back a bit, when to attack and when to play more defensively. I know we just need a couple of wickets heading into the new ball. Sometimes my confidence doesn't marry with reality, but good old Wags, indefatigable, relentless, is the man for the occasion. He gets Kohl for 67, then 20-odd runs later gets Dhawan, the big one, on 115.

Two for 222 has become four for 248 and we're in with a chance again, with a new ball to attack their lower middle order. Trent gets Rahane lbw for 18, so it's five down for 268, then two runs later, Tim gets Sharma.

Even at six for 270, they're still up for it with closer Dhoni there. He and Jadeja take the attack back to us, put on another 50, until Trent gets Jadeja caught by Ish Sodhi. Seven for 324. They need 70-odd runs, we still need three wickets, and Zaheer Khan only knows one way, putting on a quick scoring partnership with Dhoni. Wags once again rescues us, getting Khan caught by Ross. It's 349 for eight.

They need 50-odd and as long as Dhoni is there, they are good for it . . . Until Wags bowls him for 39. Sharma and Shami last another four runs, before Trent gets Sharma's edge, snaffled by BJ, and we're home, by 40 runs, in a test which is described as a roller-coaster thriller.

Eight wickets for lion-hearted Wags, Tim and Trent both taking six wickets, all 20 by the seamers, and in unfavourable conditions during that second innings when they really had no help from atmosphere or pitch and had to stick at it and show guts and belief.

In an amazing turnaround, we've won three tests in a row after going 10 tests without a win. There's some real satisfaction in a complete performance by the team, and by my contribution to it: finally leading from the front with the bat, and, as captain, under pressure, never letting the game drift, always trying to be innovative.

Having that contribution acknowledged by Martin Crowe after the game is special too.

Inevitably, it seems, the moment of triumph comes with a downer. Chris Cairns takes the opportunity to go public about the match-fixing rumours swirling around him. It's the first time I've really had to think about him since our encounter in the lobby of the Southern

Cross Hotel a couple of months ago.

The *Sunday Star-Times* reports Cairns saying it was a 'disgrace' that ICC investigators had approached his ex-wife, Carin, in South Africa, that the ICC have 'stooped to a new low'. Given Carin was married to Cairns at the time these match-fixing allegations played out, I'd have thought the ICC was just doing its job, though it does seem to be taking them a helluva long time to do it. According to Cairns, the ICC have confirmed that he's under investigation for match fixing, but have so far refused his offer to be interviewed 'anytime, anywhere'.

Cairns appeals to past cricketers who are now on the Board of New Zealand Cricket, Martin Snedden, Geoff Allott and Sir Richard Hadlee. He asks Hadlee how he would feel having his family name drawn through the mud? He asks Chief Executive David White whether he's happy 'for someone who gave sixteen years of his life to this institution and over two hundred and fifty games for New Zealand to be treated this way?'

My guess is that they are far from happy to be embroiled in this brouhaha. My guess is that they're sick to the guts at the prospect of former New Zealand test players being under suspicion for involvement in match fixing. I know I got no satisfaction from providing a statement to the ICC. Everyone is sickened, Cairnsy, in case you didn't notice.

My name isn't out there. Yet. I have a funny feeling that might not be far way. And I'm already dreading the shit-fight that might be in prospect.

I'm determined not to be distracted by the sideshow: I'm here to enjoy my cricket and to make sure we perform in the second test at Wellington and don't give our 1–0 advantage in this series away.

But we threaten to jump straight from the sublime to the ridiculous in Wellington. We're without Ross, after the birth of his second child, and our batting is always weaker for his absence. Maybe that's part of MS Dhoni's calculations when he wins the toss and puts us in.

He seems to get it right — we're six down for 86 after 35 overs (my contribution a measly eight) and another embarrassing collapse is imminent, until Jimmy Neesham and Tim Southee hit handy thirties to get us up to 192. Under the circumstances, I'll take that — it's not 45 or 65 — and since Sharma's destroyed us with six for 51, maybe pace and seam will work for us too.

Tim gets Vijay early and they're one down for two runs, and Trent chips out Pujara for 19, but they make it through to 100 for no further loss at the end of Day 1, with opener Dhawan on 71 and Sharma in as nightwatchman.

On Day 2, Tim gets an edge to BJ to deny Dhawan his century, then Jimmy bowls RG Sharma for a duck. We have them five down for 165 after 45 overs. However, the rest of the day is hard work on a flattening pitch, and Kohli, Dhoni and particularly Rahane, with a great ton, take it away from us and post 438, a lead of nearly 250.

We bat again and end Day 2 with 24 runs on the board and with Peter Fulton already back in the hutch.

Whatever fight we plan overnight doesn't look likely to eventuate at the beginning of Day 3. Our rock, Kane, goes for seven, followed not long after by Hamish. We're three down for bugger all when I walk to the crease, and try to right the ship with Tom Latham. He goes with our total at 87, and then Corey is caught and bowled by Jadeja for two and we're really in the shit at five for 94.

When BJ walks to the crease, I'm just trying to keep those 'here we go again' thoughts out of my head and stay there as long as I can, just keep going. BJ is great to bat with. I know he's a hard bastard, that if we had 11 players with his attitude, we wouldn't lose many. While he's susceptible to the first couple of balls he faces, if he gets in he's not going to give it away, and that reinforces my determination.

We bat on through Day 3. After every session we go into the changing rooms. Neither of us eats when we're batting, whether it's a 20-minute break or 40 minutes. Everyone comes and says gidday, they might ask how it's going out there, and you might talk about this or that bowler, but try and keep it relaxed, have a laugh and a joke. Some guys are quite intense, they don't really like to talk in the breaks, but the music normally goes on and everyone is trying to be laidback. After the small talk, everyone knows where BJ and I are going to be.

We'll be in the toilets talking about how the next session will play out over coffee and a durry.

At the end of Day 3, we're still five down but for a much more respectable 252. I'm still there on 114, and BJ on 52. We're actually six runs ahead, which means at least India will have to bat again, which we regard as a minor victory.

Day 4 dawns . . . It looks like the weather is going to hold for the full five days, so there's going to be no relief for us there. BJ stays for 124 and we combine for a world-record sixth-wicket partnership of 352. Jimmy Neesham, in his debut test, takes over where BJ left off.

By the tea break towards the end of Day 4, I'm exhausted, and when the twelfth man or someone comes out with an hour to go and tells me how amazing it would be if I can get through to stumps at the end of the day, I'm a bit buggered and scratchy. 'Listen,' I tell him, 'I'm on two hundred and whatever, surely I'm kinda done here, eh?'

'No, no,' he says, 'just another hour, and you go back to the hotel tonight still not out. How good would that be?'

I'm so stuffed I don't know who I'm talking to, but being not out at the end of the day and having to bat again tomorrow doesn't seem like nirvana to me right at that point. I tell him what does seem like a good idea to me is having two beers, chilled, sitting on my seat when I finally get into the changing room, whenever that is. 'Yeah, yeah, done,' he says.

At the end of Day 4, 189 overs have been bowled by the Indians, and Jimmy and I are both still there, Jimmy on 67 and me on 281.

MS shakes my hand and Jimmy and the Indian team let me walk off by myself as the crowd stands. As I enter the changing room all the boys are lined up in the aisle. At the Basin, you turn a corner and go through a door to get into the room itself and my seat is directly in front of me as I enter, right underneath the honours board. The first thing I see sitting on my seat is an ice bucket, with two cold Heinekens and a pack of fags sitting on top! You beauty! I put my bat down, take my gloves off, open a can and just hammer it.

The boys all come in and there are hugs and they all sit down close around me and have a beer, while Hess says a few words about the partnerships we've created, the resilience and character we've shown under trying circumstances, and how hard we've all worked for a moment like this. He says whatever happens tomorrow happens, but sometimes you have to acknowledge when something great has occurred and just remember it. I'm so stuffed, but it's so cool. We sit there for a good half an hour or so, then we go back to the hotel.

When I get back to my room, I order up fish and chips, then the old man rings me up. 'Where are ya?'

'Where the hell do you think I am?'

He tells me he's at the Cambridge, a pub nearby, and wants me to come down and say hello. I quickly jump in the shower and go down. Stephen Boock, one of my old man's mates, off spinner for Otago and New Zealand and current NZC president, is there as well, and I have a pint with them and head back to the hotel.

It's not until I wake up the next morning and turn on the TV that I have any real inkling what is waiting for me. Martin Crowe is on breakfast TV talking about how much a score of 300 will mean to New Zealand. No New Zealand batsman has made 300 runs. Martin Crowe was cruelly caught short at this same ground for 299 against Sri Lanka in 1991, and no one has come close since, apart from Flem, who was on 274 when he unselfishly declared against Sri Lanka at Colombo in 2003.

I didn't really know it was that big a deal, probably because milestones have never really been my gig. But it just doesn't seem that significant. I like to think that what's more important is the fact that we've batted for two and a half days to save a test match against the number one team in the world, which means that, with a day to play, we've as good as won the series. That's what I've been thinking is significant.

Then we get to the ground and everyone's asking 'How are you feeling?'

'Yeah, not too bad. A bit stiff.'

'Yeah, but how does it feel turning up at the ground on two hundred and eighty? How does that feel?'

To be honest, I was feeling a lot better before you asked.

Then we're out doing our warm-ups, our stretches, in our little circle, having a laugh and a chat, and I turn round and just for a second clock the stands and the grassy banks of the Basin. Man, there are a lot of people here! An hour before kick-off on the last day of the test match! Then I start hearing people yelling out to me. And I see the signs they're carrying and the numbers still pouring through the gate.

Back in the changing room, I have a last durry and walk out there with Jimmy. All the guys are clapping us out. As I step towards the boundary rope, I take a moment, look at the crowd, and I get it that they've come to see a bit of history. Jeez, no pressure! I don't normally get nervous, but now I am. Mainly because I just don't want to let people down. I realise that scoring 280 and saving the test is going to be an anticlimax if I don't get 300 beside my name. If I get out for anything less, this innings will be a disappointment not just for me, but for the nation.

I scratch out a few runs, and on 290 or thereabouts I nick one behind which falls short and at that point I think, well if it's not meant to be, it's not meant to be. And then I'm fine, through to 298.

On 298, part of me is thinking how ridiculous it is that after batting for the best part of two and a half days another two runs will determine so much about whether this labour is a pass or a fail. But that's part of what I love about sport, there's no fudging, no smudging. Cricket is worse — or better — than many sports. In rugby, a player can have a bad day and sometimes only he will know about it. I'm down to two runs, one hit or one miss, glory or hard-luck sympathy, and the nation is holding its breath as Zaheer Khan comes in.

The ball probably isn't there to be hit, but I try to back cut it. It's a similar shot to the one Martin Crowe got out to on 299 more than two decades ago. He tried to run his down, whereas I just try to lace it. It goes through to the fence and I'm 302.

The next five minutes I'll never forget. The crowd won't stop cheering, won't sit down.

When they do finally stop, I get out virtually straight away. And get another huge ovation all the way to the changing room. Once inside,

I'm overwhelmed by the boys, and also completely stuffed, though I've only been out there for about half an hour.

It takes me more than a moment or two to realise that I'm still captain and I've got to make a decision here. What are we doing? Can we win this game or should we just take the fact that we've won the series and grind out the last day?

I'm stuffed and make a mistake, let our innings meander on. Jimmy goes on to smash 137, which is great, and we declare at 680 for eight after 210 overs. Which means India are now 434 runs behind and have no chance of making them in the time remaining, and after three days in the field, they're weary.

The guys are really up for it, and when India bat again, we immediately have them in trouble. Dhawan is lbw to Trent for two and then Vijay edges Tim to Corey. India are two down for 10 runs and we can smell blood, particularly when Pujara goes for 17. Virat Kholi comes to the crease, gets an edge and should be gone for zero. He's given not out and there's no referrals because this is India. If we'd got them four down for bugger all, even with only two and a half hours left, we could have rolled them, but Kohli's good enough to take advantage of his luck and he gets a ton as he and RG Sharma take India safely through to stumps.

In retrospect, I feel I definitely missed a trick in not declaring as soon as I was out. That's what I'm thinking as the game comes to a close, but that negativity is quickly wiped away by the reality that we've saved the game and won a test series against the number one nation.

In the aftermath, it's difficult for me to process exactly what my own innings means, either for me or for New Zealand cricket fans. Others, like Andrew Alderson of the *New Zealand Herald*, do a better job of that than I can.

> *This was not a flirty, happy innings. This was not a sloggy half-century. This was not a forgettable limited-overs moment. This was days and days of batting to save a Test for his country. When he arrived on day five, 281 not out, so did as many*

> *New Zealanders as was possible. There were queues outside the ground just to watch him. Queues, on day five. Queues on day five of a Test in New Zealand. For one man.*

And this perspective, from outside the New Zealand bubble:

'New Zealand's summer sport is usually about taking the kids out to the grass banks with a picnic hamper to soak in the sun and watch some cricket,' wrote Abhishek Purohit for Cricinfo in a column titled 'The Sprinter Who Ran A Marathon'.

'Of course, they get behind their team when they need to. And they can make a fair amount of noise while they are at it. But to someone coming from the subcontinent, it can feel as if it's an afterthought . . .'

But not that Tuesday morning at the Basin Reserve:

> *The Basin's grass banks and wooden benches were crammed and heavy with expectation. Everything McCullum did was cheered. A leave, a block, a single. The applause when he reached the triple will stay forever with each individual present at the Basin that day. It never seemed to die down.*
>
> *It rose and fell, rose and fell, then rose again. Done with acknowledgments and celebrations, McCullum prepared to take strike next ball, but the clapping refused to stop. McCullum had to wait till his fellow countrymen had had enough of thanking him and telling him how much his effort meant to them. For once, a cricketer had the land of rugby on its feet as one.*

There's satisfaction in the draw and the series win it brings us, but the real sense of fulfilment is in the way we earned that draw and turned the match around to give ourselves a chance of winning it.

From the team's perspective, it looks like, finally, the wheel has really turned. By the end of the series against India, we've won three tests out of five and, almost as importantly, drawn the other two, which has given us two consecutive series wins.

That night two years ago, in my hotel room in Cape Town after the first innings debacle against South Africa, Mike Hesson, Bob Carter, Mike Sandle and I had talked about the kind of people we wanted in our team and the way we wanted to be viewed by our countrymen and women: we talked about making a team with soul and character, who might not always win but would always fight, would never just give it away. Two years later, we might dare to hope that we're getting there, and not just in test cricket.

With the Indian summer over, our focus has to switch to the T20 World Cup coming up in Bangladesh. I'm really up for the challenge, because I believe we have the team to win it.

I know there's a fair percentage of cricket fans who still regard Twenty20 as hit 'n' giggle, and resent the way it has changed the cricket environment. I've never been one of them, for reasons which I'm sure some will see as selfish.

14
Rich . . .

> We could have witnessed the most eventful day in cricket's history . . . one where players were bought like stocks at a share market.
>
> — Sidharth Monga, ESPN Cricinfo

Looking back, there was a day in early 2008 when the cricket world jumped on its axis — and took my world with it. With the wisdom of hindsight, you could see that Twenty20 had to happen: there was a historical imperative driving it.

On 20 February, we'd played an ODI against England at McLean Park in Napier, a see-saw thriller where we'd had to chase down 340 runs and did exactly that, but couldn't get the one run we needed to win it. An incredible draw: 680 runs and we couldn't be separated. The gambler in me couldn't begin to calculate the odds of that happening.

If all ODIs panned out like that, with one run more or less, cricket wouldn't have needed a new product. But, at the turn of the century, the English and Wales Cricket Board was looking at dwindling — and ageing — attendances for county ODIs and came up with a new format, for a much faster game that was all over in three hours, the length of your average blockbuster movie.

In New Zealand, Martin Crowe had earlier responded to the same problem with Cricket Max, a much more radical concept than the English format. Maybe that was the difference that enabled the English version, Twenty20, to stick — it was much more like a regular cricket game (no hit zones and double targets).

Twenty20 was supposed to be for domestic county competition

only, but was so popular that it inevitably began making inroads into already groaning international schedules, one or two games being tacked on to international series, usually as a warm-up or teaser for the ODIs.

Twenty20 became known colloquially, to the purists at least, as 'hit 'n' giggle', and in New Zealand it certainly began as a bit of a joke.

On 17 February 2005, we played our first international game of Twenty20 at Eden Park, as an entertaining entrée to the Australian tour. We dressed in 1980s beige and got the big hair and sideburns going. Hamish Marshall teased out a huge afro and I plastered on a moustache and painted it iridescent orange. Thirty thousand people turned up at Eden Park for this joke, and saw a sublime innings of 98 from Ricky Ponting, and, perhaps more importantly, saw a game they wanted us to win.

Afterwards, we sat in the dressing room, peeling off our silly moustaches and beige jump suits, and tried to come to terms with what had just happened out there.

It'd been a brilliant occasion, no doubt, and the Aussies had entered into the spirit of it too, with Glenn McGrath even rolling down an underarm. But with all the joviality, we were surprised how intense the demands of the game were, the pressure the format put everyone under, the urgency, not just for the batsmen, but also for the bowlers to get through their overs in the allotted time, the changeovers, the fielding. Even without the usual competitive edge, the game still provided a pretty complete test of our mental and physical resources.

We'd gone in thinking it was a bit of a laugh, but come out thinking about the size of the crowd and the noise they generated. They'd been excited by the contest, not the silly suits and afros, and it struck me then that instead of putting so much effort into making ourselves look ridiculous, maybe next time we should put more effort into actually winning it.

The next home international Twenty20 we played was against the Windies a year later. Again, it was at Eden Park in front of a huge crowd and again there was a touch of the festival about, partly because Chris Cairns had announced his retirement from international cricket.

Dylan Cleaver, in the *Herald on Sunday*, wrote:

> *Christopher Lance Cairns, the flawed genius, took his final bow at a ground where he often saved his best. He averaged 43 in Test cricket with the bat on this ground, a full 10 runs better than his overall average. He scored his first Test century here — 120 versus Zimbabwe — and took his first five-wicket bag, against Sri Lanka, on the same ground. He also played his most memorable Test innings, 158 against South Africa, on this quirky ground. So this was his ground. His evening. His crowd.*

The farewell didn't go exactly to plan — Cairnsy scored two — and the standard of cricket wasn't great, but once again the format delivered a dramatic finish, with the game tied, then decided by the first ever international bowl-out, cricket's version of the shoot-out. The first six bowlers couldn't once hit the stumps, before Shane Bond hit twice, followed by one from Scotty Styris. The crowd loved it, but it was all a bit farcical and not the most apt finish for Cairns:

'The stands were littered with banners praising Cairns,' wrote Martin Williamson for ESPN Cricinfo. 'He has graced many bigger stages, but taken part in few games with a finish like this. It was, however, rather sad that his last act was to miss the stumps twice in the bowl-out.'

Not his last act in the Twenty20 environment, unfortunately, and not nearly as sad as what was ahead of him.

From New Zealand Cricket's perspective, Twenty20 was packaging magic, appealing to a different crowd from traditional forms, a much larger demographic. And in terms of cricketing demographics, there's none larger than India. When we were mucking about in our clown suits in 2005/06, we couldn't have foreseen that the most populous cricketing nation in the world would embrace Twenty20 and give it a rock-star aura.

Two years later, almost to the day after the afros and iridescent moustaches were put away, this aberration, this joke, changed the cricketing landscape — and my personal financial situation — forever.

As spectacular as the on-field drama had been that February day in 2008 at McLean Park, the most meaningful action for international cricket was played out after the game, at the Shoreline Motel on Marine Parade, on internet pictures streaming in from Mumbai . . .

At the Hilton Towers in Mumbai, eight multi-millionaire franchise owners of the teams comprising the Twenty20 Indian Premier League were bidding for the best cricket talent in the world.

At the Shoreline Motel, we dragged the couches outside on a balmy night, ordered in pizzas and beer, set up a couple of laptops, and watched history unfold. For four of us, it was personal: Dan, Jake, Scott Styris and I were up for auction.

Like the other players who had been signed up, we'd each been offered a choice: a guaranteed pro rata contract of $200,000 for three years, or take your chances in the auction, with a reserve of $175,000. For a gambler like me, who'd never been on this kind of money before, it was no choice; risking 25K at worst to make, potentially, another 100K? Or more. Who knew?

That was the thing: no one knew. It was a new frontier and looking at it from my perspective, a boy from my background, it was hard to see any downside. We'd been gradually moving from my dad's era of an allowance that covered a pie, a pint and a punt to a truly professional environment, particularly since the players' 'strike' in 2002, but this was a huge leap above all that.

As the prices from Mumbai streamed in, it soon became apparent that the auction was pretty bizarre — there didn't seem to be much logic in some of the prices paid by the team owners. Andrew Symonds goes for US$1.35 million, and Ricky Ponting for $450,000? I mean US$450K is still staggering money, but the relativities were difficult to understand. Mahendra Dhoni for $1.5 million and Adam Gilchrist for 'only' $700K? Seriously? But any concerns about relativities were quickly overtaken by the volumes, the container-loads of dough, being dropped on these players.

We were watching slack-jawed, trying to get to grips with what it might mean for us when our names finally came up. With impeccable timing, we lost the connection. I knew Dan's manager was in Mumbai and I hassled Dan to make the call. Dan wandered off into the night with his mobile, then came back with a huge grin on his face.

'Six hundred and twenty-five thousand,' he said. 'The Delhi Daredevils.'

Jake and I were gobsmacked. 'You've gotta be joking!'

It wasn't that we underrated Dan — how could we, given he'd been our best player for so long? But Jake and I had had good seasons, and as all-rounders had thought we might be worth some decent money too. But US$625K for Dan batted 'decent money' out of the park. By our humble financial lights, this was indecent money, this was astronomical.

The trouble was, there didn't seem to be any news being posted about us. We hassled Dan again, and off he walked into the night again, then finally got a text back from his manager — Oram $650K, McCullum $700K.

I didn't believe it initially, but when it was confirmed, that I'd been sold to Kolkata Knight Riders for US$700,000, I rang Lis and she started laughing, whether from relief or the sheer improbability of it I don't know. Either way, it was probably the right response. There was nothing in my life, growing up in South Dunedin, or since, in a decade as a one-year-to-the-next professional cricketer plying his trade in New Zealand and county cricket in England and state one-dayers in Oz — the only profession I'd ever had — that prepared me for earning this kind of money.

Money can mean many things to different people. I hear that some, usually very rich, just use it to keep score. For others it means time, or travel, or it means living in a different environment or even in a bubble of your own creation. In February 2008, I wasn't sure exactly what it would mean to me. I'd also heard the cautionary tales: the problems money could create. But at first acquaintance that night, after years of trying to squirrel the stuff away in anticipation of the morning I could no longer struggle out of bed and warm my knee and back up to take the field, it looked like freedom to me, at least from that kind of anxiety.

The morning after that night in Napier when my financial situation changed irrevocably, we trained as a team, then had a coffee, but were all still in a state of shock. Even then, Jake and Dan and I were conscious that we had suddenly been painted with a different brush from the rest of the team, whose fortunes had not changed — or been made — overnight.

There was a danger that team morale could suffer, particularly since the three of us had been big advocates of 'team first' and liked to think that we lived by that credo. Suddenly, by a stroke of several Indian multi-millionaires' pens, we were among a privileged elite within the game. Or indeed, outside the game.

Our teammates knew that New Zealand Cricket had desperately wanted some New Zealand players to be up for auction, so that it lit up a pathway for our players. Justin Vaughan, the CEO at the time, had admitted that NZC couldn't afford to pay our best cricketers the sort of money we could command if we were Australian or English or Indian, and was anxious that the IPL pick up at least a couple of New Zealanders if only to prove that it was possible, that New Zealand cricketers too, if they were good enough, could aim for the stars. So in a perverse way, having the IPL pick up five New Zealanders (Scott Styris got the reserve of $175,000, and retiring Stephen Fleming, $350,000) levelled the playing field for New Zealand cricketers, and made the international game more egalitarian.

It wasn't just about the financial benefits. From the moment I first encountered Twenty20, it had pretty much been love at first sight. It suited my temperament and my batting style. In Twenty20 you had to have a crack; you couldn't sit back and think about your batting average.

Then there was the chance to play alongside legends of the game. When I got hold of the full auction results and the team rosters, I saw that I'd be sharing the changing shed at the Kolkata Knights with the likes of Ricky Ponting, Chris Gayle, Shoaib Akhtar, and Sourav Ganguly. When you're playing against these guys and trying to beat them, you try not to hold them in too much esteem, but having watched them — and others scattered about the other teams — at such close quarters, I couldn't wait to get up close and personal, to prove myself and learn what I could.

I wouldn't have to wait long. The Kolkata Knight Riders were drawn against the Royal Challengers at Bangalore for the first match-up, the game that would launch the IPL. I'd toured India a few times and thought I had some idea of what awaited me, but nothing I'd seen or done in 'real' cricket could possibly have prepared me for the experience that awaited me in Bangalore.

15

. . . And Famous

> It was the first innings of the tournament and it turned out to be the greatest innings of the tournament . . . In a sense his innings symbolised the whole IPL — in a short period of time a tournament emerged from nothing, taking the cricket world by storm. It was shown off to the world with the glitz and glamour of the opening ceremony, then this superlative innings of McCullum's exploded, lighting up T20 like no one could imagine.
>
> — John Buchanan, *The Future of Cricket: The Rise of Twenty20*

I'd been to India, but not this India. When I'd been touring with the New Zealand team the Indian fans didn't really know who anyone was apart from Fleming or Vettori or Cairns. Cricket was obviously huge, but it was all based around the Indian players, so it didn't matter who India were playing really, the opposition were just there to be knocked over by the Indian stars. In my experience, there wasn't much adulation left over for your average Black Cap.

The IPL changed that completely. The minute we turned up in the IPL, there was a ready-made fan base for all of us, because each team was attached to a city. In Kolkata, we had, instantly it seemed, five million supporters. They'd already familiarised themselves with every player in the team, because we were their team.

When the Kolkata Knight Riders arrived in Bangalore for the opening game of the IPL against the Royal Challengers, there was a stunning three-hour spectacular before the game. Until that moment, I'd had my doubts as to whether the IPL was actually going to happen.

Our practice kit was almost non-existent and the organisation seemed ragged and underfunded to my Western eyes. But when we saw the opulence that night, the sheer money and attention thrown at that opening ceremony, the doubts began to take a back seat, and anticipation of the opening match kicked in — and, for me, the fear, because we knew the tournament needed a spark to set it alight, to overcome the gainsayers, and my form in the lead-up to the match had been abysmal.

This may surprise those who think the IPL is just a frivolous money-go-round for elite cricketers, but most of my problems stemmed from trying too hard. In the nets, I was endeavouring to impress my new teammates, like batting legends Ricky Ponting and Sourav Ganguly, our captain. And I'd never before had to justify a price tag of $700,000. That brought its own pressure.

In some respects, as experienced as I was, it was like starting again: I was so nervous that I couldn't time anything. I went from trying to hit my way into form, to becoming too defensive, and no matter what I did, the timing and tempo didn't come and I kept getting cleaned out at the nets, not just by Ishant Sharma, our premier pace bowler, but also by pretty well everyone else who turned up to have a bowl. By that time, 2008, I'd shown some glimpses of what I could do, but I hadn't exactly set the world on fire. I felt I hadn't really proved myself, shown everyone that I had a right to be there. Our coach was John Buchanan, backed up by Matthew Mott, and I was surprised they stuck by me as their opening option after what they saw of me in the nets.

My state of mind wasn't helped by an incident that was going to come back and thump me.

About four days before the first match, I was having a beer with Ricky Ponting at the ITC Sonar Kolkata hotel where we were staying, when I got a call from Chris Cairns. He said he wanted to meet to discuss a business opportunity. Could I come over to his hotel?

Chris was playing in the rival Indian Cricket League, which was already under way.

The formation of the ICL had in many ways precipitated the IPL. The ICC had refused to sanction the ICL, but it had happened anyway, and that had forced the ICC's hand — to set up and sanction their own tournament: hence the IPL. The ICL had already kicked off and had been playing matches with a slate of players who, generally speaking, would not have been able to command a place in the IPL.

When I got off the phone, I told Ricky that it was Cairnsy with some sort of business proposition and excused myself.

Cairns was staying in a suite at the Taj Hotel, and he sent a car for me. When I arrived he ordered in some dinner and a bottle of red, and we caught up. Cairnsy and I had a history that had a bit of the mentor–pupil about it. He'd been one of my first idols, and had even in the past given Lis and me a bit of financial advice. Not that we took it — at the time, it was common knowledge that he'd been having a few financial issues with his fudge businesss. But that sort of detail never seemed to dent his confidence or stop him from offering advice.

What happened in that hotel room was detailed in evidence I later gave under oath at Southwark Crown Court in London. That evidence has been widely reported, but for legal reasons I cannot repeat it here. I stand by every word of it.

The encounter with Cairns didn't help my anxiety levels as the opening game loomed. I was aware of how popular cricket was, how huge the audience was, how much money was available to the Indian superstars, and I was also aware that betting, legal and illegal, and corruption, were facts of life in this vast country of teeming multitudes. It wasn't just the colours and smells and food that was exotic and different. As we approached the beginning of the IPL, I was hyper-aware of what a volatile, combustible mixture these cultures of cricket and big money and corruption were.

Given my form in the nets, I worried that if I tanked badly in the opening game my motives might be questioned, interpreted. My form in the nets got so bad that Matthew Mott decided I needed some one-on-one time, just him and me and a bowling machine. I was hopeless. After an hour, he showed his coaching chops by canning that, and instead took me to the hotel bar and ordered a beer. We just sat and talked cricket, shot the breeze, and I went to bed relatively relaxed. That session helped me turn a corner: I got a quick 40 in a warm-up match the next day, and then a 50 the day after that. I felt like I belonged at the crease again.

I'm not advocating a glass of beer as a cure-all, but Mott had the psychological smarts to see that more practice wasn't going to fix my anxieties, and that taking me under his wing socially and making a friendly connection was the right thing to do.

Despite that, after three hours of fireworks and team parades and celebrations and a lost toss, I was as nervous as all hell and had scored exactly zero off the first seven balls I faced. In Twenty20 that's almost worse than getting out. Kumar bowled the first over at me and seemed to have my measure. Whatever I tried, whether to give myself room or advancing up the pitch, I couldn't seem to get the middle of my bat on the ball, and only got to the other end when the ball glanced off my thigh pad. I stood at the other end waiting for Zaheer Khan to come at me, wondering whether I was ever going to score another run.

There were some forty thousand fans in the stadium and they'd sounded like a hundred thousand after the excitement of the launch. Now, they were much quieter. I was the party pooper. I played at and missed Zaheer's first delivery and decided that I had to take a risk: get some runs or get out — I'd be more use to the team sitting back in the hutch than staying out there using up valuable balls. His next ball I walked down the wicket and slogged across the line to leg. It's one of those four or out shots, in the air to a fielder, or over his head to the boundary. It was the latter. The crowd lifted, the first boundary of the IPL, and I was at least off the dreaded duck.

Four on the board: when Zaheer ran in to deliver his next ball, I felt more than four times better than I had the ball before. It was a clean hit to the boundary. I walked down the wicket to his next, tried to hit it over leg again, got cramped up and instead got a top edge . . . Over third man for a six. The next went for four . . . And suddenly everything had changed.

Sourav Ganguly, my skipper, had been watching all this from the other end, and must have been as relieved as I was when I finally got bat to ball. After Zaheer's over he told me I could relax now, take a deep breath. It was his subtle way of saying 'Back off'. Too late. I banged a four off Kumar's first ball, then a single, then had to wait for the next over to face the Aussie, Noffke, who replaced Zaheer. He was nervous and bowled wide down leg — five wides — then I faced three balls from him and hit two of them for six. Now the crowd were taking off too.

Zaheer came back and snared Ganguly, who was replaced by Ricky Ponting. By then I had 40 runs and was all guns blazing, but Punter told me he wanted an over to get himself in. Objectively, I could see the sense in what he was saying, particularly because I was already exhausted. The 45-degree heat and the three-hour opening ceremony, and all the nerves and anticipation, had taken their toll and I was knackered. So I took Punter's advice for a couple of overs and had eased my way through to 50 by the time the spinner, Sunil Joshi, came into the attack.

I hit Joshi for a couple of sixes, then attacked Jacques Kallis for some boundaries, then throttled back when Ricky got out, replaced by David Hussey. By the time leg-spinner Cameron White began bowling, I was into the eighties and elated that I hadn't disgraced myself. I decided to go for it. I was playing on emotion and adrenaline and don't remember much about what happened next. There were no nervous nineties, because at the end of that over I was on 99. The next time I looked at the scoreboard, there was 136 against my name and I wondered how that had happened. The next six, off Kumar, made it the highest score ever in Twenty20. The next ball was also a six. One hundred and fifty in a Twenty20 match had seemed pretty near impossible at that point, so when I got the two runs to get there, the stadium erupted. I finished with another six off Kumar, my thirteenth for the innings, for 158 runs, off 73 balls.

I walked off elated that the fireworks hadn't turned into a fizzer. And so buggered that I couldn't keep wicket when the Royal Challengers batted, which didn't matter because, despite a line-up that boasted Kallis, Dravid, Kumble and Boucher, we won easily.

My teammates and I were ecstatic, of course, but the larger significance of that innings only gradually dawned on me, through the reactions of others.

'We really needed that one spark which would set the IPL's inaugural season alight,' said Lalit Modi, who had staked everything on the IPL. 'That knock in essence was a defining moment . . . the single defining moment that told me we were there . . . To me, he was my hero — the man who fast-tracked my dream into reality, the man who was virtually unknown in India and all of a sudden a superstar.'

There were a couple of people watching back home in the wee small hours, who saw it as the beginning of a sea change for New Zealand cricketers. Justin Vaughan, the CEO of New Zealand Cricket, had played a big part in persuading the Indians to let my name go forward for the auction. For me to become the story of the night was a biggie in terms of giving NZC leverage to get more New Zealand players into the competition.

Heath Mills, the Players Association manager, knew that most New Zealanders had no idea of the magnitude of the occasion, how massively hyped and anticipated it had been in India, for a potential audience of many millions. 'For a New Zealander to go out and steal the show on IPL opening night was phenomenal.'

I can't blame other New Zealanders for not realising quite what the ramifications were: I didn't either, not even when our skipper, Sourav Ganguly, an idol in India, sat down beside me in the changing room and said to me with a smile, 'You know that things are never going to be the same for you again.'

That night after the game, there was a massive party at the downtown compound of Vijay Mallya, the money behind the Force India F1 team and the owner of the Bangalore franchise. The surrounding CBD office blocks served as light stacks for a stage set with tables of exotic food, dancing girls, enormous flower displays, music, onto which the multi-millionaire franchise owners and their entourages made grand entrances. There was Mallya himself, resplendent in shades and diamonds, Lalit Modi, IPL chairman and commissioner, who'd basically conjured up the IPL, packaged it for the broadcasters and persuaded some of the Indian plutocracy to become franchise owners. Our owner at the Kolkata Knight Riders franchise was superstar Bollywood actor Shah Rukh Khan, who floated in with his glamorous crew. You could have believed you were on the set of a big-budget movie. And after my innings, my star was shining pretty bright too, even among those supernovas.

It's amazing how quickly you learn to adapt. By the time Lis and Riley came to stay with me later in the IPL, we had to get security whenever we left the hotel lobby, and even within hotels, it could get frenetic. The first time I walked through the lobby when Lis came to stay, a few kids came up and asked, 'Can I have a photo, please?' and 'Please, an autograph?' When I said, 'No, no, sorry,' and kept walking, Lis kept her peace until we'd got wherever we were going, then turned to me and said, 'How rude is that? They're just kids, you can't just tell them to go away, surely you can let them have a photo? It would take two seconds!'

I felt that if I tried to explain to Lis why I'd kept walking, I'd sound like even more of a wanker, so next day when we walked through the lobby and the same thing happened, I stopped, signed a kid's paper and let him take a photo. Within moments, something like sixty people descended on me, just appeared from nowhere in a supposedly private hotel lobby. I was surrounded. I did my best, as they called in their friends. Finally, I had to refuse to do any more and had to push through the crowd to where Lis and Riley had been waiting for fully 15 minutes. 'Okay,' said Lis, 'I get it.'

The thing is, everyone's so polite and enthusiastic, and if you say no, they understand and just roll with it. There's no acrimony. That kind of spirit permeates the huge Indian fan base, and even most of their cricket scribes. Cricketing gods do not get out to bad shots, they're always undone either by superb bowling or sheer bad luck. So true!

Of course, it's one thing getting a reputation on the basis of one glorious innings, but quite another to live up to it, and that's been difficult, if not damn near impossible. But in the larger scheme of things, it has been a matter of great satisfaction to have played a significant part in the success of the IPL, which further cemented T20's place as an exciting, appealing and credible format for international cricket . . .

A format that I believed, as we prepared for the 2014 T20 World Cup, that New Zealand was ready to win.

16
Hit 'n' Grizzle

> I reacted badly . . . I decided I'd go out and bat the way I believed that we should be playing and bugger the team plan. I'm not proud of that; it wasn't my finest moment.
>
> — Brendon McCullum (after being sacked as vice-captain in 2009)

By 2014, there'd been four ICC World Twenty20s, won by India, Pakistan, England and the West Indies. New Zealand had never made the finals; our best result was in the inaugural tournament when we finished fourth. Since then, we'd really underperformed, finishing fifth, fifth, and seventh. But going into the T20 Worlds in Bangladesh in 2014, I'm convinced we now have the team to win it.

Over the past summer, we haven't just been performing at test level — we've really lifted in ODIs and Twenty20s. Before the Indian tour, when the Windies were here, we finished off with five ODIs and two T20s. We weren't that happy to draw the ODIs, though Corey Anderson's batting pyrotechnics at Queenstown, a world-record fastest ton, showed that we were developing the kind of batting power that anyone in the world would be afraid of. And, critically, we won both T20s against the Windies relatively comfortably.

We'd then charged straight into the ODI series against India, where we really hit our straps, winning four of the five and tying the other. That series was characterised by consistent performances from our top order: by Guppy, who got a ton in the third match; by Rosco, who got tons in the fourth and fifth matches; and by Kane, particularly, who went 71, 77, 65, 60 and 88 across the five matches, the rock on which our batting line-up was increasingly reliant.

Our ODI bowling was also developing depth, with Kyle Mills bowling as well as ever, but with new guys like Mitch McClenaghan getting four for 68 in the first, Matt Henry four for 38 in the fourth match, and Adam Milne showing pace and potential, to take a bit of pressure off Kyle and Tim and Corey, who were all still performing too.

A lot of our improvement in the ODI format has come from incorporating T20 techniques and strategies. That's something I've been pushing for some time, notably back when John Wright was coach, when I irritated him because he simply wasn't interested in deviating from the conservative. We've gradually brought the T20 mentality into our ODI approach, where the team is empowered to have a crack, and there's no sitting back and thinking about your batting average.

So, as we go into the World T20s in Bangladesh, I'm certain we have the ammunition, we have the firepower, and we have the tactics. What we don't have — and it proves crucial — is total buy-in from everyone in the team.

And there's something else that won't go away.

Our first game is against England in Chittagong on 20 March. A couple of days before that, I make a statement to the London Metropolitan Police.

This is the third time I've been through this stuff. The first time was in 2011 in India, when Dan Vettori and I spoke to the ICC ACSU representative, John Rhodes. On that occasion, Rhodes just kept rough notes, it was all very casual, no real probing, and he told us that he thought it would go away, so when it didn't go away, the ACSU had to come back in December of 2013 and do a proper interview.

Once again, I traverse the meeting with Cairns in Kolkata and his follow-up a few weeks later in Worcester, before a warm-up game on the New Zealand tour of England. I'd met him for breakfast at a café down the road from our hotel. Nothing furtive or back-room about our Cairnsy — I found him sitting in the front window of the café reading a newspaper. That afternoon I scored a ton against Worcester.

After the meeting in Kolkata, I'd belted that record score in the opening IPL match. Two meetings, two tons — maybe I should have been hiring him as a batting coach!

This time the statement is much more detailed due to the professionalism of the cops. They ask follow-up questions, they want to know precise details, like who was sitting where, a lot of stuff that had never come up in the ACSU interviews.

The fact that the Metropolitan Police have come to Bangladesh to take my statement is a worry, because clearly something is brewing, and I'm going to end up at the centre of whatever it is.

A real storm hits us in the first game. England post an imposing 172, and by the time we bat, we can hear thunder and see lightning smashing down behind the bowler's arm. The England captain, Stuart Broad, and I both want to abort the game, but the umpires want to get five overs in, so that the result can stand. Both Broady and I object, tell the umpires that no team deserves to lose when they have to play with lightning strikes around. To no avail, we're forced to bat the five overs, which is ridiculous.

Guppy gets 11, a strike rate of 22. When I come in at number three, we're so far behind on the Duckworth–Lewis that I have to go for broke, smash something like 20 off four balls, to help get us through to 52 before the umpires are forced to pull the plug. Kane's strike rate is 141 and mine is 266, and we're a bit fortunate to win a match which should never have been completed.

Then we lose our second game narrowly to South Africa, failing by two runs to reach their total of 170. This is particularly galling, because we've got the winning of the game at the beginning of the last over, only needing seven runs, with Ross, well set in the sixties, and Luke Ronchi at the crease. But Steyn gets Luke with his first ball, then beats brother Nathan with sheer pace with his next two. Nathan manages to catch up with Steyn's fourth ball and smashes it over extra cover for four. We need three runs off two balls, an equation you'd take every time in Twenty20. Steyn does his best for us, short and wide, but Nathan gets it with the bottom of his bat and is caught. One ball, three runs, Ross to face. Most times I would back Ross in this situation — he has scored his fastest 50 ever to get us to this point, but Steyn bowls full, and Ross only manages to push it back to him and is run out.

This is a tough loss to take, and means that, after getting an expected win against The Netherlands, the minnows of our group, we have to beat Sri Lanka to go on in the tournament.

When we restrict Sri Lanka to 119, with Trent getting three for 20 off his four overs, that win looks like a formality, but we make a sluggish start, Guppy going for five off 13 balls for a strike rate of 55, and then spinner Rangana Herath comes on, bowls a maiden first over, then takes five wickets for three runs — including three wickets before we've scored a run against him. Ross, me and Jimmy Neesham all go for ducks, and Kane's 42 is the only score of any respectability.

True, Sri Lanka is a very good team, going on to beat India in the final, but once again we've significantly under-achieved on Twenty20's biggest stage. We should have done better than sixth, and while I can accept the losses, what I find far more difficult to accept is what I perceive to be a continuing division in the ranks. Ross and Martin Guptill seem, still, not to want to be part of the team.

Guppy's efforts against Sri Lanka really rile me. Earlier, I'd made the team tactics very clear: I didn't care how many wickets we were down after six overs, we had to have a decent run rate by the time they brought in their spinners, otherwise Herath and company would have an opportunity to dictate terms. Guppy dawdled through to five off 13 balls and we had only 18 runs on the board after three overs. Which meant when I came in at number three, I was under huge pressure to get the scoreboard going.

It isn't just Guppy's batting. We've talked about how we need to create energy and intensity in the field, but it didn't happen. In the dressing room after the game, I give it to the whole team straight. I tell them we could have won this tournament but when you've got guys who aren't interested in representing their country, then we've got no chance. I tell them this isn't my team, it's not Mike Hesson's team, it's New Zealand's team, so if there are guys in the team who aren't giving 100 per cent, they need to look at themselves. I don't name names, but everyone knows who I'm talking about. I tell them this moment has got to be a line in the sand, and that if it happens again, I'll have no problem standing up in front of the media and telling them why the guy who has played for this team for seven or eight years and has performed individually for us is no longer a part of the team. If they're not prepared to play to the tactics that the New Zealand cricket team are playing to, they're not going to be around.

Before we get on the plane to fly home, Guppy comes up to me. 'Do you mind if I have a chat to you about what you said in the changing room?' We arrange to talk on the flight home.

I can understand Guppy's divided loyalties, to some extent. He's close to Ross and they share the same mentor, Martin Crowe, and the same agent, Leanne McGoldrick, and Guppy's wife is Leanne's daughter, Laura. It doesn't help that Leanne was once my manager.

I had seen Leanne around in my early days with the Black Caps, when she was managing some of the other guys at the time, like Cairns and Astle and McMillan and Parore. So when she approached me at a café about managing me, I was flattered. She told me that I could be captain of New Zealand one day and that she wanted to help me get there.

I developed a really good relationship with her, she took us into her home and looked after us, invited us around for dinners and treated our kids fantastically. And she did get some good commercial deals for me at the outset that I otherwise wouldn't have secured.

But after several years, I started to ask myself who the hell I thought I was, needing a manager. It's a bit of a vanity trap, which I'd fallen into before. When I was 18, my old man asked Garth Gallaway if he wanted to manage me. Fortunately, Garth told him I didn't need a manager, I needed to get out there and play.

Too many young sportspeople get sucked into thinking they need a manager when the reality is that if you're playing cricket here in New Zealand, you probably don't. For your New Zealand Cricket contract, they tell you which number you're getting, there's no negotiation.

There's no negotiation in an IPL auction and agents are expressly prohibited. You might negotiate an English county contract, but your value there is totally dependent on whether you score runs or not. You might get a couple of commercial deals here in New Zealand, but there's not a lot of negotiation or maintenance involved there — for my Puma contract, I'll pick up the phone and ask whether they're happy to roll over the contract. We're done in 15 seconds, and it's better for that relationship if it's me on the end of the phone doing that; it's better if it's personal — that's a prime reason it's lasted eight or nine years. If there's anything contractual that needs looking at, I give it to Garth.

Flem had a similar view, in fact he asked me, 'Why pay an agent, when I can help you with some of that stuff for nothing?'

Given Leanne had been so good to us, and that we'd become friends with her and her family, this wasn't a decision we took lightly, but we felt we had to start thinking with our heads not our hearts and do the right thing financially by our own family.

It was the right decision. Flem helped me a bit, but there wasn't actually that much to do. The only downside was that later, when Flem was the coach of an IPL side that picked me in the auction — for a bargain price — he faced some snide remarks about conflict of interest, that he was picking me so he could get a kickback of 10 per cent as my agent. Flem never made a cent from helping me.

Leanne went on to manage Ross and Martin Guptill, and presumably establish the same sort of close, personal relationship she'd had with me and my family.

So I can understand why Guppy's loyalties are divided, but after the T20 Worlds debacle, I've had enough. It's time to move on and I need to know that Guppy can do that.

Flying home, we're in business class, two sections of us separated by an aisle. When Guppy comes up after take-off and asks if I mind having that yarn now, there's only one place to have it, in the aisle that runs between the two sections of the team's seating. I'm conscious that everyone in the team will be able to hear at least bits and pieces of our conversation, but it's no time to hold back, the air has got to be cleared once and for all, and it's better that they hear it.

I tell him he's been caught up in his mate's fight, and I can understand the background to that, but it's not his fight. I tell him that Doug and Jesse have been dropped for their behaviour, because that behaviour was damaging the team, but what he is doing is just as damaging as what they did and he's got to work out if he wants to continue carrying on that way.

To his credit he has been outstanding since. He went away and worked on it and he has come back. I totally trust him in the environment now, 100 per cent.

When I look at the way Guppy turned it around, I regret not challenging Ross in the same way as soon as he came back into the Black Caps environment after missing the South African tour. In a way, our behaviour around him probably fed his right to feel aggrieved, helped him feel his grievance was justified.

17
Dark Forces

I believe there are dark forces at play.

— Chris Cairns

A couple of months later, in May 2014, a scenario unfolds which I've been dreading since the chance encounter with Chris Cairns in the foyer of the Southern Cross hotel last December.

Someone leaks my testimony to Ed Hawkins at the *Daily Mail* in London. Hawkins, author of *Bookie Gambler Fixer Spy*, is an authority on cricket corruption, so the leak is no brain-fade on the part of the ICC. It looks deliberate and, I suppose you'd have to say, perfectly targeted. I'm pissed off that no one at the ICC seems particularly perturbed that confidential testimony has got out in this way, but maybe it's the ICC's response to media attacks on them for doing nothing — 'Well, here's what we're doing, guys . . .'

I thought there'd be a possibility that my name would eventually be leaked, but not every bloody word of my testimony! I've got my suspicions as to how that happened, which I can't repeat here, but the leak means that Cairns and his friends know in advance exactly what I'm going to say and have lots of time to prepare a counter-argument, and to discredit me. That leak gives him the chance to start relentlessly trying to pick apart those who are going to testify against him.

That wonderful old expression about excrement hitting the fan sums up what happens next, though I get most of it second hand because I'm back at the scene of the crime — sorry, the alleged crime — the IPL, playing for Chennai Super Kings.

On Friday, 16 May, Dylan Cleaver and Andrew Alderson report

in the *New Zealand Herald* that 'investigations into cricket match-fixing allegations have taken a twist, with the revelation New Zealand captain Brendon McCullum rebuffed an approach from another player to manipulate a game. No details on dates or games have been confirmed, but multiple sources have corroborated the approach.'

David White, CEO of New Zealand Cricket, confirms that 'Lou Vincent, a former New Zealand batsman, is co-operating with the anti-corruption unit and London's Metropolitan Police as they investigate claims of spot- and match-fixing in Asia, South Africa and England'.

When reported by the media, neither my leaked testimony nor Lou's names Cairns. Mine refers to Player X, a 'former international star' and 'my hero' who approached me in 2008 regarding match fixing and money laundering. Hawkins confirms from London on National Radio that Player X is the same player named by Lou Vincent in his testimony to the ICC's ACSU.

So the cross-hairs are gradually becoming focused, and the media speculation around the identity of Player X seems extraordinarily well informed. Maybe the leak from the ICC to Hawkins came with that rider — don't name Player X. But clearly Hawkins has been told or has seen the original testimony with the names, and all the undercurrents seem to point in one direction . . .

Which is acknowledged by Chris Cairns on 19 May, when he makes a statement to Fairfax, who had until recently employed him as a columnist for the *Sunday Star-Times*:

> *I am told that Lou Vincent and Brendon McCullum have given some form of statement to the ICC/ACSU accusing me of match fixing. I have repeatedly asked the ICC/ACSU to produce copies of these statements so that I can respond. They decline to do so but seem happy to leak information to the media which they deny to me.*

I'm with him there! As expected, he defends stoutly: 'These allegations against me are a complete lie.'

And then has a heave to cow corner:

> *As for Lou Vincent, he appears to have confessed to match fixing in respect of games played in numerous countries around the world, most of which I have had no connection to. He is in a desperate position. He faces potential prosecution and in trying to negotiate a plea bargain he appears to be willing to falsely accuse me of wrongdoing.*

I seem to get off lightly, in so far as he has trouble ascribing any motive for my attempt to nobble him:

> *As for Brendon McCullum I have no understanding why he would say the things he is alleged to have said. To be clear, I have never approached Brendon, or anyone else, about match fixing or any other improper activity. I am doing everything I can to get to the bottom of these allegations.*

Cairns then threatens another defamation trial, which is pretty ballsy under the circumstances: 'I have been to court to demonstrate conclusively that I am not a match fixer before. I will have no hesitation in doing so again.'

Before finishing on what will become a familiar refrain:

> *I conclude by saying that I believe there are dark forces at play. These forces have long arms, deep pockets and great influence. I acknowledge that recently I have upset some powerful people in the world of cricket, including raising my own concerns about the health of the game. I believe I am paying the price for that now.*

I'm not sure whether I've got long enough arms or deep enough pockets to be part of these dark forces, nor can I remember Cairns raising any concerns about 'the health of the game', but perhaps I missed something. I'd agree with him that he has recently upset at least one powerful person, when he sued Lalit Modi for defamation. Is that what he's talking about, I wonder, or is he trying to link me with some conspiracy against him?

The ICC may not be making direct contact with Cairns, but London's Metropolitan Police are. As well as Lou Vincent — and most worryingly from Cairns' point of view — Scotland Yard have hauled in his lawyer in the defamation case against Modi, Andrew Fitch-Holland.

After Fitch-Holland is questioned for a second time, his lawyer, Tony Wyatt QC, reveals that 'most of the information is coming from one source, so the decision they will make when they come to decide to charge him is whether that one source is credible.'

'That one source is almost certainly Vincent,' says the *New Zealand Herald*. 'He has said he is fully co-operating with police and ICC anti-corruption investigators, and *The Daily Telegraph* yesterday described his evidence as a "treasure trove of information".'

Lou's not making any comment. Neither is the ICC: 'The ICC last night refused to shed any further light, saying it didn't "comment on corruption investigations".'

What a bloody joke! Who needs a comment from an organisation which seems to be leaking like a sieve? All the journos have to do is stand in the vicinity with a bucket.

Later that same month, Cairns is hauled back to London for a follow-up interview with the Metropolitan Police, where he's informed who the witnesses against him are and what they are saying — as if he needs that, when my stuff has already been given world circulation.

On his arrival back from London at the end of May, he calls a press conference in a side room at Auckland airport, and once again protests his innocence, attacks Lou Vincent again as a purveyor of 'despicable lies', and questions why I waited so long to give evidence to the ICC anti-corruption unit in 2011, and why, having given that evidence to them, I hadn't also given it to Lalit Modi when he was being sued for defamation by Cairns a year later.

'I have said that there are dark forces at play here,' he says, again. 'The just concluded trip to England has not persuaded me to think any differently.'

There's a gaping anomaly here that doesn't seem to have occurred to Cairnsy. If I'm part of the 'dark forces' aligned against him, which, you'd think, must include Modi, surely I would have given evidence for Modi in that defamation case? If I'd been in Modi's pocket, I'd have been in court telling the world what I'd already told the ICC, wouldn't I?

The reason I didn't is simply that no one asked me to. Modi seemed to have no idea what I'd told the ICC. I certainly didn't tell him and for once, it appears, the ICC didn't spring a leak. My attitude when I was watching that case unfold was: it's your business Cairnsy, you'll do, as always, what is best for Cairnsy — why should I volunteer to give evidence against a mate, or former mate? In South Dunedin you didn't rat on mates, and there was part of me that was uncomfortable about saying anything.

The only reason I talked to the ICC ACSU in 2011 was because it was explained to me that if I didn't report approaches for match fixing, I was equally guilty. I did what I was obliged to do under the rules that govern me as a professional cricketer as soon as I was made aware of them — no more, no less. Perhaps I should have been better informed earlier, but I've never really been one for the fine print.

So I'd watched Cairns go after Modi in 2012, astonished at his cheek, yes, but no way did I want to insert myself into that scrap. So I kept my peace . . .

Until the London police came calling back in March at Chittagong during the Twenty20 Worlds, pursuing the possibility that Cairns might have lied under oath.

The London coppers haven't decided yet whether they're going to charge Cairns. I'm hoping they don't. I could do without the aggro.

In the meantime, I've got to get my head back into cricket.

18
Winning Away

> The criticism they would invite if West Indies overhauled the target and claimed the series had the potential to frighten. But Brendon McCullum does not appear a captain who prefers the safe route.
>
> — Alagappan Muthu, ESPN Cricinfo

The West Indies at their place aren't the force they used to be, but they're still a decent test for the likes of us. History seems to be against us — New Zealand have only ever won one test in the Windies, back in 2002. Two years ago, in 2012 under Wrighty, they'd utterly cleaned us out in two tests, two Twenty20s and four out of five ODIs.

I reckon we've made a lot of progress since then, won tests and the last two series at home, but wins at home can flatter to deceive. If we've got aspirations to be a decent team, a team worth remembering in the annals of New Zealand cricket, we've got to prove we can win away.

The first test at Sabina Park in Kingston turns out to be as close to perfection as we might ever get, on paper. I win the toss, we bat first and post 508 for seven, bowl them out for 262, ram home the advantage with a quick-fire 156, then knock them over again for 216, winning by 186 runs in four days. Easy!

Well, no. After Tom Latham (83), Kane (113) and Ross (55) bat us into a strong position at the end of the first day, we lose three quick wickets, including mine, on the second morning, and at 279 for five we're close to wasting any advantage provided by winning the toss. But Jimmy Neesham and BJ come together and Jimmy's ton and BJ's 89 make the difference, get us to our first 500-plus total away from home in eight years, and set up the match for us.

By that stage, the pitch is taking turn. We'd anticipated that and gone in with two spinners, Ish Sodhi and debutant Mark Craig, who, when selected, had prompted a chorus of 'Who?'

Before the team was announced to the media, I was in a car with Hess when he took a call that left him a bit taken aback. 'Bugger,' he said, or words to that effect, 'Jeets has turned us down.'

We'd gone back to Jeetan Patel and given him one last shot, but for entirely understandable reasons he'd decided against the tour. He had an English county deal in place and would have been jeopardising that for a last hurrah with the Black Caps. Which meant that we were desperate for another spinner. We had Ish, a leggie who turned the ball away from the right-hander, so we needed someone who could turn it away from the left-hander.

There weren't many obvious options — in fact it came down to a choice between my brother, Nathan, and this guy from Otago who I'd played a club game with before the last Windies tour to New Zealand. I'd also played a warm-up game with him at Lincoln, and been impressed not just with his bowling, but also with his batting and fielding. Okay, it's a huge jump from club cricket to international, particularly in foreign conditions, but . . . When in doubt, take the aggressive option. So Mark Craig was in. So much for nepotism.

Picking both Mark and Ish for this first test was a big punt, but they're brilliant, holding their own in the Windies' first innings, as their efforts and Tim's four for 19 in unhelpful conditions for pace bowling gives us a big lead of nearly 250 runs going into our second turn at bat.

That advantage proves critical as we get skittled for 156 in our second, with only Tom Latham able to put a score together, a 73 for a fine double.

In the Windies' second, Tim once again knocks the top off them, taking out the dangerous Chris Gayle and Powell, before Mark Craig and

Ish Sodhi do their thing. Mark ends up taking eight for 188 and becomes one of the few Black Caps to earn Player of the Match on test debut.

In the second test, at Port of Spain, our run of eight tests without defeat comes to an end. Mostly, it's down to a pretty inept batting display in the first innings after winning the toss. A paltry 221, with Tom Latham getting the only substantial score, means that instead of setting up the win, as in the first test, our first innings puts us on the back foot.

When the Windies put a total of 460 on the board, with tons by Brathwaite and Bravo, the rest of the match becomes an exercise in trying to avoid a loss.

In that respect, we fight hard to the end, and that's pleasing, at least.

I open, when Hamish goes down crook, but fail at the top, and after some resistance from Tom and Kane and Ross (36, 52 and 36), we're eight down for 212, before Mark Craig sticks with BJ. They put on a partnership of 99 runs, which, as the rain showers threaten, gives us some hope of saving the game by pushing it well into the fifth day and making the Windies bat again. Mark makes 67.

They only need 93 runs, and after a rain delay Chris Gayle takes the weather out of the equation by smashing 80 of those runs at a strike rate of 173. After five days of attrition cricket, we get a Twenty20 finish from one of the most spectacular batsmen ever.

So we lose after fighting hard for five days, making them at least work for a result which some may have thought was in the bag after our batting failure on the first day.

In many ways, this test epitomises a key element of what we've tried to do since that discussion in the hotel room in Cape Town: show character, show some soul, and if we do get beaten, make it bloody hard, don't roll over, fight to the end, make them earn it.

Even if it's the kind of loss I can live with, it's still a loss, and the series decider at Barbados now shapes as a measure of how far we've progressed. I'm desperate for an away series win, because it would mean that we'd done something we haven't been able to do for more than a decade — it's been 12 years, in fact, since we last beat a top-eight nation in an away series.

The third test goes down to the final hour of the fifth day and I'm sweating on it because I've made a declaration which is variously described as 'brave', 'generous' and 'foolish'.

We bat first and get a middling 293, courtesy mainly of Jimmy Neesham's 78 and thirties and forties from Kane, Ross, Mark Craig and me. Their first innings edges us by 24 runs, which effectively turns it into a second innings contest.

Kane steps up and anchors our second with a big ton (161 not out) which is huge in the context of a game in which no one up to that point had even scored an 80. Jimmy supports him with a 50 and, thanks to the two of them, I've got some options in front of me at the end of Day 4. Do I declare overnight, or bat on into the fifth day and make the game safe for at least a draw? If I declare overnight, I'm giving the Windies 98 overs to get 308 runs.

We've been behind for so long in this game, that it's tempting to take the safe option, particularly since the series is riding on this match. We've also seen in the last test what Chris Gayle can do to a tempting target on the fifth day — do I let fear, of one player in particular, and fear of losing, dictate my choices?

For me, this is what being a captain in test cricket is all about. Can you dare to win and take the risk of losing that comes with it? Do you have the courage to back your chances? Back your teammates? Give the opposition a chance, yes, but back your own players? It's squeaky bum time.

One of the things in the back of my mind is that if you make a decision which is a proactive one, it empowers your team. If we go back out there tomorrow and bat on until we get bowled out, funnily enough even though we'll have more runs on the board, it might mean that we have more chance of losing. It's a signal to everyone that we'll be happy with a draw. While if we proactively declare, that says to the opposition, 'We're coming after you.' In a subconscious way it puts you back in control of the game, and it makes them think — 'Hell, what are they doing here? They're coming after us!'

I don't agonise overnight about declarations in this situation, I don't make too many calculations. Basically, when I come off the field, I look around the dressing room, and make a decision on gut instinct. I don't lay all the facts out on the table, make all the equations about what if: instead I look around at my players, try to catch their eyes. Right, he's in. Or he's not. You can tell just by looking at them — do they look away, or are they giving me that 'I want a crack' look?

I will have dropped hints during the last session too, because everyone knows what's coming. I might go to certain players, say something like, 'Jeez, clear day tomorrow, imagine how sweet the beer would taste tomorrow night after we bowl these guys out.' I listen to what they say, watch how they're saying it. They'll give me signs as to whether they think that is true or not. There are always going to be those who haven't even thought about it. There are those who are hoping you are going to say it, and there are those who are hoping you are not going to say it. Those that don't want you to say it are usually the coaches! But the important guys, like Southee and Boult, are usually in — they want to have a crack, they want to try to win test matches.

The time I do sit down and do the numbers is when we're on the other end of a declaration, or when we're behind a game. So if we're needing 500, I might say, 'All right boys, this is how we are going to do it. We've got four and a half sessions to get five hundred', or whatever it is. You go: 'If we score a hundred in this session, a hundred here and a hundred here, then we will get two hundred in the last.' I try to take the emotion, the fear, away from the task in front of us, and paint the little path forward. When it is the other way around, though, I act out of pure instinct, governed by what I'm seeing in the eyes of my players.

At Barbados, those eyes are telling me they want to have a crack, so I tell them we'll declare in the morning. If the Windies are good enough to get three runs an over on the last day of a test with the series on the line, they deserve it. It's done and dusted before we leave the dressing room, even though the opposition — and everyone outside the team — won't know till next morning.

And, as usual, I get back to my hotel room and the texts start coming in — all saying, invariably, *Don't give them a sniff! Close it out!*

I'm used to that.

So I turn up with a group of mates on the last day of a test match, of a series, after all the hard work, after 14 days of hard-fought cricket in a different country, having no idea whether at the end of that day we're going to win or lose or draw. How good is that? That is why you play. How sweet would it be, you say to them, if we're sitting together in the dressing room at the end of the day having actually got this thing done?

I speak to the team a lot, but it's never big emotional motivational talk, it's always about bringing it back to what we can control. That, under pressure, we take the aggressive option, that if we tick off this, this, this and this, that if we just make sure we are concentrating on each ball, that if we execute as best we can, we'll take care of it.

It all seems pretty cruisy, to begin with. Tim and Trent assert themselves as one of the best new ball attacks in world cricket. Trent is swinging the ball both ways, and has them one down for seven runs — Brathwaite shoulders arms to an in-swinger which cannons off his pads into the stumps. Edwards then edges him to Ross in the slips and they're two down for 23. Tim chips in with the big one, Chris Gayle, who's looked relatively sedate until then, and they're three for 31 and we're looking good. Chanderpaul and Bravo are establishing a dangerous partnership when Mark Craig gets Chanderpaul stumped. Four for 81. Tim Southee is bowling beautifully to their middle order and gets Ramdin at 122 and then Bravo on 40 at 129.

At six for 129, we are looking the best of chances but, typically for this series, nothing comes easily, and the Windies' tail shows remarkable resolve. Mark Craig gets Roach cheaply, but Jason Holder and Shane Shillingford put on a 70-plus partnership, and gradually the dynamic changes, as the Windies get out to seven down for 220, 88 runs short of victory. The decisive moment comes as the test counts down to the final hour, when Mark bowls Holder for 52 and we can attack their last two batsmen, Benn and Taylor. Wags has Benn caught, and the *coup de grâce* comes, suitably, from Trent Boult, who traps Taylor lbw. There are minutes left to the close of play.

It's the proudest I've been, playing for New Zealand, and one of the most memorable series I've been a part of. I was awful with bat in hand, but just seeing the development of different guys and the way that when the pressure was on we were able to respond, the way we were able to stay in the game when things were not going well, was encouraging. They actually dominated us for long periods and it was so pleasing that we were able to weather that storm, kept finding ways to claw our way back in, kept showing those fighting characteristics we've talked a lot about within the group and which we want to be known for outside the group.

A big part of being able to do that was Kane's ton on a turning, bouncing pitch, for which he was awarded Man of the Match. With 413 runs at an average of 82.60 he also took Man of the Series.

It's satisfying watching him become a world-class batsman, but also seeing the way, with each series it seems, another young player is introduced, and almost immediately finds his test match feet. Mark Craig was only on tour because Dan had retired and Jeets pulled out, yet he's had an amazing series with both ball and bat. It's made for an awesome bowling attack. Tom Latham seems to have solved one half of the opening riddle, and Jimmy Neesham has made a huge contribution to this series win, our third in a row.

The fact that these young guys are almost immediately finding their feet is a tribute to the stability of the environment, and Mike 'Roman' Sandle has had a huge amount to do with that. His first tour as manager was with Wrighty on our last tour of the Windies, and he's learnt from that shambles, and is great at making people feel welcome and valued.

This time, we actually embraced the places we went to, embraced the fact that they were culturally so different to us. We got on really well with the West Indies boys, which I think helped a lot. We went around to Chris Gayle's house for one of his parties, and throughout the tour we made a point of catching up with some of the guys in their team, the ones we had a relationship with through the IPL. They were really good to us and introduced us to the way they lived, with the result that we had a bloody good time in these really cool places, like Jamaica, Trinidad and Barbados.

We might be nowhere near the finished product, but that's part of the excitement — finding out how much better we can be. Something special? Maybe that's gradually moving from a dream or hope to a reasonable expectation . . . On the cricket front at least.

What happens next could, I suppose, be seen as a continuation of the strange dynamic of my recent past as a professional cricketer: excitement, aspiration and satisfaction on the field beyond anything I've ever experienced, while off the field it seems like one shit-fight after another.

19

Fair Facts and Foul

The Metropolitan Police have contacted their New Zealand counterparts about Chris Cairns' conduct towards Brendon McCullum, a potential witness in his impending perjury trial. *The Herald* understands Metropolitan Police officers, who will lay a charge of perjury against Cairns when he flies to London next week, contacted police here with concerns about a story in a Sunday newspaper that was the subject of a High Court injunction, believing it could be seen as undermining a potential trial witness.

— Dylan Cleaver, Jared Savage, *New Zealand Herald*

A couple of months later, in September of 2014, after another too brief respite at home, I'm back in India for the Champions League. This is the Twenty20 championship for the top provincial or state teams from around the world, the Big Bash in Oz and the South African, English and Caribbean T20 comps, including the Northern Knights from New Zealand. I'm playing for the Chennai Super Kings, who qualified as one of the top three teams in the IPL.

On 12 September, I hear the news that Chris Cairns will be charged with perjury by the Crown in London, who are alleging that Cairns lied under oath in the defamation case against Lalit Modi when he said that he 'never ever cheated at cricket' and nor would he 'ever contemplate doing such a thing'. Back then, the jury had agreed with him and awarded him damages of about NZ$180,000 and court costs of approximately $775,000. Now, the Crown is concerned that Cairns sold the jury a pup. My testimony has been taken by the London cops and I'm likely to be a Crown witness.

The very next day — what a coincidence! — I'm woken at my hotel (it's night-time in India) by a phone call from Simon Plumb, a journalist with, inevitably, a Fairfax paper, the *Sunday Star-Times*. He tells me he's seen an email from me to Kerry Schwalger in 2012 which alluded to my having prior knowledge of the decision to appoint me as New Zealand captain in place of Ross. This is in the period before the first test at Galle in Sri Lanka when the team was imploding around Ross, a time when I'd had to have been a complete fool not to realise that if New Zealand Cricket sacked Ross, I'd be the next in line.

It's like the Parker Affair all over again, but this time the whole thing is more sinister.

The call isn't entirely unexpected. I terminated my contract with Kerry Schwalger earlier, around March, partly because it was impossible to arrange enough time together to justify the monthly retainer I was paying him, and partly because some of his communications to me were becoming quite bizarre. I told Kerry I'd pay him as and when I used him. He agreed and we left it at that, no hard feelings.

There've been a couple of indications since that my break with Kerry might not be as clean as I'd hoped.

On 20 May, the day after Cairns is quoted in the *Sunday Star-Times* talking about the 'dark forces' lining up against him, I'd received an outlandish, irrational email from Kerry Schwalger, now calling himself Kerry Kruise, based in 'gorgeous Santa Monica'. He said his organisation had been fielding calls about me: 'Apparently they want to know all sorts of things about you!' He expressed concern that his reputation would be 'dragged through the mud for being complicit in any wrong-doings' that I may have been involved in.

He didn't say who 'they' were, the persons or organisations that wanted to know this information, but I had my suspicions.

I emailed him back, reassuring him that I'd done nothing illegal and reminded him of the confidentiality clause in the contract between us, and hoped it would go away.

Shortly after that, I had a conversation in Christchurch with a mutual mate of mine and Cairns', who dropped the name Kerry Schwalger into the conversation and said that Cairnsy had been speaking to Schwalger. I did wonder what the hell Cairns was doing speaking to Schwalger, but perhaps it was entirely innocent, and Cairns wanted to employ him. At that stage, Cairns hadn't been charged with anything.

But in early September, a week before Cairns is charged and Simon Plumb calls me in India, I begin hearing reports that Kerry has been contacted by media, or by people associated with Cairns, for information about our relationship.

Once again, I email Kerry and seek his reassurance that he won't breach the trust and confidence I'd placed in him, not to mention the contractual obligations between us.

In return, on 6 September I get an email from him which doesn't do much to allay my fears. I'd heard that he'd had some sort of breakdown since we stopped working together, but I had no idea how serious that had been. He said he'd been in Ward A of the 'Auckland Mental Health Unit' for the past month, having spent the first five days in the Intensive Care Unit. Initially he claimed not to have had any communication with anyone, and that it was his ex-partner who was threatening to expose all his files. But then towards the end of the email, he asks me to call him so he can 'explain in detail the current situation with all parties who are desperately trying to woo me with what they think are lavish gifts/promises & the like . . .'.

That freaks me. Call me naive but I find it hard to believe that there are people out there who are bidding for confidential emails between me and an advisor, particularly when the advisor concerned is so obviously in an extremely fragile mental state. Then again . . .

In the reports I'm hearing, it appears Cairns, Fairfax and John Parker are all in the bidding mix. Or maybe one party has bought the emails and they are circulating them. That kind of makes sense, because Fairfax journalist Mark Geenty was among the names on Parker's email list.

What doesn't surprise me is that Fairfax is part of this shadowy group aligned around Cairns, trying to exploit Kerry's relationship with me.

The media lines seem to have been drawn some time ago. The *Sunday Star-Times* seems intent on becoming Cairns' mouthpiece — Cairns was a columnist for that paper, owned by Fairfax Media.

I'd been an original investor and advisor — and initially a director, albeit briefly — in a company called CricHQ, which invents and markets a digital platform for cricket scoring. The company is quite successful but at one point needed additional investment. I was stunned when Flem, who was one of the directors, told me he'd pitched the company to Fairfax, who said they were interested in investing.

From my understanding, Fairfax were prime movers behind some of the allegations about New Zealand cricketers with conflicts of interest, yet here was Flem out there giving them chapter and verse on exactly who was involved and in what capacity. I asked Flem whether he had any doubts about the legitimacy of Fairfax's interest, whether it was just a fishing expedition for information. Flem said he had no doubts at all. That might have been naive. The Fairfax interest in investing in CricHQ came to exactly nothing, but the information that organisation gained from that little manoeuvre kept surfacing in their media outlets.

One example was Mark Reason's distressing newspaper column, the one I read in the foyer of the Southern Cross hotel, where he opined that I was playing cricket for the Black Caps just so that I could get on the tour to India and further my profile for a particular business interest.

Genius move by Fairfax, you'd have to say! But also, an indication of what I'm up against trying to protect my private correspondence with Kerry Schwalger.

Over in India, I sense that now Cairns is going to be charged, now that I'm going to be a prime witness against him in a criminal trial, the ante is going to be upped.

I'm trying to keep my composure about what seems to be happening behind the scenes, when Simon Plumb wakes me and tells me that he has all my emails from Kerry, and he's going to run a story in tomorrow's *Sunday Star-Times* about Ross and about all this other information Kerry has invented for them, presumably to help hike the price: that I beat Lis, that I trashed a hotel room in Brisbane, that I take methamphetamine and human growth hormone, and that I bet on cricket and am involved in match fixing.

I refuse to comment and immediately phone Garth Gallaway, who takes the call from me at about two o'clock on a Saturday afternoon. At about 3 pm on 13 September, he phones Jonathan Milne, the editor of the *Sunday Star-Times*, and explains to him that the information contained in emails between me and Kerry Schwalger is governed by strict contractual confidentiality and, regardless of the contract, is privileged by nature of the relationship of trusted advisor and client. He tells Milne that what the paper is doing is cheap and poor journalism. Milne argues that it's very good journalism and refuses to back down. Garth asks him to advise him by 5 pm if they intend to go ahead and publish any of the material, because he would need to apply for a High Court injunction to stop him. Milne assures Garth he will let Garth know if he's going to publish, but by 7 pm Garth has heard nothing and phones a High Court judge about 30 minutes before kick-off between the All Blacks and South Africa at Westpac Stadium in Wellington. Garth applies for and obtains an interim injunction, orally.

The following morning, the *Sunday Star-Times* runs a story by Simon Plumb titled 'Special: Cricketer Gags Paper — McCullum: The Story He Wants Hidden'. It's worth repeating some of it, because it reveals who's really driving this attack on my integrity:

> *New Zealand cricket captain Brendon McCullum last night went to the High Court to stop the* Sunday Star-Times *publishing a story that could play out in Chris Cairns' perjury case in London . . .*
>
> *Cairns confirmed to the* Sunday Star-Times *yesterday that his legal team was analysing 'information' involving McCullum and his former mental skills coach, Kerry Schwalger. The injunction prevents the newspaper revealing startling details about that professional relationship and others involving the Black Caps environment.*

There's actually nothing in the Schwalger emails that is relevant to the Cairns perjury case. He's not mentioned once, and I'm pretty sure I never discussed Cairns with him in any capacity. What there is, though, is a lot of splenetic stuff about fellow players and others within my immediate environment who would be embarrassed by having their names published. So would I be, because none of the venting does me great credit, to put it mildly. But how many of us, particularly those of us working in a high-pressure performance environment, don't have these kinds of thoughts? Perhaps I was foolish to put them in writing and trust Kerry Schwalger — Lis gave me enough warnings about him — and I made a major misjudgement of character, but I was paying the man a monthly retainer for the privilege, for him to be there for me, to help me deal with the day-to-day frustrations as the Black Caps fell apart under Ross's captaincy.

At that time, Ross was no doubt conferring with his confidants and referring to me in less than complimentary terms. Maybe he was clever enough not to do it by email. But whatever he said or wrote in those confidential, private relationships is his own business, not mine.

Surely the larger question in relation to what Cairns and his cohorts are doing is this: at what point does this kind of cheque-book 'investigative journalism' tip over into becoming a mouthpiece for a former employee who has been charged with a criminal offence? At what point do threats to publish this stuff become part of an attempt to bully and intimidate a potential witness?

In case there is any doubt, Cairns clarifies the new rules of engagement between him and me. A photo published by the *New Zealand Herald* on Friday, 12 September, shows Cairns carrying a clear plastic folder entitled 'BMC Emails'. Cairns is quoted as saying that his legal team are analysing 'information involving McCullum' and that he hoped that 'significant additional information will be flushed out that will help people to better assess the situation, as well as the character and motives of the parties involved'. The clear message I take from this is: Back off, or else.

I'm not the only one getting that message. The *Herald* also reports that the London Metropolitan Police are 'so concerned about a trial witness being potentially undermined that they contacted their counterparts in New Zealand'.

I don't have any idea what the 'dark forces' opposing Cairns are, but I'm beginning to get a graphic idea of the kinds of bouncers Cairns is lining up for me.

I know I've got to put this out of my mind and concentrate on cricket, stick it all in the non-cricket bag and zip it up tight, not let it inhibit my performance.

I can do that, mostly. But even when I do, subconsciously I know in my waters that there are people out there who are biding their time, looking for an opportunity to circumvent the injunction and get this private correspondence into the public arena. It casts a shadow over everything.

I can understand why Cairns now sees me as the enemy. The bit I don't understand is why such a powerful media organisation should be giving him so much oxygen.

I've heard the old joke — just because you're paranoid doesn't mean they aren't out to get you. It doesn't seem so funny any more.

20
RIP Phil

All your preparation, all you have ever thought about in cricket, just throw it out the window for this game.

— Gilbert Enoka

The bulging discs in my spine and the degeneration of my knee keep reminding me that I'm not bulletproof, that every sportsman lives on borrowed time to keep on playing. But it's not life and death.

That's where we all stood as professional cricketers before 25 November 2014, when Phil Hughes, on 63 not out for New South Wales in a Sheffield Shield game against South Australia at the SCG, faced a delivery from 22-year-old fast bowler Sean Abbott. It was a head-height bouncer which Phil tried to hook. He was too quick and was through the shot before the ball arrived. His head was side on to the ball as he completed the shot, tilting away, exposing a gap between his old-style helmet and his neck. The ball hit him behind and slightly below the left ear, near the junction of the brain and the spine. It broke an artery and the brain stem area was flooded with blood and began compressing. Phil staggered a couple of steps, put his hands on his knees for a moment, then fell face down on the pitch. Two days later, at St Vincent's Hospital, he was pronounced dead, from catastrophic head injury.

I was in Sharjah in the United Arab Emirates when the first news came through that Phil had been hit and was in intensive care. The Black Caps were about to begin the third and last test against red-hot Pakistan, which the month before had demolished Australia 2–0 at the same venues as we were playing. We'd looked like going the same way as the Aussies, when we lost the first test badly.

Pakistan had won a big toss in that first test at Abu Dhabi, and made the most of it with three of their batsmen scoring tons on their way to a massive 566 for three declared. I'd opened with Tom Latham, who held us together with 103, the only really significant score in a total of 262. Pakistan elected to bat again, and it was much like a continuation of their first innings, until they declared at 175 for two, 479 ahead. We managed to stretch it into the final day, but with a top score of 39 — me — we were never a chance of recovering from that huge first innings deficit.

My post-match interview, where I said that we had the potential to come back to win the series, looked a pretty forlorn hope in the light of the stats from that first test. It was the biggest test win by Pakistan against us in terms of the number of runs, and we'd only been able to take five wickets in the whole game. The win made Misbah-ul-Haq Pakistan's most successful test-winning captain ever.

But I knew we'd been in this situation before in recent history and had been able to bounce back. Just a few months ago in the West Indies, we'd lost the second test heavily in Trinidad and came back to take the series with that fighting win in the third at Barbados. But I had to concede that a comeback against this Pakistan team on the turning UAE pitches was a much bigger ask.

We'd gone in with a plan, with which we persevered in the second test at Dubai. We felt we needed to play both all-rounders and both spinners, which meant I had to shift up to open. I won the toss, and we built a first innings of 403 around Tom Latham's second ton in the series. It wasn't quite enough to put Pakistan under pressure, and when Sarfraz Ahmed did a Latham and anchored Pakistan's innings, our lead was a slender 10 runs, which turned it into a second innings contest.

Ross delivered with a century, and at 250 for nine before lunch on Day 5, I declared. I knew that if we wanted to win and square the series, I had to keep them interested, give them a chance to win, so they'd play their shots and not just close the game down. Conversely,

I had to give us enough time to bowl them out. At one stage we had them four down for 75 and we were looking likely, but Asad Shafiq, Younis Khan and Sarfraz Ahmed dug in to get the draw.

We take a lot out of that game, the fact that we'd competed and had Pakistan hanging on at the end. It was a huge turnaround from the first test, and gives us real impetus going into the third. We haven't lost a test series since the West Indies in 2012, and we desperately want to preserve that record by getting a win at Sharjah to level the series. And I have a card up my sleeve that I now get to play — Dan Vettori.

He's still playing wonderfully well in ODIs for us and has never officially retired from tests, even though he hasn't played any since mid-2012 or indeed any first-class matches since December 2013. But I'm convinced he'd be really useful for us on these pitches, and I knew he was coming over to play a couple of warm-up matches for New Zealand A before the ODIs with us, so I texted him to see if he was interested in playing a test for us while he was here. He was initially reluctant, and I understood that — he's been beleaguered with injuries and has to nurse a fragile Achilles and watch his workload — and he doesn't want to do anything to jeopardise his chances of playing in the upcoming ODI World Cup at home. But I emphasised that he'd be our third spinner, so he wouldn't be carrying it all on his shoulders as he used to, and finally he agreed to play.

So we go into the third test with Dan batting at six in place of Jimmy, and giving us a third spinning option in addition to Mark and Ish. It's great to have him back in the test environment even if it is probably a one-off. His family — mother, father, wife and children — is here to clap him as he leads us out onto the field, after I lose the toss and Pakistan pad up.

They're 281 for three at the end of the day. By that time, we know Phil is in intensive care, fighting for his life. Next morning, the 27th, we hear that he's lost that fight.

I wouldn't claim to be a close mate of Phil's, but I had opened with him playing my solitary game for Sydney in the Big Bash. We'd got on really well in those few days together and, after that, every time we played against each other internationally or domestically we would always catch up and have a few beers. Kane had played him at age-group and knew him really well. Even the guys in the team who didn't know him at all could imagine what Phil's family were going through.

There's also the realisation that it could have been any one of us. None of us ever anticipated that someone could die from a cricket ball, not in this day and age. You want your fast bowlers roaring in, having a hard attitude, intimidating, ready to exploit any lack of bottle or technique, but not at the expense of someone's life. Cricket was meant to be a game, not a life or death struggle. It hits everyone hard that, for Phil, it had become exactly that.

That morning, my initial attitude is we shouldn't be playing. That's mainly because I look around the room and no one wants to play cricket. It's lost all meaning. There's no other international cricket going on at the time, so ours is the only game affected midway through. Maybe that makes it more important for the broadcasters that we continue.

Roman, Hess and me speak to the match referee, Andy Pycroft. Both umpires are Australian. They're broken, in their rooms, they're no good. We tell Andy our guys are no good either and we don't want to play. We get New Zealand Cricket on the phone, David White. He's very supportive of our stance and he gets on the phone to the ICC and the ICC speaks to Andy and the umpires. I don't know where the Pakistanis sit with all of it, but I understand some of their guys don't want to play either. In the end it's agreed that we'll have one day off and see what happens.

The day off allows us all to work out some sort of coping strategy. That night most of the team are in my room. I ring Gilbert Enoka and tell him I don't know what to do. Since leading the side, I've had a clear vision of what I thought we should do, but Phil's death finds me wanting. I tell him we've got a group of men here who are broken, it doesn't feel right to continue playing, but there's a good chance we'll have to.

Gilbert is outstanding, says don't judge anything that anyone does during this week, just let people grieve in their own way, get over it in their own way and concentrate on themselves rather than the team when they need to, but try to bring everyone together and have a few laughs if you can. 'All your preparation, all you have ever thought about in cricket, just throw it out the window for this game.'

So that's what we do. That night we find some beers from somewhere and most of the team spend time in my room. We know we've got to be at the ground the next day for what is supposed to be Day 3 of the test, but we don't actually think we're going to be playing.

But when we turn up at the ground next day, we find that the game is going ahead, like it or lump it. It's probably the right call, but it doesn't seem right at the time.

I make it clear to everyone, harking back to Gilbert's advice, that there won't be any harsh judgement on any player's performance and there'll be no consequences for failure. We just have to do the best we can, to honour Phil and the game itself.

So we play the rest of the test in a virtually empty stadium with our heads in a strange place. Instead of caring about our performances or the result, we simply don't.

Thanks to Phil, there's a release of many of the external factors that can creep in and influence a player. Instinct takes over — just playing and being 'in the moment'.

For me, the result of that 'uncaring' no-consequence play is a bit of a revelation. In many ways what Gilbert told us squares with some of the exercises I'd been trying to do with Kerry Schwalger — take the conscious mind out of the equation, neutralise it so you can let your natural reflexes take over.

I've suspected for some time that if you get hung up on your performance and the end result, it paralyses your ability to play instinctively. Somehow, you have to be able to care a great deal but play as if you don't. Not an easy contradiction to execute in practice, but we absolutely nail it for the rest of that test under these most peculiar and tragic circumstances.

From 281 for three at the end of Day 1, and 311 for five at drinks in the first session of what is effectively Day 2, Pakistan lose their last six

Getty

One headline read: 'Test slipped through fingers'. I've got my head in my hands as I put down a catch in the first test against the West Indies at University Oval, Dunedin in December 2013.

THE TRIPLE

Right: In full flight on my way to 302 against India at the Basin Reserve in 2014. Below: The magic moment.

Opposite page, top: Five minutes I'll never forget . . . the crowd won't stop cheering, won't sit down. Bottom: In the dressing room with the boys at the end of play.

Photosport

Getty

Getty

Photosport

Getty

My one and only test wicket came in the second test against Pakistan in Dubai, November 2014. Sarfraz Ahmed, caught and bowled McCullum 112.

Photosport

Heading for a double century in the third test against Pakistan in Sharjah, 2014.

Getty

A New Zealand record 74-ball test century against Sri Lanka at Hagley Oval, Christchurch in December 2014.

Getty

Leading New Zealand off Hagley Oval after our convincing win over Sri Lanka in the opening match of the 2015 ICC World Cup.

Photosport

On the way to a New Zealand and World Cup record 18-ball 50 against England at Westpac Stadium in Wellington.

Photosport

With the Chappell–Hadlee Trophy after our win over Australia in the World Cup match at Eden Park.

Getty

I managed 59 as we chased down 298 to edge South Africa in the World Cup semi-final at Eden Park.

Getty

With Grant Elliott after our nail-biting victory against South Africa. Grant's superb 84 set us up for the win and a place in the World Cup final against Australia.

Getty

Above: I make the right call at the coin toss before the World Cup final against Australia at the MCG.

Photosport

Right: Not the way I wanted my 2015 World Cup campaign to end.

wickets for 40 runs, and that opens the door for us — their total of 351 is serviceable, but not match-winning, if our batting is good enough.

Our batting is better than good. We put together 690 runs, the biggest total ever by New Zealand, and the second-highest score against Pakistan by any team. The core is a double ton from me and a much finer 192 from Kane, but there are significant contributions right down the batting order: Ross's 50, Corey's 50, Mark's 65, Tim's 50 and even Ish's 22 at the end. All at an average of five runs an over, with 22 sixes, a new record in a test innings.

Man of the Match, Mark Craig, who has taken seven for 94 in their first innings, gets another three in their second innings and with Trent's four for 38 stalls a great Pakistani fightback centred around Asad Shafiq's 137. Pakistan are all out for 259, and we've crushed them by an innings and 80 runs and squared the series. All in four days.

Dan, who's taken a critical wicket in each innings, leads us off, for what will be his final test. Typically, selflessly, he doesn't say anything publicly about this being the end, but instead talks about the team's experience.

'It's been a very hard test match to play and we're lucky that we've had Brendon and Mike Hesson and Mike Sandle, our manager, to lead us and really help the guys get through it, because a lot of guys knew Phillip very well and we felt like he was one of us, and we mourned him as a teammate.'

This test is New Zealand's first win against Pakistan in Asia in 18 years.

Beyond the stats, it means we drew a series which we looked to have lost, that after an abysmal start we were able to fight back to at least parity against the team that had Australia on the ropes under the same conditions just weeks before. It means that what we are trying to do is working, not just at home in familiar conditions but wherever, in whatever conditions. We're developing a team which is multifaceted, that's able to triumph no matter what is thrown at it.

The effect of Phil's death on what happened didn't go unnoticed by those who witnessed it. Cricinfo saw it this way:

> *The Kiwis were badly affected by the incident and didn't even celebrate any of their achievements. A remarkable thing to note here is that they barely applauded a wicket. Consider this: just the two bouncers bowled today and no close-in fielders in front of the wicket! Takes some doing and still they won the game in four days to level the series 1–1. McCullum deserves all the credit for masterminding such a performance from his side. Also full marks and hats off to the Kiwis for the spirit they have shown throughout the series. Certainly an example set for all the other sides to follow and act upon. Long live their attitude!*

We appreciate the plaudits, but the big thing I take away from this test is the way Phil's death affected our mindset and the way we played in the rest of the match. It was so strange, yet felt so right, that after Phil's death, we didn't really care any more about the result. The fact that nothing we could or couldn't do on the field really mattered, in comparison to what had happened to Phil, had an amazingly liberating effect. Not only did we play without fear of losing, we played almost without care — it was in some ways the most carefree cricket we've ever played, certainly at test level. The team had drawn strength from one another, and Gilbert Enoka's 'no consequences' brought a 'joy of life' in a cricketing sense that was richly ironic but, nevertheless, liberating.

For me, it reinforces the essence of why you're there, the need to enjoy what you're doing, and to always feel that what you're doing out there, winning or losing, honours the game itself. That can't be allowed to become empty gestures and sound bites.

21

The Power of XI

Most teams would commit one man to this errand, some might send two. But here was more than a third of New Zealand's fielding resources tearing after it; in each other's slipstream like a track cycling outfit, even though this ball seemed destined for the fence. Somehow, between the four of them, they found a way to haul it in, one man scooping it back from the rope, another plucking it up and returning it. Each of the four fielders then high-fived the others — even the two that had not touched the ball. Seven high-fives in all. One run saved. It has been like this all series. The New Zealand XI has fielded like they have had twice that number on the ground. It has been like this for all of the past year, with bat and ball as well. New Zealand commit men to the pursuit of the seemingly impossible. Somehow, someone scoops it back. Somehow they find a way.

— Andrew Fidel Fernando, ESPN Cricinfo

The insight from Phil Hughes's tragedy doesn't end in Sharjah. In fact, as time goes by, I realise that the change of perspective is going to be there for the rest of my time playing test cricket for New Zealand and I think we become a much better side as a result.

Against Sri Lanka on Boxing Day, 2014 at Hagley Oval in Christchurch — the first international cricket in that city since the quake — I lose the toss and Angelo Mathews decides to insert us on a greenish wicket. That looks like paying off, when we're three down for 88, despite a patient opening partnership of 37 from Tom Latham and

Hamish Rutherford. That might not sound like a huge partnership, but it was invaluable, as Hess makes clear later.

'When you have roles, you might not get a hundred every game, but you have to play the way the team requires. That gets the best out of the group. The way our openers batted the first hour against Sri Lanka after losing the toss was them fulfilling a role. They might not have made a lot of runs individually, but it was important for the team.'

It is a good base for what happens next: I belt 195 runs off 134 balls, including 18 fours and 11 sixes. I get out trying to bring up the double ton with a six.

At the close of play, I find Garth Gallaway in the carpark. He's finished his commentating stint and is struggling to get his car started. I offer to drive him home and on the way he tells me that I had lots of time to get to 200 and still beat Nathan Astle's record for the fastest test 200 ever, and also Bradman's record in terms of minutes taken. He looks at me and says, 'But, none of that matters, does it?' Na, I tell him, had to be done.

If you go back over the tapes of my finest moments with the bat pre-Sharjah and post Sharjah, there's a big difference. Before Sharjah, I'd celebrate with the best of them, get quite emotional, wave the bat about, maybe do the odd dance, look a bit like David Warner on Valium. But after Sharjah, my moments of success were acknowledged in a more muted way, because what Phil's death has taught me is that these successes don't *really* matter. What matters is that you're out there with your mates, able to play. Value every minute and honour the game that allows you to do it.

That permeates everything we do now. After the news came through that Phil had died, and we were told we had to complete that test, there was no way we were going to sledge anyone. We arrived at that point because of what happened to Phil and it cut pretty deep. So why should we go back to sledging now? It's not about being 'nice guys' or trying to curry favour with the media, it's actually about being honest about why we're out there.

Our total of 441 probably isn't as much as we might have hoped for in the end, but when the Tim and Trent show, backed up by Jimmy Neesham and Wags, knock Sri Lanka over for 138, it looks like being plenty, and given they've only lasted 43 overs, there's no question that I'll enforce the follow-on.

Sri Lanka try to prove me wrong by batting a hell of a lot better the second time, on the back of a big 152 from opener Karunaratne, but Tim and Trent stick to their guns, taking eight for 200 between them, and leaving us 107 to get for the win. Which we do, for the loss of our openers.

That brings 2014 to a close, a year in which the Black Caps have registered five test wins, a big jump from my first year as captain when we went something like seven tests without a win.

The team performance is topped off by some landmark personal achievements. That 195 makes me the first Black Cap to score 1000 test runs in a calendar year. Tim and Trent have taken 33 and 34 wickets respectively, and are both within the top 10 international rankings. Ross is in the top 10 for batting, and Kane is closing fast. There are plenty of others who have made significant contributions throughout the year — Mark Craig in the West Indies and the UAE, Wags in Barbados particularly, Tom Latham in the UAE, and Jimmy Neesham. Then there's BJ, who has made 40 dismissals, more than any other international wicketkeeper this past year. He's the hub at the centre of our fielding effort.

We now have a new year to confront, where the focus is about to shift to the ODI World Cup. Hess refutes any suggestion we're looking too far ahead. 'All we're thinking about is the next test at the Basin Reserve. We're not even thinking about the World Cup.'

I'm not sure that's completely true, judging from the way we begin the second test against Sri Lanka on 3 January 2015.

We lack focus batting and bowling in the first innings and end up well and truly under the pump, 135 runs behind after Kumar Sangakkara finally comes right with a double ton.

Our second innings doesn't initially promise any relief. By the time we wipe out the deficit, we're five wickets down and so far behind the game that even I wouldn't have given odds on our being able to get out of it with a draw. And yet — and this proves how far we've come — we somehow find a way back into the game, not just to make a contest out of what seems like a walkover, but to win it.

We're certainly helped by the Sri Lankan fielding. Kane is dropped three times and really makes them pay, surpassing Sangakkara's masterly knock with his first double ton, 242. It's almost as if we're witnessing a passing of the baton at the end of the old king's reign to his successor. BJ once again supports what begins as a rescue operation with a big ton, and by tea on the fourth day, Kane and BJ's tenacity and brilliance give me some cards to play. Neither of them look like getting out, and we could simply bat out Day 4 and into Day 5 and make sure we don't lose. A draw will give us the series one-nil.

But, again, it's dare to win. When I look into the eyes of my players, I see what I need to see. I believe they're up for it, they want to have a crack, so I pull the pin at 524 for five on Day 4, leaving Sri Lanka more than a day to get 389. The pitch is still a good batting track and I need to give them a target which tempts them to have a go. Any more runs to chase, any less time to get them, would encourage them to shut up shop.

My only uncertainty is around Kane. He's heading for 250 and looks like he could get 400, the way he's going. He knows that, but when I talk to him, his focus is utterly on doing what we need to do to win the game. I can't help but think what other players in his situation would have said to me. What a man.

Sri Lanka end Day 4 on 45 for one, which gives them a day to get 344 runs, with all their big guns intact, while we still need nine wickets. I get back to the hotel to the usual barrage of texts. *You're one up in the series, why'd you give them a sniff? If Sangakkara or Mathews get set, Sri Lanka will get the runs . . .* And so on.

I'd like to repeat to these people our mantra about playing aggressive cricket, that it isn't just words. That we want to keep progressing the game, looking for results. That you remember test wins but you don't necessarily remember draws. That you want to achieve special things along the way, and a lot of hard work goes into that. And that, even with all that hard work, you still have to be prepared to take a punt, be prepared to lose to risk a win. That if the opposition are good enough, they're good enough, and you'll be humble enough to accept the loss with good grace.

Next day, Day 5, the temptation ploy seems to work. Six of Sri Lanka's top eight batsmen fall to aggressive strokes. Trent kicks off with Prasad's wicket, then 10 runs later gets the big one, Sangakkara, for five, and we're in the match. The turning point comes before lunch, when Kane plucks a screamer from the sky at gully to send back Angelo Mathews. That makes them five down for 110 at lunch and we know that if we hang tough, we'll get there.

In the afternoon session, Mark does exactly that, and gets Jayawardene, Chandimal and Herath for bugger all on a wicket that isn't doing a lot, and we win the test surprisingly comfortably, by 193 runs, and take the series two-nil.

Sri Lankan captain Angelo Mathews puts our win down to our fielding. It's true that they dropped key chances and we held ours — some of them, like Kane's to dismiss Mathews in the second innings, and Trent's at backward point to dismiss Sangakkara in the first, truly spectacular. Those were definitely turning points in a tight match, big guns falling to sharp chances. But it wasn't just about the spectacular catches, as Andrew Fidel Fernando reported for Cricinfo in the quote at the head of this chapter.

Reading stuff like that is so cool. It means the work we've put in is paying off. We're developing confidence in both batting and bowling: we've got class batsmen who can get big scores under pressure, and bowlers who can take 20 wickets on pretty much any surface. This time, Kane is Man of the Match, with 69 in the first innings and a match-changing 242 not out in the second. But he couldn't have done it if BJ hadn't stayed with him, and we wouldn't have got home on the last day if Mark Craig hadn't taken four wickets on a pitch which wasn't a big turner.

Fernando gets it:

> *New Zealand have had many heroes recently, from McCullum and his triple-hundred last year, to Mark Craig's 10-wicket haul at Sharjah, and now Williamson's double-ton at the Basin Reserve. No one will have a plaque unveiled in their honour for cutting off a boundary, or receive the keys to the city for pouching safely at slip, but New Zealand amplify the threat of the collective like no other side, and their opponents will continue to discover that can be the difference between victory and defeat.*

New Zealand amplify the threat of the collective like no other side . . .

I can't put it so beautifully, but it's great to see what we're trying to do being recognised by some pundits, that the team-first culture is sticking, that even though we were one-nil up, we'd still press — and by so doing take a risk of losing — to try to go two up. That we try to be proactive, aggressive, even at the risk of a result not going our way.

Its seems like a long time ago that we sat down in Cape Town and worked out what we needed to do, but it's actually less than 24 months. Internally, it's now a nicely structured team — we've got great management and support people around us, and we've got a team of guys who are not necessarily old, but who are very experienced now, emotionally pretty level-headed, and strong leaders.

The soul we aspired to in Cape Town is starting to manifest itself in fighting characteristics, and there are signs that we're getting the respect we also talked about back then, not just from our opponents, but from the people we're ultimately out there representing, the New Zealand public.

After that devastating loss in Cape Town, Hess, Mike Sandle, Bob Carter and I talked about two aspects: what we do and how we're viewed. We can be happy with what we've done so far, and we can take some satisfaction from the changes in public perception those performances have engendered. I think we've got rid of the prima donna stuff, and the public are starting to see us as a team of pretty humble guys who are known to respect the game and play it in the right manner — hard, but within the spirit of the game.

It's a fantastic beginning to 2015, a year with an ODI World Cup hosted by New Zealand and Australia, then a tour to England in winter and a tour to Oz in prospect at the end of the year. How good is that? Another date, in October with the criminal court at Southwark in London, seems so far away I can almost put it out of my mind.

22
Prelude

> We've also been pretty consistent in how we've gone about things in terms of selection, in terms of the way we want to play the game, and in terms of the people we think fit that mix. We've given them time to try and grow into the game. By doing that you end up playing for the team, rather than trying to just stay in the team. When you're fighting for your place all the time the team aspect can be neglected, and we certainly don't do that in this group.
>
> — Mike Hesson

For most of my tenure as captain, I've been most concerned about building a Black Caps team to play test cricket, but in and around all these tours and test matches, there've been a stream of One Day Internationals.

In the UAE, for example, after that climactic third test played in the shadow of Phil Hughes's death, there'd been two T20s, shared, then no fewer than five ODIs, mostly tight and tough, which we'd won 3/2 under Kane's captaincy, while I rested for the next round. That ODI series win was arguably as important a result as the drawn test series, given what was on the horizon.

The eleventh Cricket World Cup is scheduled to be played in Australia and New Zealand in February and March of 2015. We've been talking about it and doing promotions for it for at least a year, but we've spent much longer trying to build a team capable of not just competing for it, but winning it.

As much as I love test cricket and regard it, as the name suggests, as the ultimate examination of a cricketer, I've also fully embraced the shorter formats of the game. In some ways, at least from a captain's point of view, the pace and compression of the ODIs and T20s make them even more challenging. There's no time to recover from catastrophic mistakes, as our World T20 campaign at the beginning of last year proved. We know going into the World Cup that we have to get personnel and strategy dead right.

Hess and I actually wrote out our team for the World Cup 15 months ago. We first worked out the likely venues, the kinds of conditions we'd be playing in, and what sort of skill-sets we'd need to play under those conditions. We selected our top team, then replacements for key areas, down to our third choices in each position. We knew there'd be attrition through injuries and other circumstances and that we had to have cover for every contingency.

'Other circumstances' covered the loss of Jesse Ryder, for instance. We had Jimmy Neesham as our third all-rounder, so it made sense to try him out as an opener in place of Jesse, to see if that was a way we could get him into the top team. I was batting at number five at the time.

In terms of tactics, we tried to get away from the conservative style we'd played under John Wright — conserve wickets for 35 overs and have a big punt in the last 15. Jesse — like Guppy — had had a free rein: 'Just go and whack it, mate. Don't think about anything else, just go and pump it!'

So when Jimmy was tried at opener, we gave him the same message: 'Just go and play — don't think about it. Don't play like an opener or how you think an opener should bat, just go and whack it.' As it turned out, he didn't deal with it that well. We were asking him to be more aggressive, and he just couldn't be.

Hess is a great planner, and is really good at being able to forecast different situations and teams — his knowledge and preparation have had a lot to do with our successes away from home, and it has been fascinating to watch him now turn his radar onto home conditions. He's also level-headed and consistent in the way he selects. He'll give players time to grow into the environment and what's expected of them, and wants them to play for the team rather than playing to try to stay in the team. There's a critical difference. The team requirements are always paramount. Players have to buy into what we are trying to do as a team. Selector Bruce Edgar deserves a lot of credit here too.

When Jimmy didn't come off as an opener, we had to change tack and shift me up to open — I was the next option on the list. That meant we needed a number five, and the name after mine at number five had always been Grant Elliott.

We didn't think we needed to have Grant there through all the preparatory stuff because we were so certain of what we were going to get from him under home conditions. Hess and I both believe that Grant would have been a highly successful player in international cricket if he hadn't gone to Bangladesh for the T20 Worlds last March. He got dropped after that and he never got the opportunity to play again, but we know that his stats and performances everywhere outside the subcontinent are outstanding. We also know he's a big-match player, a guy who delivers in those games.

Dan Vettori is another interesting case, because we weren't sure he was going to hold together physically, so we had to try other spinners, but always knowing who our first choice was if he was still standing.

There were line decisions made by Hess and Bruce Edgar, with input from me, like the choice between Kyle Mills and Matt Henry. We sat around and debated the merits of those two players for ages. It came down to an acceptance that whoever that choice was, he was unlikely to play unless there were injuries. So if we have Matt in the squad not playing much, then we need him, how is he going to go after sitting on the sidelines for five weeks, say, given he hasn't played much international cricket? With Millsy, we know what we are going to get. He's vastly experienced, and even if he has to sit on the sideline for most of the tournament, he's still going to be great around the group. In the end, that choice would work for us, because when we're forced to bring Matt Henry in for the semi-final, he's been playing domestic cricket and is match fit.

The World Cup will open with New Zealand versus Sir Lanka at Hagley Oval on 14 February. Before that, we get a last chance to put theory into practice. Between 11 and 29 January, we play Sri Lanka no less than seven times, winning four, losing two, including the last one, with one being washed out. I thought it was too much against the same team, particularly when we had to front up against them again in the opening match of the Cup. But it does get us match hardened against some superstar ODI batsmen — we're not going to face a more intimidating line-up than Dilshan, Sangakkara, Jayawardene and Mathews. And it does give different guys the opportunity to step up under pressure.

We want our batsmen to be confident that we can set a target or chase one down, that we've got power and suppleness throughout, able to kick out to a quick start, stabilise or accelerate through the middle, and close under pressure, if needed.

In the first ODI against Sri Lanka, Jayawardene gets a ton, but we chase successfully, after my 22-ball 51 at the top makes sure we're under no run-rate pressure, and Corey, mainly, gets us home with a patient 81.

In the second at Seddon Park, we try to set a target. My 117 from 99 should be the basis of a good total, but our middle order comes down with a rash of run-outs — four in a row — and our total of 248 is easily dealt to, mainly by Dilshan, who, like me, is always going to get runs quickly if he stays in.

After the third is washed out, Sri Lanka sets a challenging total of 276 in the fourth. This time, we fail at the top of the innings, and at various times don't look like getting there, but Kane powers our chase with a fine ton, aided and abetted by Grant and Corey and Luke. After Kane is dismissed, we still need 25 runs off the last 18 balls, but Luke smites 24 off one Perera over, and that's the game.

This is a signature performance for the team, because the impetus in the game swings back and forth several times. At one stage Sri Lanka looks like setting a total of over 300, but our bowlers hang in there and take six wickets in the last six overs — Tim and Mitchell conceding only eight runs from the last three overs at the death — to leave us with an achievable total. By then we'd lost our best bowler, Adam Milne, who'd gone off with a side strain after getting Sangakkara and Mathews with successive balls, then getting a faint edge off Jayawardene, which the umpire didn't pick up.

The fifth and sixth matches end in what looks like comfortable wins on the scoreboard, but each has different dynamics, and brings different players to the fore.

For instance, the fifth at Dunedin is remarkable for the way in which, after having our top knocked off cheaply, at five down for 93, with me and Martin and Kane and Ross and Corey all back in the hutch for bugger all, Grant Elliott and Luke Ronchi step up in a record-setting sixth-wicket stand, which grows rapidly from rescue mission to all-out assault. Grant hits a composed 104 while Luke smashes his way to 170. They're both still there at the end, sharing a world-record ODI sixth-wicket partnership. The target of 360 is never threatened, despite another ton from Dilshan.

This is another signature match, in that it sends a real message about the kind of batting power we have down the lower middle order. It also proves to any lingering doubters that the selection decision of Grant Elliott is the right one.

The sixth match puts another piece of the batting puzzle in place. Ross hasn't been scoring many, but in this match he and Kane just miss out on tons, to set a total of 315. And once again, Corey delivers with both bat and ball, making 40 runs and taking four wickets for 52 off his 10.

That win makes the series safe, and maybe we let the focus slip in the last game, which I sit out. Sangakkara comes good with a ton, supported by Dilshan, and we fall 34 runs short of their total, despite solid contributions from Kane (again, the Man of the Series) and Luke and Dan and Kyle.

It's disappointing to surrender the initiative or momentum against the team we're shortly going to open the World Cup against, but it can also be seen as a timely reminder of Sri Lanka's batting power.

We then win two matches against Pakistan, the first reasonably comfortably after Ross and Grant chase down a low total — Grant has taken three for 26 off five overs with his medium pace, to give us another viable bowling option.

In the second ODI against Pakistan, we set a huge total, 369, courtesy of a 76 at the top by Martin and centuries from Kane and Ross. Pakistan don't get within coo-ee.

That match finishes 10 days before our World Cup opener, and we couldn't feel more ready. The warm-up matches have served their purpose in showing us we're not just a one- or two-trick pony. We have found a lot of different ways to win and a lot of different players have shown that they have the power and poise to do the job.

Our bowling has pace, penetration and control, through Tim and Trent and Adam at the top, supported by Corey, and by Grant's medium pace, while Dan is, well, Dan. Unique.

Of our batting line-up, Martin and Ross have left it late to find some runs, but you might argue they've timed it perfectly. And everyone else down through the order has made runs, some going big, at one stage or another.

But whether we're ready or not, the World Cup is upon us.

23
Something Special

> The toss was lost, drizzle was falling, it was time to go out and face the new ball. The Prime Minister was in attendance, there was pomp and ceremony. It was the opening match of a World Cup. All that would have been enough to break the resolve of a lesser man. Instead, there was a lesson in how to grasp a moment: Brendon McCullum style. He was on strike after four balls, preparing to face Nuwan Kulasekara with rain still hanging in the air. The bat hammered the popping crease then was raised like a battle-axe, his knees flexed and his eyes widened. A split second later, the ball was drilled over cover . . . The next ball he faced, his first from Lasith Malinga, was punched sweetly off the back foot through the covers. McCullum's powers are unlikely to stretch to parting the clouds, but as he started to unleash, the thick morning cloud cover, which had threatened to keep everyone in suspense a little longer, began to lift. Christchurch's biggest sporting occasion since an earthquake in 2011 devastated the city took shape . . .
>
> — Andrew McGlashan, ESPN Cricinfo

The day before the opening match against Sri Lanka at Hagley Oval, I gather the guys around me for a final few words. It's the Clayton's pep talk. I tell them I'm not going to give them a motivational speech, because there's nothing they need to hear. It's just another game: we go out there and do the business. I know we're ready.

We know it's not just another game — hell, we've been so focused on this tournament for so long, worked so hard to be ready for it.

I think we can win it but I have some concerns — not about our abilities, though I know whoever wins it will need a bit of luck. My concerns are around how we're going to deal with the expectation, because the public is going to get right in behind us, particularly if we start well. If we are not level emotionally or if we are training too hard or if we are putting too much pressure on ourselves, we are going to succumb when the big moments come. So I keep telling the guys, and myself. Just go and enjoy yourself. Have a crack.

We've already covered the strategy we want to employ. We know the Sri Lankans so well after seven ODIs against them, their strengths and weaknesses. We have huge respect particularly for their batting strength — Kumar Sangakkara's last four innings against us are 76, 9, 81 and 113 not out.

The morning is overcast, and it looks like there's a bit of rain around. I think there'll be some swing, so when I go out for the spin of the coin, our plan is to bowl first.

Some people prefer to chase or they prefer to set, but I try not to have a preference and just react to the conditions of the day. Historically, it's probably true to say that the Black Caps preferred to bowl first because we didn't really believe in ourselves under pressure with the bat. But I back our batting and have deliberately installed an attitude of 'it doesn't really matter'. Just as well, because Angelo Mathews wins the toss and puts us in.

This is it. The end of hype, the beginning of history, we hope. New Zealand has made the semi-finals a few times, notably back in '92, the last time we co-hosted the tournament. We need to at least match that for a pass-mark. The added element this time is the introduction of knockout quarter-finals.

We're in arguably the tougher of the two pools, A, with four other 'majors' — Australia, Sri Lanka, England and Bangladesh, plus two minnows, Afghanistan and Scotland. Five into four doesn't go, so one of us big boys is going to miss out on the quarter-finals. In Pool B, the four majors, India, South Africa, Pakistan and the Windies, should all go through at the expense of three minnows, Ireland, Zimbabwe and the UAE.

Not making the quarter-finals is unimaginable for us, but equally so for the other majors in our pool: Sri Lanka, winner in 1996, runner-up in 2007 and 2011; England, semi-finalists twice and runner-up three times; and Australia, six World Cup finals for five wins. On history alone, you'd say it's between Bangladesh and ourselves for the chop after pool play. And our recent record against them isn't that great — they've won their last seven ODIs against us. But surely, in our own backyard . . .

It's a long tournament, and there are a lot of well-intentioned words about staying in the moment and not getting too far ahead of ourselves, and taking one game at a time. Objectively, the opening game against Sri Lanka is not make or break: we could probably afford to lose against one of the majors in our pool and still make the quarters.

Bugger all that. I want to make a statement that we are up to the occasion, not overwhelmed by it. And I want to set a run rate that gives the rest of the batting order time to settle. I'm conscious of the last T20 Worlds, when we got away so slowly against them that we were under scoring pressure when their spinners came on. That had ended our tournament.

I take a four off the first ball I face, then belt Malinga's fourth over for 22 and it's all going to plan. I'm on 65 off 47 balls by the time they bring on their best bowler, spinner Rangana Herath. I take him on, dance down the pitch, don't quite get all of it and I'm caught at mid-on. I'm disappointed, but we're 111 for one wicket after only 15 overs — well ahead of the game — which allows Guppy and Kane to accumulate nicely, until Guppy goes for 49 at 136.

Our crisis comes at 193, when Kane is caught unexpectedly for 57 and on the same score we lose Ross. But Corey, one of our youngest, comes in and plays the innings that matters — 75 from 46 balls, supported by the veterans, Grant and Luke.

We think 331 should be defendable, but it doesn't seem quite so intimidating when Dilshan takes to our pace attack. I bring Dan on early to contain things, and almost immediately he does the trick, catching Dilshan. Dan has sweated blood to get to this tournament, after his Achilles injury — thank god we've got him.

But I can't bowl Dan for 50 overs, and after Dilshan goes, Thirimanne and Sangakkara settle in and at 120 for one off 21 overs, Sri Lanka are looking likely. I throw the dice and keep Trent on, even though he, like Adam and Tim, is getting a bit of a hammering. He responds brilliantly, snaking a full out-swinger into Thirimanne's stumps.

New batsman Jayawardene has had problems with Dan historically, so I bring Dan back and with his fifth ball he gets an edge to Luke. Next over, Trent swings one the other way and gets Sangakkara plumb in front. Sri Lanka have gone from one down for 123 to four down for 129, and with Adam coming back with real hostility and pace in his second spell, and Corey keeping the pressure on, it's far too big a mountain for them to climb.

It's a big win for us, both in terms of the margin — 98 runs — and in terms of the psychological boost we, and the New Zealand public, get from it.

That might be the first time I say it, in the dressing room afterward, 'Enjoy the ride, boys!'

That ride, against Scotland at Dunedin, gets a little bumpier than it should be.

Winning the toss is a big advantage, and Trent rams it home with a wicket with each of his first two balls. Tim's also on a hat-trick in the fifth over, before Scotland fights back, with a good partnership by Machan and Berrington. But Corey gets both of them, and then he and Dan wrap up their lower order.

A total of 143 was never going to be enough, even though we bend over backwards to help them by playing some pretty wayward shots and losing seven wickets on the way.

The next big focus for us is England at Wellington. They've been smashed by Australia in their opener at Melbourne and really need to beat us to stay in the hunt for a quarter-final.

The toss is the only thing they win. Eoin Morgan decides to bat first, and unwittingly sets the stage for one of the finest exhibitions of swing bowling ever seen in an ODI. Tim Southee's figures, seven for 33, are the third best in World Cup history and the best by a New Zealander.

I'm able to set an aggressive field throughout their innings, starting with four slips and keeping three or four there beyond the first 10-over power play. That's a tribute to Tim of course, but also to the unrelenting pressure from Trent, then Dan and Adam Milne, who also takes a great outfield catch to dismiss the England captain and snuff out any hope of a fightback.

England's total is 20 runs less than Scotland's, but we're determined to make a better chase of it and not give England a sniff.

I take 18 off Stuart Broad's first over, and 49 off two overs from Steven Finn — including four sixes in a row — on the way to a World Cup record 18-ball 50. I'm on 77 off 24 balls in the eighth over when I'm bowled by a Woakes full toss. Bugger. That would have been a very quick ton. But it's already over for England.

The innings lasts 12 overs and, while I have some sympathy for the wonderful ever-optimistic England supporters who have travelled so far for so little cricket from their team, it's an electrifying result for us.

If Sri Lanka was a good strong lift-off to the tournament, this game shoots us into the stratosphere.

Enjoy the ride? Hell, yes! Airports, restaurants, hotel lobbies — wherever we go, people are amazing. I tell the guys: 'How cool is this? If someone wants a photo, do it with a smile on your face.' This is not going to last forever and we don't want to be like those pricks we've all seen before, who win a few games and then all of a sudden carry on like they're King Dick.

We're pretty much guaranteed a place in the quarters if we beat Australia at Eden Park.

We're hoping they might be a wee bit underdone — after skittling England in Melbourne, they've had to wait a week before their next match against Bangladesh in Brisbane, only to have it abandoned without a ball being bowled: points shared. That illustrates the need to bank points at every opportunity, because the Aussies would have been counting on the full quota from that game. That could easily happen to us.

As a result, and with England going so badly, we know that even if we lose this one, we're still a good shot to go on to the quarters, but that's not our attitude: we're on a roll and want to keep it going, make a statement.

My schedule around the actual cricket is pretty intense as well — a lot of functions, speaking engagements and the like on behalf of the team and sponsors. Hess and Roman and I try to carry as much of that burden as we can, so the rest of the guys don't have to. It can be a pain when it's right before a game, but our attitude is to embrace all that too; we'll only get to do it once.

The night before the game against Aussie, we have to attend a function at Sky City. Both prime ministers speak. Tony Abbott is pretty boring, but John Key is outstanding. Then Michael Clarke and I get up on stage and do a little Q&A, in front of a huge audience. Flem later tells me about a conversation he had with Darren 'Boof' Lehmann, the Aussie coach. Flem remarked to him the game should be a great match. 'If your boys turn up', says Boof.

Michael Atherton has described Eden Park as 'a bear pit'. He last played there in the 1990s, when 'something liquid' was thrown on him while he was fielding on the boundary. Maybe the crowd is better behaved now, but on the night of 28 February, the lights somehow make a magic circle out of what in daylight can be a soulless concrete bowl, and it becomes a broiling close-packed amphitheatre, where lions and Christians wouldn't be out of place.

Aussies aren't easily intimidated, however, and their openers, Finch and Warner, happily belt our pace bowlers around, and make their pre-game statements about the ease of hitting the tiny boundaries in New Zealand look so true. Tim bowls Aaron Finch for 14, but at 51 for one after six overs, the game is getting away from us and I have to bring in Dan to at least put a brake on the scoring rate.

Dan delivers almost immediately, despite one of the most attacking batsmen in the world, David Warner, trying to get after him on what Shane Warne describes as a pitch with 'zero spin' surrounded by 'tiny' boundaries. That first sequence of dot balls Dan bowls to Warner changes the game. Warner simply can't get him away, and the flying opener is suddenly grounded.

Dan then applies a straitjacket to Watson that induces a miscue to Tim at deep mid-wicket — two for 80. Warner's still thrashing on the end of Dan's line, his run rate halved, and it's probably down to Dan that Tim gets him lbw in the next over. Three for 80, and the whole dynamic has changed.

The Aussies are under scoreboard pressure — or, more accurately, believe that they are. Another team might not see it that way, might play more carefully to see Dan off. But Steve Smith gets a faint edge to Dan's faster, flatter ball, and they're four down for 95.

With Dan tying them in knots at one end, I can bring Trent back to attack them at the other. To incredible roars of approval from the packed house, he absolutely rips the guts out of the Aussie middle and lower order, bowls Maxwell for five, Marsh for six, gets Clarke and Johnson caught for seven and eight respectively, then bowls Starc for nine. If they weren't Australians you'd probably feel sorry for them, because at nine down for 106, it's not really a game. All that hot air about tiny boundaries and massive totals!

But Brad Haddin, my old training colleague at NSW, does a great rescue job, getting them to 151, in league with Pat Cummins. That makes it a game, though there's no way it should be a winning total.

I take a Mitchell Johnson corker on the forearm in the third over. The ball hits the fleshy part, not the bone, so there's instant swelling but no real damage that I know of. Apart from that discomfort, no real worries as I smash 50 off 24 balls and it looks like we're going to canter home. But it's funny how often innings seem to replicate one another, and you can't always tell what a decent score on any pitch is until the other side has tried to bat on it. After I get caught out at mid-off, I watch our fall of wickets take on an alarming similarity to Oz's.

One for 40 (Guppy, gone for 11) becomes two for 78 when I go, and we're looking as sweet as Oz were at two for 80. Then their left-arm quick, Mitchell Starc, rips out Ross and Grant in short order and we're four down for 79. Kane and Corey stabilise things through to 131, and we're looking good again, until Starc comes back and gets Luke for six, Pat Cummins chips in with Dan for two, and then, when Kane takes a single off the second ball of Starc's next over, Starc skittles Adam and Tim for ducks with successive balls.

In what seems like no time at all, we've gone from sitting pretty to sitting ducks, nine down for 146, and still six runs short, with Trent out there facing fire-breathing Starc, and Kane stranded at the other end, helpless to avert this mayhem.

Where am I when this drama's unfolding? Out there in front of the dressing room with some of the team, anxiously watching every twist and turn, not daring to change position and somehow hex things? Never. I never watch live. What does it matter if I'm out front or not? I'm better off in the changing room, trying to stay nice and relaxed, not give off too many emotions, so I can support the boys who are going out to bat.

There's a TV screen in there of course, but it's on a slight delay and with the sound off it's next to useless, which is fine. The doors are open and I can hear the crowd, so I know exactly what's happened before it's confirmed by the TV screen. I've spent so much time in that dressing room over the years that I can tell from the crowd reaction whether it's a six, four, two or one, a wicket or a wide.

Once our last batsman, Trent, has gone out to face triumph or disaster, I retreat to the dunnies, out of range of the smoke detectors, and start working my way through a packet of fags.

Out in the middle, Trent manages to get his bat on Starc's hat-trick ball, and is able to leave the last.

Kane is on the horns of a dilemma, illustrated perfectly by what happened to Adam and Tim when he took a run early in Starc's last over — they both got cleaned out. Kane has to get six runs without exposing Trent. One option would be to try to run two on what is a small field. Another option would be to hit a couple of fours. Or . . . While we're still mulling the options, Kane being Kane just steps down the pitch to Pat Cummins, one of the fastest bowlers in the world, and smashes him back over his head for a six. Job done.

George Binoy described the match for Cricinfo:

> *This was the match the 2015 World Cup was crying out for, a competitive contest between two major sides, and the co-hosts played out a thriller in front of a packed and partisan Auckland crowd. The game had everything: perfect weather, a full house, a flurry of early boundaries followed by eye-popping collapses, sensational swing bowling, clever spin bowling, and perhaps the calmest batsman in the world hitting one of the fastest bowlers in the world for a straight six to seal a one-wicket victory for New Zealand. When Kane Williamson put Pat Cummins back over his head to win the match, and the Chappell-Hadlee Trophy with it, more than 40,000 stomachs unknotted at Eden Park, and even this most staid of cricketers allowed himself a fist-pump to celebrate.*

And, too, some guy in the bowels of Eden Park, leaping in the air, fist pumping, bugger the sore arm, before remembering he'd better extinguish the durry he's holding before it sets off the fire alarms.

When we began the tournament we wanted to not have to worry about anything. We've done all our preparation; we've done all our work. We hardly train because we've done all our training. We don't go to the gym because we've done all our gym work. If we were racehorses, you'd say we were tapering, so that we're fresh and up for it on race-day.

Practically, for us, that translates into a helluva good time, to keep any sense of pressure at bay. We have fun, we play a lot of golf. Three days before the game against Afghanistan in Napier, we play the Cape Kidnappers course, followed by an epic dinner at the Elephant Hill winery.

We also polish off Afghanistan by six wickets. The Dan and Trent double act makes sure they don't bat out their 50 overs, so once again we're chasing a small total — though, in fairness to Afghanistan, their 186 is 35 more runs than Oz managed against us, 43 more than Scotland and 63 more than England. One pleasing element of our chase is Martin Guptill's 57, his first significant score of the World Cup.

His selection had been controversial for some pundits, due to a dry spell — his last ODI ton was back in January of 2014. But it has never been an issue for us — we know exactly what he can bring at the top of the order and in the field, and his commitment to the team has been 100 per cent since our clearing of the air on the plane back from the T20 Worlds. Against Afghanistan he looks on the cusp of coming right, and he emphatically — and crucially — confirms that form resurgence against Bangladesh in our final pool game.

We go into that game knowing we haven't won against them for five years, and we're determined to put that right. As usual, I lose the toss, they bat, and we go after them with the ball. But this time, finally, we strike a team able to bat through 50 overs against our attack and set us a big target — 288 — thanks mainly to an unbeaten 128 from Mohammad Mahmudullah.

The Bangladeshi captain, Shakib Al Hasan, throws the dice and opens with himself and another left-arm spinner, and gets both me and Kane in the fifth over, but Guppy takes the attack to him and he and Ross hold the innings together, adding 131 for the third wicket. Ross's 56 isn't his most fluent innings, but with Grant Elliott he gives Corey and Tim Southee a launch pad, and we make it to 289 with three wickets and an over to spare. Guppy's 105 is obviously pivotal to the win, but it's also a huge lift for the team, given what's ahead of us.

Bangladesh have done us a big favour, because it's exactly the searching examination we need going into the knockout stage of the tournament. For the first time in the tournament we've struck a team we couldn't blast out, who set us a sizeable number to chase.

It's the first time there've been knockout quarter-finals. We can't think about being three matches away from glory, we've got to think in terms of being one match away from becoming spectators.

Six out of six gives us top ranking in Pool A, and the way it shakes out means we're up against the Windies at the Cake Tin in Wellington in the quarter-final, which becomes the stage for one of the most memorable individual performances of any World Cup — and I'm not talking about me winning the toss for once!

Bowling first has worked for us thus far: apart from the first game against Sri Lanka, we've been chasing, so it's been a winning formula, even if it has been largely a product of my bad luck with the coin toss. That 'formula' has given rise to a question in some commentators' minds as to whether we're overly reliant on our bowlers to set a soft target for our vulnerable batting line-up. But there's no question in my mind: it looks a good wicket and we should take the positive option.

We've learnt to our cost that an hour's madness can cost a test match, but in ODIs, it can come down to a moment. Poor Marlon Samuels drops a straightforward chance at square leg off Martin Guptill in the first over, and it must surely rank as one of the costliest grasses in World Cup history, as Guppy soars to a ton, a double ton and finishes unbeaten on 237, the highest World Cup score of all time and the second-highest in all ODIs ever.

The barely credible stats tell the story: 163 balls, 24 fours, 11 sixes, his first half-century off 64 balls, his hundred from 111, his second hundred from just 41, and by himself he scores 92 of our 153 off the last 10 overs.

Samuels' botched catch characterises the Windies' fielding effort as a whole — except for a superb running catch by Jason Holder to get rid of me. Kane also goes cheaply, so one of the other satisfactions from a team point of view is that two batsmen who've been struggling for runs, apart from the Bangladesh game, succeed when they need to. Ross supports Guppy perfectly, feeding him the strike, getting 42 runs in a third-wicket stand of 143, before making way for Grant and Corey to come in and have a blast.

But if there's one opener who can match Guppy, it's Chris Gayle, and he lights up the Windies' reply. He's got a bad back so he just stands and delivers, whacking it for sixes and fours through the on side, before Adam Milne bowls him.

One of the other big batting hopes for the Windies, Marlon Samuels, the villain who let Guppy off the hook, is caught spectacularly by

Dan the veteran, leaping high on the boundary to get a hand up to save what would otherwise have been a six. Cricket can be cruel. In the end, the Windies' batting line-up makes 250, just 13 more than Guppy on his own.

We're through to our seventh World Cup semis. The others didn't have knockout quarter-finals, but irrespective of that, those results, apart from 1992, probably represented a fair return on the talents of the respective New Zealand teams. But this time we believe we're better than that, and we're no longer alone in that belief.

Sambit Bal, Editor-in-chief of ESPN Cricinfo, writes: 'Anything is possible with this team now.'

And that's exactly the way we feel.

24
So Near . . .

> . . . the New Zealanders' arms went up and around the shoulder of their mates on either side, drawing each other together so tight there was no daylight in between. And there they were, a group of powerfully built men in their black kit (in itself a statement of authority) standing tall in solidarity, like a band of brothers, with a tribal energy about them. It was an arresting and powerful image, a visual representation of their World Cup campaign.
>
> — Sambit Bal, ESPN Cricinfo

There's no doubt the best four teams make it through to the semis: all the quarters are one-sided. Bangladesh fall over 100 runs short against India at Melbourne, Australia lose only four wickets in beating Pakistan's total in Adelaide, and South Africa monster Sri Lanka in Sydney, skittling them for 131, then overtaking that total for the loss of only one wicket. That last result is particularly ominous, because South Africa will be our opponent in the semi-final at Eden Park on 24 March.

While we can look back on our World Cup finishes and acknowledge that, with the possible exception of 1992, they were a reasonable reflection of our talents, South Africa are the perennial under-achievers. They've been the top-ranked ODI team for long periods yet, like us before the quarter-finals, have never won a knock-out match at the World Cup.

One of their semi-final losses in particular, against Australia in 1999, is the stuff of choking history, right up there with Greg Norman and a certain aquatic . . . well, best to leave the list right there. On that occasion, South Africa entered the final over at 205 for nine, needing a further nine runs to win. Lance Klusener took fours off Damien Fleming's first two balls to bring the teams level. South Africa had to win the game to progress, so needed one run off four balls. Allan 'White Lightning' Donald was at the other end — all he had to do was watch and not lose his wicket. Steve Waugh brought his whole field up inside the circle to prevent the single. Klusener mishit Fleming's next ball, no run, though Donald was backing up so far he was nearly run out. Donald was more careful next ball, so careful that when Klusener mishit again and set off for the winning single, Donald was ball-watching and missed the call, then dropped his bat and was run out by a mile. One mad moment and the tournament was gone.

That history has been mashed into headlines like 'Knockout Hoodoo', in the lead-up to the match at Eden Park, and there's a lot said by the South African team about how ready they are to finally deliver on what their talents have long deserved.

There's also a bit of bad odour with us left over from four years ago, when Scotty Styris and Millsy, who'd come on as twelfth man, gave batsman Faf du Plessis a real spray. Both Kiwis were fined and it wasn't a great endorsement of the game, but attempts to revive that antagonism before this game fall on deaf ears — on our side anyway. I've played with Faf in the IPL and know him to be a great fella, an absolute champion bloke, and I'm determined that, win or lose, there'll be no repetition of that kind of stuff. In fact, before the game, when we're out in the middle warming up, I make a point of saying to their captain, AB, that both teams get on great and have enormous respect for one another, so win or lose let's all have a beer together after the game.

That respect is justified. When we analyse their team, it's hard to find any weaknesses. There's the obvious firepower of Steyn and Morkel and Philander, while Tahir is one of the best leggies going around. Even part-time offie JP Duminy has also been really effective in ODIs. They bat deep and explosively, with legends like Amla and AB de Villiers consistently ranked the best in the world. AB also leads their fielding efforts, and they're the one team, I think, that can genuinely challenge us as the best fielding unit out there.

AB wins the toss, decides to bat. The stats in this tournament favour the team batting first, but we've been the exception to prove the rule and hope to do it again. There's been rain overnight and it's a warm, steamy, humid Auckland day.

One area where we've had an advantage is the first five overs. South Africa haven't been getting off to explosive starts — no 50-plus opening stands so far in this World Cup, averaging in fact only 16.25. We need to keep that stat going, get wickets early, put whatever pressure we can on their middle order, particularly AB, who is, with Chris Gayle I suppose, the single biggest threat in World cricket when it comes to changing a game with the bat.

We do that. Once again, Trent, the top wicket-taker in the tournament, does the trick and bowls Amla for 10 in the fourth over. When he gets de Kock to nick it to Tim four overs later, they're two down for 31 and you'd have to say it's pretty much going to plan. We've lost Adam Milne to injury, but that's not as damaging as it might have been because Matt Henry steps in, fit and ready after featuring in domestic cricket, just as we planned.

But du Plessis, who's been thoroughly worked over by Trent, keeps his cool this time, and patiently rebuilds the innings with the support of Rossouw. It takes them 25 overs to get to the 100 mark, but they're gradually increasing the tempo, and given the firepower to come, we're desperate for a wicket. Corey's getting hit and becoming expensive at 12 runs per over, but it's a price we're prepared to pay when he gets Rossouw to lift one into Guppy's safe mitts: 114 for three.

That brings AB to the crease and he and du Plessis lift the tempo inexorably. While their first 100 took 145 balls, their third 50 comes up in just 46. At drinks after 33 overs, they're 162 for three, with Faf on 63 and AB set on 26. I can feel the complexion of the game changing and pull what levers I can, but AB is dropped on 38, and nothing quite works. Three balls after he's dropped, AB is on 50. Six balls after that, he top-edges and the ball drops between three fielders.

They hit the 200-runs mark off 217 balls in the thirty-seventh over, and it looks like we'll be chasing a huge total — some projections are

350 plus. Faf is 82 and AB is rapidly catching him, on 60, and we're haemorrhaging runs and I'm not sure how the hell we get to apply a tourniquet. We're still giving everything in the field and not bowling badly, controlling everything we can possibly control, but sometimes you come up against guys who play significant hands, and that's what's happening — all we can do is try to hang in there. For the first time in the tournament, I feel the game being taken away from us. The score keeps accelerating and AB is revealing why he's rated the best in the world.

With 12 overs to go, they're 216 for three and I'm looking heavenward for inspiration as AB scores at will and there doesn't seem to be a lot we can do to stop South Africa posting a really big total . . .

Behold! Way up beyond the arc of the floodlights, there's salvation: huge black clouds, which duly deliver a deluge. I'm later asked what I'm thinking when I feel the first drops. Keep raining!

As the rain fades and the covers are removed, the Duckworth–Lewis reset means we've lost seven overs. There's no doubt this penalises South Africa, because they've got wickets in hand which would have served them well across the last 12 overs, but when Faf and AB come back out, they've only got five overs left to wreak mayhem.

Faf is looking good for a ton, but golden arm Corey does it again with his second ball, and he's gone for 82. But at four down for 217 in the thirty-eighth, he has really set it up for South Africa.

David Miller comes to the crease and he and AB cut loose. Fortunately, perhaps, Miller gets most of the strike, but he's no mean hitter himself and races to 49 off 18 balls, before edging Corey to Luke. JP Duminy gets to play a cameo, and AB only adds five to his rain-delayed total, before the 43 overs run out.

The total posted of 281, adjusted to 298, is daunting given we've only got 43 overs to get it, but it's considerably less than what we might have been chasing without the rain. It's still a huge chase — there's only been one bigger successful chase at this ground and that was off the full 50 overs.

I walk to the crease knowing I've got to explode out of the blocks, stop South Africa from applying any runs-per-over pressure on us if I possibly can. If we allow the South Africans to get a choke-hold on us, the run rate will escalate and we'll be under huge pressure. We've got a lot of really good players who can operate at a run rate of five or six an over, but once we get up to seven and eight an over it gets more difficult for them. Guys like Grant are outstanding chasers at five or six an over, but when it gets above that, it doesn't mean they can't do it, but it becomes a big ask.

I get onto Dale Steyn's fourth ball and drive it over cover for a six. Six balls and 18 runs later, I'm well under way. I take 25 off Steyn's third over, during which my 50 comes up off 22 balls.

'McCullum has shredded attacks before in this tournament,' writes Andrew McGlashan for ESPN Cricinfo, 'but given the occasion and the bowlers in front of him it almost defied belief.'

Except that on 59, I pull Morkel to mid-on where Dale Steyn gets a little revenge by taking the catch. Still, at one for 71 after just six overs, it's mission completed in terms of getting us off to a cracker. The required run rate has come down from almost seven an over to a run a ball, and I walk off hopeful that our middle order can bat without huge scoreboard pressure. There might be some slippage in the required run rate, but if it's anywhere near that with 10 or 15 overs to go, we're a better than even chance, even with their bowling line-up.

Unfortunately, we lose our way when Kane goes for just six, then there's a mix-up between Ross and Guppy which results in Guppy being run out, then Ross gets caught down leg-side off Duminy. We've crashed to four for 149 and the pendulum swings back in favour of South Africa, and I can sense the anxiety around the ground, that this might be the end of the magic carpet ride for us.

On the positive side, we're halfway there with six wickets in hand and nearly 30 overs, which allows Grant and Corey to settle in without making any rash moves, just take the singles, and pick off the loose ones to the short boundaries.

At drinks in the twenty-sixth over, we're going well at 174, with both Grant and Corey well established. Our 200 comes up in the thirty-first over, and we're looking a good chance at 99 runs off 78 balls. Corey posts his 50 off 47 balls, just before Grant gets his 50 off 53, and when we get to 250 without losing a wicket, the mathematical equation is definitely in our favour — we only need 49 runs off 36 balls. Wickets, though, are the key, and it seems that just as we clamber our way to a position of relative safety, South Africa counter-punch with a wicket.

Corey falls almost immediately, ending a stand of 103 with Grant, then Steyn comes back to get Luke cheaply, and it's squeaky bum time as Dan walks to the wicket. I can't imagine a better player for the occasion, and Dan proves his worth with his unorthodox nurdling and glancing, trying to get runs and get Grant on strike . . .

But inevitably with such high stakes, things get pretty hairy. Grant is almost caught off the last ball of the penultimate over, and we begin the last over still needing 12 runs and with Dan on strike. It's a question of who will hold their nerve. The stadium is holding its breath, as Steyn begins his run in.

Earlier in the tournament, Steyn was quoted as saying: 'If the team needs two wickets, I'll take those wickets. If the opposition needs five runs off the last over, I'll make sure they only get two. Whatever it takes.'

You'd have to take the man at his word. He's done the job before on us and he's not ranked number one ODI bowler for nothing. Dan is desperate to get Grant on strike. He swings, misses, but takes off anyway. Grant's on to it and charges to the striker's end before the keeper de Kock can throw down the wicket. Eleven runs off five balls. Grant can't do better than a single off Steyn's second ball, so Dan's back on strike. Ten runs off four balls. Steyn needs treatment for a calf injury, which prolongs the agony for me and forty thousand others at the ground and countless millions glued to their TV sets around the world.

I'm in my usual position in the dunnies at the back of the dressing room, smoking and listening to the crowd. This time I'm not alone. Two Indian caterers, the guys who're looking after us for our food in the changing room, join me. Like me, they can't bear to watch. One of them says, 'I'm really sorry Mr McCullum, but may I please have a cigarette? I am so nervous.' So the three of us pile into my packet of fags.

Outside, Steyn comes right and charges in. Dan does what Dan does best: finds a way. He glances a ball behind square on the off and it finds the gap. Six runs needed off three balls. Dan and Grant have a chat. When Dan can't get his bat to the next delivery, he takes off for a bye and, once again, there's nothing South Africa can do about it. Dan has done exactly what he needed to do: put Grant on strike for the winning and the losing of the game and a place in the final. Five runs off two balls. Effectively — though I'm not sure whether Grant knows this — four runs for a tie would be enough, since we finished with more points than South Africa in the pool play and would take it on the count-back.

Grant was a controversial selection in the squad, but we knew we might need his composure and experience for just such an occasion. But we couldn't have imagined that he'd find himself facing his former countrymen with the power of triumph or disaster over them in his hands.

Grant simply takes all the equations, count-backs, and even the last ball of the match out of the reckoning by pulling Steyn gloriously over mid-on for six.

I never thought I'd hear a roar like the one Eden Park delivered when Kane finished off the Aussies with a six, but this is at least its equal. Everyone goes nuts.

In the bowels of the stadium, the two Indian caterers — I wish I knew their names — jump on me and the three of us dance round the dunnies together, then I rush through to the dressing room and out to the front. The boys are ecstatic, but out in the middle, Grant is perhaps the only one who's still composed. After a huge victory pump and a hug with Dan, he bends down to a shattered Dale Steyn and offers him a hand up.

That moment encapsulates what is best about sport. Delight in your win but feel for the vanquished. Know how easily the roles could have been reversed. Know that another time they will be. That's what's so cruel and clear about sport: you win or you lose. The margins may be as tight as the proverbial, but it's still win or lose, triumph or despair and there isn't really much anyone can say to the South Africans to ease their grief. Yes, many say it's the best one-day match they've ever seen, and certainly it's the most exciting high-stakes match I've ever been involved with, but that's scant consolation to the splendid team who make such a legendary match, but lose it.

AB's after-match interviews are heart-rending and gracious, and I can't help that feeling of 'there but for the grace of whomever, go I', and hope that I would be similarly classy if the circumstances were reversed — as they so easily could have been.

And they are *so* classy. AB and I had agreed the teams would have a beer together after the game, but with the level of emotion they're going through, I'm thinking, Jeez, they're not going to be up for that. Within half an hour every single one of them — every management person, every player, everyone — arrives. You can tell they're broken, but they all come in and they spend a good hour or hour and a half in the changing room having a few beers with us. They are bloody great, and that is one of the coolest moments of the tournament.

Next day, we read the reports and look forward to the result of the other semi-final on the Thursday. I'm quoted as saying that I wouldn't mind facing either Australia or India in the final, and that I back my side to beat either team. Then, when the Aussies polish off India, amassing 328 at the SCG before bowling India out with nearly a hundred runs to spare, I'm pleased. It's the perfect final for us, the chance to beat Australia in their own lair.

I'm quoted as saying, 'Hope they're all dreaming as much as we are.' The Aussie response to that would probably be: Dream on, Kiwis. Though if it was Brad Haddin doing the verbals, he'd be mixing in some choice adjectives.

After a game like the one against South Africa, an anticlimax is always on the cards, but when that next game happens to be the final of the World Cup in Melbourne against Australia, it's much harder to take.

Our preparation gives no indication — to me, anyway — that we're not up for it. True, we've not played outside our home patches in this tournament, but we're ready for a trip, ready to go and take on the Aussies in their own backyard. We'd recced the MCG months ago with just this scenario in mind. The media stuff about the size of the boundaries is just Aussie bullshit and bluster — we've played on grounds all over the world and this isn't the first time we've been confronted with a differently dimensioned stadium. We couldn't be more ready than we are. In the lead-up to the final, we try to embrace the excitement and anticipation, but not get too emotionally hyped.

Yet when I get on strike to Starc in his first over, I forget one of the basics: watch the bloody ball! Two loose swishes, then I get cleaned out.

One down for one isn't the start we wanted, but of itself it doesn't spell disaster for our chances, even though it's embarrassing when I get back to the dressing room and realise I've made the most basic of cricketing mistakes.

We've proven we can overcome a bad start. But at three for 39 off 12 overs, after Guppy and Kane go cheaply, we're definitely in trouble, both in terms of wickets lost and run rate.

Starc and his mates are bowling quickly and accurately. Ross and Grant have to put their heads down and try to rescue the situation, set a platform to enable us to bat out the 50 and at least post a score we can bowl at. They do pretty well, put together a stand of 111, before Ross, who's been a bit scratchy throughout, edges James Faulkner to Haddin, who lets his gloves do the talking for once and takes a great catch down leg. At 150 for four after 35 we're still in the game, though.

Despite our start, and even though the Aussie bowlers are a class act, the two Mitchells particularly, I feel we can still get to 250 plus and make them sweat for it. Nine times out of ten in this situation, we'll do that. This time, the pressure of the situation gets to us, must do — the idea, after so many months of the prize being a long way off, then some way off, and it's now sitting there right in front of us. What's worked for us has been not thinking about it, just playing. But now, we start thinking about it too much, wanting it too much. Jeez, we're within touching distance of the World Cup!

Corey goes two balls later to Faulkner for zero, followed by Luke one run later in Starc's next over for zero, and then Dan not long after that to Johnson for nine. We've lost our middle order for 17 runs, and at 167 for seven after 40, we're almost done. To dispel any doubts, Grant's great lone knock comes to an end four runs later — another catch to Haddin off the innocuous Faulkner.

Any repose for Haddin's mouth is only temporary — his constant verbal sprays threaten to dehydrate him as the wickets tumble. Tim smashes one, then goes walkabout and is run out, and that about sums up our innings.

Even so, between innings I still believe we have the winning of it. We've got 183 runs on the board and I'm sure we can rock and roll them. This Aussie batting line-up is relatively inexperienced and I tell the guys we've spooked them once and we can do it again, that if we can get among them early, our 183 is going to be worth 220 or 230, and we'll see how they go under pressure. I'm picking they'll come out hyped by nerves and really aggressive, and that'll play into our hands. But I also know that to defend a score like that, everything has to fall for us.

It doesn't. As usual in the Lucky Country, luck is in short supply for non-dinky dis. We have them one down for two runs, when Trent catches Aaron Finch off his own bowling. Warner's on the attack and, for once, I play the defensive card and take out the second slip. The very next ball goes right through there at catchable height. My fault, but also a product of not having enough runs on the board. Dan pulls a muscle and it really hampers his bowling; he can only get through five overs. But despite all that, the moment that seals the match comes when Matt Henry gets one through a nervous Steve Smith. The ball rolls into the stumps, but the bails don't come off.

These games spin on a moment, and that's the moment. If we'd got Smith, we were in the game, massively. Warner falls on 63. If they'd been three down for that score, with Michael Clarke nervous, scratchy and out of sorts, we were in with a real crack. As it is, Smith and Clarke consolidate and, under no run-rate or wicket pressure, see it through.

It looks like a hiding, and I suppose it is in the end. They took their chances and we didn't. No fairytale ending for us. As well as Australia played, we've saved our worst for last and that's particularly disappointing. Australia stepped up on the day that mattered and were too good for us. It's never great getting second, but you've got to doff your cap to the winner.

Afterwards, I take a lot of satisfaction from the fact that we gave ourselves the opportunity to win the World Cup, and also from the way we played throughout, the brand of cricket we played, the commitment of the guys, the entertainment and excitement we brought to the tournament, and the pride Kiwis had in what we were doing. It's been one hell of a ride, and something we'll remember for the rest of our lives.

With the example of South Africa fresh in my mind, I want to be as gracious in defeat as they were. And I'm grateful that some of the journalists and commentators pick up on that. Brydon Coverdale, writing for ESPN Cricinfo, says:

> *As Michael Clarke and his teammates held the World Cup aloft on the MCG outfield on Sunday night, the New Zealanders stood and clapped politely. Then they filed away one by one, ready to head indoors to commiserate. Brendon McCullum was the last man standing, the last one watching the Australians and applauding. It could have been no other way.*
>
> *There is no such award but if a prize existed for Captain of the Tournament, McCullum would have been the only possible winner. His approach has been infectious, his aggressive style responsible not only for New Zealand reaching their first World Cup final, but for dragging the entire nation with them on the journey. And he has done it with incomparable class.*
>
> *That continued during and after a loss that must have been heart-breaking. As Clarke walked off having been dismissed for 74, with Australia nine runs from victory in his last ODI, McCullum was the first to run over and shake Clarke's hand.*

Dignified to the end, McCullum refused to offer excuses for his team's loss.

It has been magic, absolute magic. I'm hoping that, even though we fell at the last hurdle, some of those moments along the way will stay alive in the memories of young Kiwi cricketers, inspire them, show them what is possible. If that happens, it'll be a legacy of which I and the men I played alongside, and all those who helped behind the scenes, will be so proud. I've always wanted to be part of something special with the Black Caps, with New Zealanders. I didn't really know what that might be. Now I know, and I'm so glad that I didn't walk away from that possibility, that I've managed to stick around through thick and thin to be a part of it.

25
Plain English

> At Lord's these past five days, a burst of sunshine has emerged from the clouds that have recently hovered over English cricket. The feel-good factor is back . . . England and New Zealand contested something close to a perfect Test match, a game that swayed in the breeze of sport's unpredictability. It was clear that the players enjoyed it, though one group rather more than the other when the end result was confirmed.
>
> — Mark Nicholas, ESPN Cricinfo

Shortly after the end of the World Cup, I'm back in India for the 2015 IPL, and it's only there that I begin to get an idea of the kind of reverberations for the world of cricket that the Black Caps' magic ride has created.

I've had a strong profile in India since the launch of the IPL, but most of the time what you do in international cricket doesn't make a great deal of difference to the Indians, it's all about what you do in the IPL. This time, it's different. It seems to me from the reaction, as I travel around, that New Zealand might have been the Indians' second-favourite team. There seems to be recognition for my captaincy, rather than for being just a basher.

The wash-up from the World Cup seems also to have had an effect on some of the international players around me. Mike Hussey seems intrigued by our take on it, tells me that he always felt sick with nerves and dread on the way to a big cricket match and remarks that the New Zealand team's attitude seemed very different. I explain to him that for me it has always been that I just can't wait to go and have a game of cricket — what's the worst that can happen? And that was the attitude I wanted the Black Caps to have.

It turns out to be a pretty reasonable IPL season for me, but the down-side of that is a late arrival for me, Trent, Tim and Kane in England in May for a two-test series. We miss both warm-up games, against Somerset and Worcestershire, won in our absence. It's not ideal to go into a test series with no meaningful red ball cricket for over five months but, as Hess says, we don't have much choice. It's been this way for the last eight years, so we just have to adjust as best we can.

In England, even more so than in India, I find a quite amazing response to what we did at the World Cup.

Some of that has to do with the state of English cricket, and the fact that we arrive at a difficult time. England's World Cup campaign was disastrous, the coach has resigned, and there's an ongoing public stoush between Kevin Pietersen and the selectors. Alastair Cook, the England captain, looks like the weight of the world has descended on his shoulders after one win in their last four series. I remember how that feels!

So we're basking in quite a bit of adulation, especially from the commentary teams, which is pretty cool because they seem to appreciate the way we'd played — not just that we'd played aggressively, but also for the way we'd carried ourselves and the spirit we brought to the games. That such a traditional set-up, the home of cricket, is looking at us in a positive light means a lot.

With England at a low ebb, there's a perception that they are ripe for the plucking, but when we lose the first test at Lord's from what seems to be an impregnable position, my captaincy stocks fall quite dramatically with some critics. There's nothing like cricket for that roller-coaster ride from cock-of-the-hoop to feather duster!

It's actually a great test, which starts well for us. My first act is to win the toss and put England in. And there's an immediate pay-off — England are four for 30 in short order, with Cook, Lyth, Ballance and Bell all out. On debut, Matt Henry is brilliantly complementing the Tim and Trent show. But then Joe Root and Ben Stokes just miss their tons, and both Buttler and Moeen Ali play good hands to resuscitate England and get them through to 389.

Then we seemingly set up the game with 523 in response, with a ton from Kane (132) and good contributions from Guppy, Tom Latham, Ross, me and BJ, giving us a first innings lead of 134. So far, so good.

When England bat again, we once again have their top order under pressure, at two for 25, then three for 74 with Lyth, Ballance and Bell back in the dressing room. But Cook is still there, and with Joe Root and then Ben Stokes supporting him, the English captain puts together a huge ton in the context of the match. His 162 is classic Cook, a ton off about 300 balls. But it's another magnificent knock from Ben Stokes that really hurts us. His maiden century, the fastest in Lord's history, anchors a total of 478 — which would have been considerably more without Trent's wonderful bowling on the morning of the fifth day.

Between innings, as we pad up, we've still got to fancy our chances, if we get away to a good start.

Being two down for no runs is not that start. It does have a certain statistical symmetry to it — it's the first time in cricketing history apparently that two openers who've both scored fifties in their first innings both score ducks in the second — but that's no comfort to me, and it quickly gets worse, when Ross joins Guppy and Tom back in the dressing room. Three down for 12 runs. Suddenly England have all the momentum, and we're looking to try to consolidate. If we can manage that, maybe we can have a second launch at the total later in the day.

Given that, we decide that BJ will go in ahead of me at number five, try to shore things up, take a bit of sting out of their attack. One factor in that decision is my feeling that my defence is not quite where it should be for test cricket after coming straight from the IPL. I realise that'll confirm some of the criticisms about my arriving late from the IPL, but that's the reality of the demands of the different formats and contests and it's too late to revisit the pros and cons of that when you're walking out to face.

In any case, the strategy works, to a degree. BJ puts his head down and he and Kane work assiduously to rebuild our innings. But, on 27, Kane is caught by Joe Root off Stokes and when I come to the wicket, my first ball from Stokes is later described as a 'murderous in-swinger'. He swings it miles back into me and it hits my glove, onto my pad and rolls into the stumps. What do you do? Trudge back the way you've come, with a first-ball duck against your name, as the crowd rises in anticipation.

Ben Stokes is on a hat-trick, which Corey avoids, but at drinks, halfway through the penultimate session, we're five down for 75. By tea, he and BJ have taken us through to 134 for five, and we're looking good for at least a draw.

We begin that final session with BJ on 36 and Corey on 51. With the two of them there, BJ the rock, and Corey scoring so freely, anything is still possible, but when BJ edges Wood to keeper Buttler, the wheels fall off alarmingly quickly. Corey is gone soon after for 67, and seven for 174 becomes 200 for nine at drinks. By then any prospect of winning is gone and we're hanging on for the draw — dashed when Trent tees off to Broad and is caught by Moeen Ali, to a rapturous reception by a capacity crowd at Lord's.

We're still 9.3 overs short of stumps and safety.

Some of the stats from the match aren't kind, and neither are some of the New Zealand critics.

It's the highest first innings score by New Zealand in a losing test, and only the fourteenth time in test history that a team has scored 500 plus in a first innings and still lost. It also maintains a sad record for New Zealand second innings at Lord's: scores include 220, 219, 131 and 68, and an average of 17.92 runs per wicket in the fourth innings in seven tests there.

While the English enjoy it, as the Mark Nicholas quote at the start of this chapter illustrates, other critics, like Jarrod Kimber, are more than slightly peeved that a game we had controlled had slipped away: 'This was their time. They saw it. They grabbed at it. They fumbled. They had it taken away. They won't go to Headingley confident or in charge. They will go 1–0 down.'

My captaincy also gets a grilling from a by now predictable source.

Under the heading 'NZ hero Brendon McCullum is absolutely, positively not a great captain', Mark Reason articulates for the *Sunday Star-Times* a point of view which probably garners a fair bit of mindless support: 'At Lord's Brendon McCullum threw away a series win because he is too in love with his own attacking image.'

Ian Chappell is quoted at length by Reason. Using Chappell of all past captains to beat me over the head is a bit strange. He is often described as one of the most aggressive captains ever, and is also described as a captain who, like me, is accused of having fashioned his team in his own image, a team who became known in some quarters as 'the ugly Australians'. Yes, he took over an Aussie team at a low ebb and through self-belief and a team-first ethos he created a team that never lost a series but, then again, he did have the likes of Thomson and Lillee, Greg Chappell, Doug Walters, Rod Marsh, et cetera, to help execute his plans.

Reason seems increasingly to see himself as a lone prophet in the wilderness, pointing the bone at me:

> *. . . If enough people said the same thing, then it had to be true. The man was a genius.*
>
> *Only McCullum is not a genius. For all the positives that he has brought to the New Zealand captaincy, McCullum is fundamentally lacking in that other Chappell virtue, common sense. In the rush of adrenalin, as he dives over the boundary ropes, flicking the ball back with a heroic sweep of the arm, McCullum cannot see past his own bravado.*

I reckon that statement is worth examining in some detail, because it seems to me to be the very opposite of the team-first, emotionally stable ethos Hess and I and Mike Sandle and the team leaders have been trying to instil. It's interesting how far from reality some observers' perceptions can be.

Objectively, I can't see much 'bravado' or lack of Chappellian common sense if you look at my captaincy in this test.

I won the toss, put England in and they lost four early wickets.

They got a reasonable first innings score, but we got over 500 in our first turn to bat. Clearly, someone got that right.

Then they batted very well in their second innings, Stokes amazingly so. We didn't, but it wasn't because we were full of false bravado. In fact, my decision to send BJ in ahead of myself because his defence was better could be read as a conservative, even cautious move. That tactic might even have worked if I hadn't got out to a wonderful first ball from Stokes, which I tried to defend.

Which match was Reason watching?

This time, Mark Reason is not alone in giving me stick, but at least most of the other critics have some basis in fact. Many of them seem to be critical of my after-match comments. The *New Zealand Herald* editorialises that I'm more worried about winning the PR battle and being the media darling than trying to win the game. Clearly, my after-match comments are far too positive for some:

'To England's credit they were too good for us in the crucial stages but I'm still really proud of our guys and the way we kept going,' I said. 'I thought it was a fantastic test to be a part of, to play five days in front of full houses at Lord's and for it to come down to the final ten overs is a testament to how good it was.'

I also say that the result hurts, a lot. That bit seems to get lost. But you can't have a fair-weather commitment to team strategy and only laud it when you win. There's criticism for losing too easily, for being cavalier about it, for 'letting the test go' and then not being remorseful enough afterwards. For the record, this is what I actually say, as well as the above:

> *'It hurts a lot, I won't lie. At the same time there's an element of pride that we continue to play a style of cricket that gives us our greatest chance. There will be times when teams can stand up to you and withstand the pressure and come out on top. You just have to doff the cap, say well played and make sure next time you get the chance you go hard again and ask the same question. Who knows, at Headingley we may see a different result but I'm sure our guys will continue to play the same style.'*

To be fair, that's appreciated by most of the critics, such as Andrew McGlashan at ESPN Cricinfo:

> *It has been a fine time for New Zealand cricket of late and much of that comes from a kind approach to the game. If the spirit of cricket is based on respect — for the game itself, the opponent and for yourself — McCullum's team illustrate it better than any other. There is no ugly face, no sign of unpleasant words and no hint of deceit. Instead, there is an overwhelming generosity of spirit. England batsmen were congratulated on their achievements by firm New Zealand handshakes. Friendship was the theme of the contest, albeit with no quarter given in the heat of battle.*

There's another really important element to this 'generosity of spirit'. You've got to look at both sides, for goodness' sake. Ben Stokes came out, had a crack, and played like a genius. There are players in the world who, when they come off, it doesn't matter what you do, you can't stop them. Stokes was that player that day. He was the difference. Acknowledge that.

And as we pack out of our London hotel and head up to Leeds for the second test, it's worth remembering something else I said:

'Emotionally our guys are really steady and that's allowed us to be able to play some good cricket so that will be the message, no knee-jerk reaction to a performance like this because we were pretty good for most of it.'

26
Sweet Spot

> McCullum's team sent a message: their style came with risk, but not at casino-like odds. Better to play with freedom and be a desirable global commodity than beg for scraps of attention and pity.
>
> — Andrew Alderson, *New Zealand Herald*

The second test in a dour, sometimes icy, Yorkshire couldn't be more different from that ecstatic summer festival mood at Lord's, yet there are some weird parallels.

The winner of the toss — in this case Cook — decides to bowl. And, initially, as at Lord's, that decision seems vindicated: we're two down for two runs, then three for 68, before our middle and lower order fights back — just as Joe Root and Ben Stokes did at Lord's — with Luke Ronchi on debut getting 88 priceless runs, supported by forties from me and Mark Craig. At eight down for 281, we're hoping to get to 300, but Mark and Matt Henry get us through that barrier to 310, then Trent manages 15 with Mark to make sure we finish on exactly 350 — a score we'd have taken when we were inserted on a rainy, cold Leeds morning the day before.

That rain pretty much wiped out the morning session of Day 1 and came back in the afternoon to make a disjointed first day that didn't help our batsmen settle in and get their innings going. Yet despite all that, we'd scored almost 300 in that first day, absolutely pumped it and really advanced the game, despite all the time lost to rain.

Day 2 and the first part of Day 3 aren't blighted by rain, and England also make exactly 350 — another total I'd have readily accepted when

England were one down for 177, then two for 215. This time, after Cook's 75 and Lyth's 107, there are no other substantial contributions, the rest of their top and middle order being ripped out by Trent and Tim, who ends up with four wickets.

So, effectively, the game begins again just before lunch on Day 3. I keep telling the boys what a great achievement it'll be if we can win a test, how few teams come over here and beat England in their own conditions.

Guppy and Tom get us safely through to lunch, but immediately after, we lose two quick wickets, Tom and Kane, and we're rocked back on our haunches at two for 23. This time, Ross and Guppy stop the rot, and take us through to 122, before Ross is caught by Stokes off Wood just short of his half century. Nineteen runs later, Wood also gets Guppy, so it's down to BJ and me to try to get a total we can bowl to.

One scribe reckons Cook was giggling at slip in anticipation of a short flurry from me. In the first innings I'd hit a six off the first ball I'd faced. This time, I go into my shell a bit and don't score a run off the first six balls. BJ is flowing at the other end, and I see my job as supporting him to try to get us to a score to put us beyond reach of England. Defensively, I'm still not picking up the ball as well as I should, but I manage to eke out 55 runs from 98 balls, which is pretty sedate for me. But when I go, leg before to Wood, at 262, the innings is still in the balance.

BJ gives us, once again, the innings we need, putting together a stand of 53 with Luke (a 31 to go with his great first innings) and the same again, exactly, with Mark, before finally being caught by Joe Root off Jimmy Anderson for 120.

It's not just the quantity of BJ's runs that keeps us in the game, but the speed he's got them at. His 100 comes off just 136 balls and he and Luke take 50 off 40 to give us well over 300 runs from just over two sessions. It's that scoring rate, maintained by BJ and Mark into Day 4, that begins to give me options, despite losing the best part of a day to rain.

At seven down for 368, we might be grateful for 400, but Mark's remarkable late-innings batting anchors a run-a-ball 40 from Tim and then 12 from Matt before I declare at 454, with Mark unbeaten on 58.

That declaration is a no-brainer — we've got to win this test to draw the series, and we need to give ourselves time to bowl them out, and allow for the ongoing threat of rain. If the rain stays away, England have the best part of five sessions to get 455, which must be enticing for them too.

England make a solid start, and Cook is doing his limpet impression, when Trent gets Lyth for 27, and that opens the door, because he seems to have poor Gary Ballance on toast. Two for 61 quickly becomes four for 62, when Mark spins out Bell (who, like Ballance, is having a dreadful series) and Joe Root.

At that stage, we're looking sweet, but England stabilises, with Cook holding down one end and the dangerous Ben Stokes getting set at the other. With fresh memories of what these two did to us at Lord's, I decide to gamble.

It's quite windy and Mark is drifting it with the breeze but then spinning it away, so Cook's able to play down the line to him — if it beats him then it just goes past him, and if Mark gets too straight Cook is able to whip him. I decide Kane might be a better option.

Kane can be a bit of a golden arm, he's just got a knack, and I know he's got Cook out a few times by just sliding it into him. Kane is a bit skiddier than Mark and doesn't turn it as much, so I reckon if Kane uses the drift and Cook plays the line and misses it, he's going to be a sitter for leg before.

I can't say it goes exactly to plan: instead of getting Cook lbw, Kane induces a nick from Ben Stokes, which is gloved by Luke.

We go to lunch with England at 102 for five and the game in the balance, Cook on 40 and wicketkeeper Buttler yet to score. We've got two sessions to get five England wickets, and Cook has to be the key.

I persist with Kane and it finally works: on 56 Cook plays the line, misses, and the ball skids into his pads. Cook 56, lbw Williamson, England six down for 141.

From there, we still have to really work for everything we get. Ali falls relatively cheaply, but Broad stays with Buttler, until he's bowled by golden arm Kane.

At tea, England are 206 for eight with Buttler on 40 and Wood on 10. At Lord's, we were 134 for five at the same stage, and couldn't save the game, so we'll be disappointed if we can't get the two wickets we need in one whole session. But as long as Buttler is there, they have a hope of saving it.

Wood hangs around until 230, then on 17 he nicks Tim to Mark in slips. Jimmy Anderson then stays with Buttler for six overs until Mark gets Buttler leg before for a fine rearguard action 73.

So England are finally all out for 255, 19 overs short of batting it out. Job done. Phew.

This has to be one of the most satisfying wins I've ever been a part of, particularly when you drill down into the dynamics of the match and the series.

To level the series and preserve our two-year unbeaten run by scoring 804 runs at close to five an over after being two down for not much in both innings, to skittle England twice with a combination of pace and spin, to take the catches we did, and to do all this while we lost the best part of a day to rain, shows not just the talent of this team but its character. It's our first away win against England in 16 years, and only our second ever at Headingley.

The big thing for me is that we didn't blink. We didn't retreat into our shells after the loss at Lord's and abandon our playing style and philosophy. We showed guts and we showed belief.

After the game, Hess talks about our aggressive mindset, and puts it in a nutshell:

'It is challenging if it doesn't work out because you can get exposed, but if you truly believe the way you play gives you the best chances of success then, regardless of the situation, you need to stick to your guns.'

I look back at how we came from one down against Pakistan last year to draw the series in really testing conditions in the UAE, and now we've done the same in the very different conditions of England.

As we head into a five-game ODI series it's great to see that appreciation reflected in the England team and the media. George Dobell's report for ESPN Cricinfo is representative:

> *One factor that must not be overlooked in the coming days is that England lost this Test — and drew this series — against a fine side. It is no disgrace to lose to a team of New Zealand's ability and many will celebrate that they were rewarded for the appealing manner in which they played. They provide proof that cricket can be played with passion and aggression without resorting to sledging and threats. They have been a breath of fresh air in a beautiful sport that has, of late, sometimes looked a little ugly, and their spirit improved England's.*

There's also a lot of laudatory personal stuff about this team being built in my image. All of which is hugely gratifying, but it kinda misses the larger point, a point which former Black Cap fast bowler Iain O'Brien makes brilliantly on ESPN Cricinfo:

> *While McCullum, as captain, is in charge, I don't see it quite as clear-cut as New Zealand playing just like Brendon does.*
>
> *I'm looking a little deeper and at the same time reflecting back to 2005, a team McCullum was a big part of. Trying to take a game deep didn't work for us. We weren't good enough, we would run out of steam. And since we didn't play as many Tests as some other teams, we couldn't learn to develop that Test match fitness (physical, mental, and emotional) that is so necessary for success.*
>
> *To contrast that, then: to an extent, what we're seeing this New Zealand team do is say, let us win in four days. Let us not go out there to grind them down, let us go out there and take the game to them. Not to absorb the pressure but to force it back. Let us attack as much as possible. Make them make the mistakes.*

> *This style — it's actually not a style. It is a product of the players New Zealand are producing. Not the product of one person's vision.*

We would've loved to have seen a couple of the ODIs given up for a third and deciding test, but in England's eyes, we haven't been worthy of a three-test series — maybe that will change. As Andrew Alderson suggests in ESPN Cricinfo:

> *They [New Zealand] are No. 4 in the rankings, and it is not hyperbole to suggest their revolutionary brand could be a bargaining chip for extra away Tests. Who wouldn't want to play New Zealand? Win and you defeat one of the world's most dashing teams; lose and you've witnessed cricket at a tempo difficult to emulate but spectacular to watch. A team that can score 1547 runs at 4.27 per over and deliver 40 wickets through pace and spin, as New Zealand did across the two Tests, provides captivating entertainment . . . Four slips and a gully? No problem. Eight batsmen out of ten hitting sixes in the second innings at Headingley? Voila. Pitch the ball up and let it swing? Too easy. Attrition is out, aggression is in.*
>
> *The usually objective sanctuary of the English media box ooh-ed and aah-ed as New Zealand unleashed their arsenal of skills.*

The second test result prompted England captain Alastair Cook to say, 'If you were a boxing promoter you'd be asking for a rematch right now.'

They say imitation is the greatest form of flattery, and in the ODI series a rejuvenated England play the way we did at the World Cup.

They make a real statement in the first match at Edgbaston. At five down for 195 and more than 20 overs to go, England could batten down the hatches, but Jos Buttler ups the tempo if anything, hitting 129 off 77, and with the support of Rashid's 69 off 50 there's nothing our relatively inexperienced bowling attack can do to stem the flow. Trent takes four for 55, a stunning return in the context of an innings where 408 runs have been plundered, and where the other bowlers' figures make pretty grim reading.

There's only one approach to chasing a total like that, and when Steve Finn bowls me for 10 off four balls, we're on the back foot, compounded by Guppy going pretty cheaply. Only Ross makes it past 50, narrowly, and we're all done at 198, losing by 210 runs, a figure that used to be a competitive total in ODIs when I first began playing them.

That first ODI establishes a template for the rest of the series — batsmen ascendant in some huge totals, matched by crowds and enthusiasm, as we travel round the country.

We win at The Oval by a mere 13 runs after almost getting to 400 ourselves and take a 2–1 lead in the series with a narrow win at Southampton. Then England chase down 349 at Nottingham, and the series comes down to a decider at Durham where, unfortunately for us, on a grey day and slow pitch, rain and its inevitable partners, Messrs Duckworth and Lewis, intervene once again. Jonny Bairstow, replacing injured Jos Buttler, plays the winning hand, an unbeaten 83 off 60 balls.

I'm not surprised at England's resurgence. The England ODI captain, Eoin Morgan, is a great mate. He'd had a terrible World Cup, but he's a genuine talent and was always going to come back. He was the reason I signed for Middlesex. I knew he was the right man for England, and I'm pleased he's getting the accolades for winning a stunning series.

And what a series. There have been more runs scored than in any previous five-match ODI series, at a higher run rate, and the crowds have flocked to see the action. While the Back Caps may have finished on the wrong side of the win/lose ledger, according to many of the critics, we leave English cricket in a much better place than we found it a couple of months ago.

We're delighted, but we're buggered. We knew when we put all our eggs in the World Cup basket in terms of training and peaking that there'd be a hangover for a few months after. And we're still feeling it. We've lost key people to injury, bowlers particularly, and by the end of the tour, we're out on our feet.

There are a lot of personal achievements to reflect on. Kane gets Man of the Series. The 1038 runs scored by Ross against England are the most by any New Zealand batsman — he became the first New Zealand batsman to score 1000 ODI runs against England during his innings of 47 in the last game. Kane has scored 1037 ODI runs in 2015, the most by any batsman. During his innings of 50 at Chester-le-Street, he became the first batsman to score 1000 ODI runs this year. He's trailed by Guppy (980), Ross (929) and a certain Kumar Sangakkara (862).

Over and above all that, though, is the memory of what has been a brilliant tour and series. As Mark Nicholas writes for ESPN Cricinfo: 'Not since the glorious Ashes summer of 2005 has cricket been so interesting to people who aren't interested. They simply cannot believe that the game could be played at such breakneck speed and with such gay abandon.'

I'm not sure about the gay abandon but, yes, the pace has been incredible — and has taken its toll. But the memories of this tour are the kind that fortify the soul in difficult times, and I fear there's a bit of that right in front of me.

When we were in London, I never got down to Southwark, but that's the next destination in my cricketing journey. I've gotta say, a criminal court is not the kind of arena I'd ever thought cricket would take me to.

27

Trial and Tribulation

> Cairns' team made much of the 'shifting sands' of McCullum's statements, accusing him of misconstruing an innocent conversation and later dovetailing his evidence with Lou Vincent's.
>
> — Jared Savage, *New Zealand Herald*

The prospect of the Cairns trial has hung over everything I've done for at least the past year. The demands and sheer excitement of the cricket we've been playing have helped me keep that black cloud on the distant horizon, but now it's right above me.

My mate Garth Gallaway made it clear at the time Cairns was charged with perjury that I couldn't be compelled to testify, that I couldn't be subpoenaed from over there, that I'd fulfilled my obligations as a professional cricketer by reporting the Cairns approach to the ICC. He said that if I wanted to, I could walk away from having anything to do with the trial.

I've definitely thought about how much easier it would be for me and Lis and the family to do that, rather than putting us through the wringer by going to London. I would feel justified to some degree by the way the ICC have cocked the whole thing up with their leaks and mismanagement, but I know that in the end it's not about the ICC, it's about cricket, and if I walked away from this trial, I couldn't live with myself — in my mind that'd make me the worst kind of hypocrite. I can't go round espousing the spirit of the game, then disappear down my bolt-hole when the going gets a bit tough. I don't think I've got any option but to stand up in that witness dock, but I dread it.

It's weird, though. In September, I'm with Mike Hesson in my best bib and tucker being honoured with the New Zealand Order of Merit for services to cricket at Government House by the Governor-General, who uses words like 'leadership' and 'inspiration' and 'world class'.

I'm stoked for Hess as much as myself. His stoicism and resolve in the face of the most trenchant criticism, much of it personal, has been Herculean. I've watched it all from close quarters and had enough of it myself to know how difficult it is to just shrug it off and keep going, make good plans, stay the course.

A month later, I'm in my best bib and tucker in the witness stand at the Southwark Crown Court in London, for services to cricket (in my mind at least), facing a barrister who uses words like 'cheat' and 'liar' and 'match fixing'.

I'm a fish out of water in both arenas, but I'll take the kind words of Governor-General Sir Jerry Mateparae any day, over the loaded questions of Orlando Pownall QC, Cairns' lawyer. Sir Jerry makes Mike and I feel like we've achieved something special for cricket and for New Zealand, whereas Pownall makes me feel like I'm the one on trial for trying to turn cricket into a rigged circus.

Even the lead-up to the trial is stressful.

Back when Cairns was charged, Garth also explained to me that if I agreed to testify, I'd inevitably become a target, that under the adversarial system of justice Cairns' only real defence, his only play, was to try to discredit me and the other Crown witnesses.

I already had more than an inkling of what that might mean. The ICC plastered a big target on my back when they leaked my testimony to Ed Hawkins of the *Daily Mail*, so that every man and his dog knew in detail exactly what my evidence was going to be.

Cairns hadn't been charged at that stage but he must have known the writing was on the wall and started talking about 'dark forces' aligned against him. Then Cairns posed for the media so that a clear plastic folder he was carrying was in shot. The file was titled *BMC* with my name and Schwalger's clearly visible. Cairns was quoted as saying that he hoped 'significant additional information will be flushed out that will help people to better assess the situation, as well as the character and motives of the parties involved'.

Since then, nothing has changed. The Schwalger emails don't have anything to do with Cairns, he's not mentioned once, but I'm advised by the Crown in London that Cairns is trying to get them admitted as evidence because he believes they'll help discredit me as a witness. This isn't the only element that makes the lead-up to the trial so stressful.

Christchurch was Cairns' old stamping ground; he still has a lot of mates around town. Some of them were people I considered my mates too. The information they have would have been highly relevant to proceedings in Southwark. These people either refused to come forward or wouldn't cooperate when asked directly.

Okay, that's their choice, but they're not my friends any more; I simply don't want to be around them. It's a bit like a divorce — people feel they have to make a choice, and some did. I guess most of them have known him longer than they've known me. So it goes.

There are other more innocent decisions which have unforeseen consequences when I get to court.

My good mate Flem tries to steer well clear of anything controversial. He tells the Metropolitan Police that he's 'a bit foggy' on whether or not I had told him about Cairns approaching me about match fixing. Maybe he was trying to stay out of the whole thing, which I understand, but he inadvertently gives Cairns' barrister Orlando Pownall another stick to beat me with in cross-examination. 'You say you told Stephen Fleming? How is it that he can't recall your doing that? Wouldn't that sort of revelation about his former teammate be something Fleming would remember?' And so on and so forth.

The ICC's role in this isn't so innocent, given what must have been a deliberate leak of my testimony, but their original interview was an innocent enough cock-up. It had been so casual, partly because the ACSU officer who was conducting the interview, John Rhodes, didn't think it would go anywhere. When the ICC realised that my testimony might be important, Rhodes came back for another go, but they still didn't have an interviewer who was as experienced as the London cops who did the third interview.

So there were bound to be discrepancies between the three interviews. Big deal, I thought, but I discovered in the witness stand that these barristers are like hens, when they discover a seemingly insignificant blemish on another hen. Their job seems to be to peck away until they have blood.

Garth has tried to prepare me for what's about to happen, but I must be pretty naive.

'I'm really looking forward to this,' I tell him as we walk across Thames on the footbridge near our hotel on the morning I take the stand. 'It's not often you get a chance to stand up, to do the right thing.'

Because I'm a witness, I don't see any of the trial, apart from when I give evidence myself. So I don't see or hear Lou Vincent's testimony, just read about it in the papers like everyone else.

I can't help but feel sorry for the poor bastard. A self-confessed liar, cheat and scoundrel, yes, but when he finally stands up in Southwark, he's a vulnerable, fragile man who is, I believe, belatedly trying to do the right thing. From all the reports, he gets absolutely pilloried by Cairns' defence counsel and then by the judge.

What happens to Lou makes me wonder about the adversarial system. It seems that in court, if you have made mistakes in your life, you can never redeem yourself, you can never recover from them. Tell one lie and you're forever a liar. It's like the old joke about the village goat. Except that Lou got involved with a lot of goats.

But my name is Brendon Barrie McCullum, and when I stand in the dock and say my name and swear to tell the truth, I look across to Cairnsy, sitting in his glass case like a display item, composed and corporate in his dark suit and impregnable sense of entitlement, and wonder which one of us is on trial here and how the hell did it come to this, the two of us on opposite sides in a grotty criminal courtroom in London?

Maybe it shouldn't surprise me. As a cricketer, Cairns loved to attack the game and could change it with both bat and ball, one of the few. Outrageously talented from very young, a prodigy from a famous and much-loved father, he was cricketing royalty when I first played for the Black Caps, and always projected a sense of entitlement. Perhaps that was — and is still — part of the problem: he feels bulletproof.

I feel far from bulletproof. On the bench in front of us, head submerged under a huge white wig, eyes hidden behind reflecting glasses, body robed in red, a man called Nigel Sweeney is peering at me. I'm told he's the judge who put Rolf Harris away: perhaps he specialises in Australasians. He doesn't say anything much to me, but Pownall, Cairns' tall, suave barrister, has plenty to say once he gets stuck into cross-examining me.

He calls me 'McCollum', and keeps referring to 'Brand McCollum', this commercial entity that I'm supposed to somehow be protecting by giving evidence against his client. 'Brand McCollum' can't be that successful if Pownall can't even get the name right, and it can't be that huge a commercial entity if it doesn't even have an agent acting for it, but I don't bother correcting him, because it quickly becomes apparent that in Pownall's eyes, I have a few other potential blemishes he can peck away at.

One is the three-year delay between 2008, when Cairns twice approached me, and 2011, when I first reported those approaches to John Rhodes of the ACSU. I admit to Pownall that I was wrong not to report the conversations immediately. When he asks me whether I was fully aware of my responsibilities to do so, I admit that I was, and that I don't know why it took me so long. I do mention that where I was brought up, we don't rat on mates. Misguided — wrong in this case — but there we are. I hadn't exactly kept it secret and had mentioned it to my skipper at the time, Dan, and others who were about to confirm in evidence that I'd done so.

I answer the questions put to me, but later wonder if I've made clear enough a fine distinction that mattered at the time: that I was aware that I had to report to the ICC any approaches regarding match fixing, yes, but not that if I didn't report that approach I'd be equally culpable.

I'd been alerted to that dictum by Rhodes at a seminar the day before. Dan Vettori, my skipper at the time, hadn't known about that rule either. As soon as we knew we'd be equally culpable if we didn't report it, we'd sought out John Rhodes in his hotel room and told him all about it.

The second thing that seems to agitate Pownall is what he calls 'the shifting sands' of my three statements. They undoubtedly become more detailed as they go along, I can see that, but that's surely explained by the calibre of the interviewer, and the dawning realisation by the ICC that something serious might come from these allegations, so they'd better do a proper interview.

I actually feel sand-bagged by the ICC, that the ACSU officer, John Rhodes, didn't tape that first interview with Dan and me, made sketchy notes, and then didn't do much better when he came back in December of 2013. When the Metropolitan Police interviewed me, it was much more detailed and professional. That's the difference.

It's difficult not to resent the ICC for the way I'm hauled over the coals by Pownall about this, fielding his imputations that I've lied, that I've developed and embroidered the story as I went along (for reasons that are never really articulated, but which apparently have something to do with 'Brand McCollum').

The third thing that concerns Pownall is that I didn't testify against Cairns when he sued Lalit Modi for libel. If I knew Cairns was lying under oath in that trial, why hadn't I made myself available to Modi's defence and said so?

Telling Pownall that it was none of my business and, again, that where I was brought up, you don't rat on mates, doesn't seem to impress him much. I'm not sure he appreciates the difference between doing what you're obliged to do as a professional cricketer (report the match-fixing approach to the ICC) and volunteering to give evidence against a former friend in a case at the other end of the world that has nothing to do with you.

There's not much else. I've got no idea at this stage what Judge Nigel Sweeney makes of it, I'm just really grateful to be told, eventually, by Pownall, that he's got no further questions.

Later that night, Lis and Garth and I have a quiet drink, in celebration of nothing other than the fact that the whole bloody ordeal is over.

It's not, of course. Far from it, but my teammates are already in Australia for a tour which I've been looking forward to for a long time, one of the highlights of my cricketing life.

28
The Lucky Country

> Bad luck. It's one of those flip phrases you hear at times of failure. Often luck has actually had nothing to do with it. But this Trans-Tasmanian summer it has been much more literally true of New Zealand. You couldn't even say luck has deserted them, for that indicates they once had it. That hasn't been the case since they landed in Australia in October. This summer they have been Black Cats more than Black Caps.
>
> — Brydon Coverdale, ESPN Cricinfo

When we're badly beaten in the first test against Australia in Brisbane, there seems to be a consensus that we're underdone going in. And perhaps we are, though it's not due to lack of planning.

We thought that by the time we got to the Gabba on 5 November, we'd have completed a comprehensive series of warm-up games which would bring us out of a patchy New Zealand spring and fully assimilate us to Aussie conditions. We knew we'd need to be sorted and match fit for test cricket at the home of such a combative opponent and we put in place a programme which would get us there.

I missed the first game, a day/night ODI against a strong Prime Minister's XI in Canberra on 23 October. When we amassed over 300 against the likes of Peter Siddle, then skittled them for 205, with Trent and Jimmy Neesham bowling well against a strong line-up, including Khawaja, Burns and Voges, our tour seemed to get away to a promising start. The promise, however, might have been more of threat — the pink ball swung prodigiously at night when the Australians batted.

Next day at the same venue, we began a two-day game against, essentially, the same team, called Cricket Australia XI. This time, no pink ball, no night-time swinging and, crucially, the first appearance of words which from then on through to Adelaide were to preface every scoreboard and come back to haunt us: *Australia won the toss and elected to bat.*

Unlike the night before, Burns (retired 102), Khawaja (not out 111), Voges (retired 33) and Mitch Marsh (not out 18) had very little problems with our attack. Our pacemen, Trent, Matt, Doug and Jimmy, took one wicket between them while conceding nearly 200 runs, and if there hadn't been retirements, the figures would have been much worse. Mark Craig got one for 105. When we batted, the Australian bowlers found wickets hard to come by too. Kane and I got fifties and retired, and most of the line-up got some time in the middle. Coming away from that game, I guess you could say we'd made the best of what was a dead pitch.

Our preparation was supposed to be topped off by a three-day match in Sydney, against another strong line-up. But the pitch at Blacktown in Sydney was even drier and deader than the ones in Canberra.

We lost the toss and at the end of Day 1, the Cricket Australia XI was 350, with both Aaron Finch and Ryan Carters on huge not outs, and our bowlers absolutely buggered. Tim had gone off with an upset stomach after three overs, so for the rest of the day our bowlers got flogged. I was concerned at the way a couple of deliveries had reared off the deteriorating pitch when we took the second new ball, so on Day 2 we didn't use our pace bowlers. It got so bad that I bowled 10 overs! We finally took a wicket — Carters' — 20 minutes before lunch, and they declared at one for 503, a record stand for all first-class cricket in Australia. Great.

That was the end of the game. Hess and I decided it was both dangerous and pointless to send our guys out to bat on a pitch where the ball was taking hunks out of the surface, a surface which, we thought, would have no resemblance to the pitch we'd be playing on in Brisbane.

'We've just had two days here and haven't gained a lot out of it from a preparation point of view,' said Hess, 'other than time on our feet, which is always useful.'

I think he was being kind. He also said that the pitch wasn't up to first-class standard, which was the crux of it. We were told that because of the recent weather, they hadn't been able to grow any grass. It didn't seem that different from any other spring in Sydney, in my experience. You don't tour Australia and expect any favours, but to be served up a pitch like that in the home of cricket was, let's say, less than generous.

But there's also the element of luck. As one Aussie scribe pointed out, on Australia's recent Ashes tour of England — whether by good fortune or design — Australia won the toss and got the chance to bat first in all their pre-series warm-up games.

We head for Brisbane a couple of days early, a bit pissed off that we haven't had a decent three-day contest in normal Aussie conditions, but determined to put it behind us and switch on for the first test.

As it turns out, maybe batting at Blacktown on that first day would have been a better preparation for Brisbane than we thought.

We'd anticipated the Gabba pitch would be reasonably sporting on the first day at least, but it's a batting highway which Australia are good enough to take full advantage of, after I lose what I call a 70/30 toss — if you win the toss, you're a 70 per cent chance of winning the game.

It's pretty dispiriting, even for a player with my approach towards trying to enjoy the contest, when you realise halfway through the first session of a five-day test that the best you're playing for already is a draw.

Oz are 161 by the time they lose their first wicket. By drinks they're 305 for one, and at the end of the day they've scored 389 runs for the loss of two — Burns for 71 and Warner for an explosive 163.

Day 2 doesn't get any better. By lunch they're 482 for the further loss of Steve Smith and they declare before tea at 556 for four, when Khawaja is finally out for 174, caught off Kane, with Voges still there on 83.

Understandably, our bowlers' numbers make for pretty ugly reading, no matter what interpretation I put on them — unwanted tons by Trent (127 runs for one wicket), Doug (none for 107) and Mark (none for 156). Jimmy might have joined them but his back gives out and

New Zealand Herald/Jason Oxenham

Left: Chris Cairns with the much-publicised 'BMC Emails' folder outside his Auckland home in February 2014.

Below: Arriving at Southwark Crown Court to give evidence in the Cairns trial in October 2015 with my solicitor, friend and mentor, Garth Gallaway.

Getty

Getty

Being invested as an Officer of the New Zealand Order of Merit for services to cricket by the Governor-General, Lt Gen The Rt Hon Sir Jerry Mateparae at Government House in Wellington, September 2015.

Photosport

Announcing my retirement from all forms of international cricket in December 2015. Mike Hesson and David White are alongside me.

Photosport

I lead the Black Caps out onto the Basin Reserve at the start of the first test against Australia, February 2016. It was my 100th consecutive test for New Zealand.

Getty

The Australians form a guard of honour at Hagley Oval as I walk out to bat in my final test, February 2016.

Photosport

Acknowledging the crowd after recording the fastest century in the history of test cricket. The milestone mark came up off 54 balls.

Getty

Above: With 'Hess' at the end of my final test. It had, as they say, been a great ride. Below: With Kane and a final moment of reflection in the dressing room.

Photosport

Photosport

Hagley Park, Christchurch, 24 February 2016. The whole group together at the close of play on my international career.

Photosport

Getty

With Maya, who brought the coin out to the middle in honour of my 100th consecutive test, and with Riley, who performed the same duty for my final test.

Getty

With Lis and our children, Maya, Evie (in Lis's arms) and Riley during the formalities after the final test.

Photosport

With my beautiful wife Lis at the ANZ New Zealand Cricket Awards in Auckland, February 2016.

he can only bowl 10 or so overs. Tim is the best of them, at one for 70, but the fact that Mark has to bowl so many overs on the first day of a test indicates how ineffective our pacemen are. There's no swing, bugger all movement off the pitch early on, and Trent particularly seems short of pace and rhythm. Sir Richard Hadlee has been talking up Tim and Trent as our best opening combination ever — and they have been — but it's a bad time to have an off day.

Guppy and Tom give us a solid start. We're one for 56 when Guppy goes, and two for 102 when Tom is caught off Starc just short of his half century. That's a base for a substantial score, particularly with Kane set, but when Ross, who's been unable to get a decent bat in the warm-ups, goes for a seven-ball duck, followed by me for six and Jimmy for three, we're in the shit at five for 118.

What follows is the best century I've seen from a New Zealand batsman. Kane is magnificent in the face of the pace and hostility of the two Mitchells, Starc and Johnson. But it's a bit of a lone hand. BJ stays with him for a partnership of 60-odd, then Mark for 50-odd, and Doug and Tim do their best, but it's a shame that one of our top-order batsmen couldn't have stayed with him and given us the big total we needed. When Kane finally nicks one to Nevill off Starc, he's on 140 and our total is a disappointing 317, 239 runs behind.

There's worse, as Oz begin their second innings. Tim has injured his lower back and can't bowl, and Jimmy's re-injured his back and is labouring. What remains of our attack is caned, as Warner and Burns simply kick on from their first innings. By tea on Day 3 they're 86, and they're scoring at will. Burns beats Warner to his ton, off 102 balls, and it's just a slog towards the inevitable declaration, which comes at the beginning of Day 4, leaving us two days to make over 500 runs.

We've at least got the batting practice we'd wanted! It's a rain-interrupted day and we've managed this sort of salvage operation before so we're not without hope. Guppy and Tom give us a reasonable start again, and at two for 130 before tea, with Kane and Ross looking set and more rain looming, we're a chance of holding on.

The first big wicket comes shortly after. Kane's scoring quickly, 50 off 55 balls, but is given lbw to Lyon on 59, getting some spin out of his pacemen's foot marks, and we're three for 136.

The heavens open at tea and no more play is possible, so Ross and I come out on Day 5, still hoping we can get out with a draw and start again in Perth.

Ross goes quickly, but I'm seeing the ball well and scoring at a run a ball. Then Jimmy goes for three, completing an unhappy test. BJ and I have done the job before and we're up for it, but not this time. On 242, he's given lbw to Lyon and one run later I'm sawn off on 80 by umpire Nigel Llong, whose name will loom large again on this tour.

Llong raises his finger to an appeal for a catch by Steve Smith off Mitch Marsh, a ball which replays confirm I clearly didn't hit. But already on this tour, luck is a difficult commodity for us; we've used up our reviews. Another nine balls and we would have had two reviews reinstated.

That's the end of our resistance. Beaten by heaps, one down in the series, in front of paltry crowds.

After that opening-day rout, there's some satisfaction from having taken the match into a fifth day, but on analysis, the figures are once again pretty ugly, particularly for our bowlers. Trent ends with match figures of two for 188, Doug nought for 170, Jimmy one for 111 and Mark three for 234, with those wickets coming when Oz were on the slog towards a declaration. These in a game where Starc took six for 120-odd, and spinner Mark Lyon four for just over 100.

Post match, I make as many positive noises as I can, but the second test in Perth is just four days away and I know, even given our record for coming back in a series, the task in front of us is huge.

The second test in Perth turns into such a brutal examination of wills that it ends the career of one of the best fast bowlers of my generation.

Once again, I lose the toss, and once again it's a bad one to lose, another 70/30, as the pitch at the WACA proves to have as much life and pace as the Nullarbor. The Australian batting — and unfortunately, our bowling returns — replicate their first innings at Brisbane. Only worse.

By lunch, Oz are 105 for one, Warner is in full noise, and we already know, with four days and two sessions ahead of us, that the wicket will be a road to nowhere for our bowlers for at least the first two days and the best we can hope for is a draw.

Day 1 ends with Oz on 416 for two, and we're facing a battle of attrition in the West Australian heat to salvage anything.

Day 2, and Oz finally declare before tea, nine down for 559, three runs more than they got in Brisbane. Warner (253) and Khawaja (121) have gone huge, while on our side, Trent, Matt Henry and Mark all get the kind of tons they don't want, while both Tim (who's recovered from his lower back injury) and Doug are in the eighties. This time, though, you'd have to say they don't bowl that badly on a pitch that gives them nothing — its only purpose seems to be for batsmen to boost their averages.

So we pad up before tea on Day 2, with plenty to lose and nothing to win.

But this time, our first innings at bat doesn't follow the Brisbane script, thanks to a monumental innings from Ross (290) and another big ton from Kane (166), who is being acknowledged by the Aussies as the best batsman in the world. This time, it's the Aussie bowlers who are put through the wringer, as Ross bats on and on through Day 3 to finish on 235.

On Day 4, Ross carries on, looking good for 300, until he's caught off Lyon for 290. It's still the highest test innings ever by an overseas batsman in Australia, which is remarkable when you think of all the legends who have tried to bring their best games to test the Aussies.

We're finally all out just before lunch on Day 4 for 624 runs, a lead of 65.

It's a huge change of dynamic for the Aussies, just being kept in the field for almost two days. This time, their bowlers' figures are bleeding heavily, with Starc and Hazlewood and Lyon all going for tons, and the worst of them, Mitchell Johnson, going for a very tired and dispirited-looking 157 runs. That evening, he confirms that the Perth pitch has finished any desire to continue, he's had enough, this will be his last test.

For the rest of Day 4 and Day 5, the run-fest continues, with Steve

Smith and Adam Voges making tons before Oz declares after lunch, at 385 for seven, leaving us the impossible task of making 320 in a session and a bit. Mercifully, rain washes out a fair bit of the time available and we're all put out of our misery.

At the end of the match, I ask the guys to form a guard of honour for Mitchell Johnson, knowing as I do so that, for quite different reasons, I've just about had enough too.

29
The Jury's Out

> We have heard, for example, from Mr Bitch-Bistle, a man who by his own admission is a liar, a humbug, a hypocrite, a vagabond, a loathsome spotted reptile and a self-confessed chicken strangler. You may choose to believe, if you wish, the transparent tissue of odious lies which streamed from his disgusting, beady, slavering lips. That is, Ladies and Gentlemen of the jury, entirely a matter for you . . .
>
> — Peter Cook, in wig and gown, giving directions to the jury at *The Secret Policeman's Ball* in 1979

A few days after the end of the Perth test, we play a West Australian XI at the WACA. It's a day/night two-dayer, with the primary objective of giving us a chance to get used to the pink ball before the third test in Adelaide.

The ball may be different, the lights may be on and the stakes much reduced, but some things stay the same — the Aussies win the toss and elect to bat. That's pretty much Day 1. Wags takes advantage of Trent's absence with a back niggle to take five wickets.

On Day 2, we get to bat against the pink ball. When it's my turn at the crease, something snaps. I run at every ball and whack a wild 49 off 28 balls. Hess must be alarmed at what he sees. When I charge, miss with a wild swipe and get stumped, he finds me out the back where I'm having a durry, trying to calm myself down. 'You okay?'

'I'm done, mate,' I tell him.

Hess knows I've been struggling, but it seems like a sudden and emotional decision. He asks me if I'm sure I want to retire.

It *is* quite sudden and emotional, but I'm sure. I had visions of playing the T20 Worlds in early 2016, then giving away the shorter-format stuff for the Black Caps and just playing tests, but I've come to the end of my tether. I just know in my waters I've had enough.

He's bloody good about it, says he can't pretend to know what I've been through, and asks me if I can stir myself for a couple more fights. I tell him I've got a couple more fights in me, I think. I can get through the rest of this summer's test programme, but that'll be it.

Partly it's the attritional warfare that the first two tests have turned into, on pitches that have done nothing for the game, just inflated the averages of, mostly, the Aussie top order, who've had the advantage of batting first. They've been games that have tested the patience of both the players and the few spectators who've turned up to watch them, and have ground the fast bowlers into the dust, and, in Mitchell Johnson's case, into retirement. Dull games in truth, which the Aussie cricketing public has had the good sense to stay away from.

But it's not just what's been happening on the field.

In the month since I gave evidence at Southwark Crown Court, the Cairns case has dragged on, a wound to cricket that keeps bleeding like a stuck pig.

It's been all over the media in Oz, as the other witnesses, such as Dan Vettori, Shane Bond, Chris Harris, Andre Adams, Kyle Mills, Ricky Ponting and David White, have given evidence by video, and then Cairns himself.

All this has led to constant speculation by media and social media, and, of course, because I'm one of the three prime witnesses for the prosecution, my name is constantly at the forefront of speculation as to Cairns' guilt or innocence, and my possible motivations for giving evidence. Some of the conjecture has been ridiculous, and from people who should know better, and some of it is downright nasty.

At the head of that queue is, naturally, The Voice of Reason in the *Sunday Star-Times*. On 22 November his column is headed 'Everyone is looking over their shoulder with Chris Cairns trial'. The column finishes by saying:

> *Nothing has changed. Justice Sweeney, the presiding judge in the Cairns trial, has previously said, 'You have shown no remorse for your crimes at all. Your reputation now lies in ruins. You have been stripped of all your honours but you have no-one to blame but yourself.'*
>
> *In fact, Sweeney spoke the words in sentencing Rolf Harris. But he could just as easily have been talking about a figure at the heart of New Zealand cricket. Precisely who the guilty figure is, we don't yet know. The jury's still out on that one.*

I'm accustomed to Reason stretching the chewing gum, but this is plain loco. Someone 'at the heart of New Zealand cricket' is akin to a convicted paedophile and rapist? Who could that be, I wonder? The CEO of New Zealand Cricket, David White? Or me, the Black Caps captain? None of the other witnesses in the case could be construed as being 'at the heart of New Zealand cricket'. I feel like ringing him up and saying, 'Come on mate, if you really think that, name names. Who are you talking about? Put your money where your poison pen is.'

I've tried desperately hard to keep my head locked into the very demanding cricket right in front of me, but to be honest, it's impossible to ignore the fallout from the trial completely, and it's been chipping away at me like Chinese water torture right through the Australian tour.

Knowing that John Rhodes is, ironically, the ACSU officer on this tour doesn't help. He manages to avoid me completely, despite orders from his boss, Sir Ronnie Flanagan, to seek me out and apologise for the ICC shortcomings in the evidence presented by the ICC at the trial.

The day before the game against the West Australians, the evidence finally comes to an end and Judge Nigel Sweeney begins his summing up and gives his directions to the jury. The more I read about what he's telling the jurors, the more my heart sinks.

Sweeney tells the jury, among other things, that they have to believe two out of the three main witnesses against Cairns in order to find him guilty. Sweeney then goes on to completely and utterly discredit two of those witnesses, Lou Vincent and his ex-wife, Elly. Paraphrasing Sweeney, Elly was presumably so drunk she didn't know what she was saying, and Lou's evidence, though he has been banned from cricket for life for match fixing, can be written off in respect of anything he's said about Cairns as the rambling lies of a troubled soul.

From the moment Sweeney rubbishes Lou and Elly's evidence, the die is cast.

I had no idea if Sweeney is obliged by some rule of evidence to tell the jury that they have to believe two out of the three of us, or if that's his own idiosyncratic interpretation. I have since been told that in the UK Sweeney was obliged to instruct the jury that there had to be two corroborating witnesses in cases of perjury. From a common-sense point of view, what happens if the jury disbelieve Lou and Elly, but believe me? What happens if they believe me and don't believe Cairns?

Sweeney, to my uneducated ears, appears to be telling the jury that if they believe me and disbelieve Cairns, they still cannot convict him, if they also disbelieve Lou and Elly.

I simply don't understand why the jury cannot disregard Lou and Elly's evidence if they don't believe it, and still reach a verdict based on whether they believe me or Cairns.

I'm not saying that would happen — in my opinion, Sweeney casts aspersions on my evidence too — but if I'd known at the outset what the equation was going to be, two out of three, it would have been a fairly compelling reason not to bother going to London, not to put myself and my family through this crap.

In fact, as the trial developed, I'd been disconcerted to realise that I was the prime witness. Before the trial the police and prosecution had often expressed to me their complete confidence that they had evidence that was going to nail Cairns. I got the impression they had some sort of smoking gun, and that while my evidence was still important, it was a comparatively minor part of the prosecution case. If I'd known that I was basically all they had, it might have been another reason to think twice about doing it.

If my heart sinks on reading that direction, it plunges into my cricket boots when I read the judge's directions to the jury about the 'previous good character' of Cairns, apart from 'keeping money in cash to avoid tax'. His 'previous good character' isn't a defence as such, says Sweeney, but it does count in his favour, in that it supports his credibility and points to him being less likely to have committed an offence.

Jesus wept.

We travel to Adelaide to get ready for the pink ball test starting on Friday, 27 November. I should be excited to be a part of this piece of history, and excited about our chances of winning this test and drawing the series. To be in this position after the debacle at Brisbane is another endorsement of the character of the team, and we're confident that we can do as we did in the West Indies and in the UAE, and finish over the top of them.

I'm trying to be excited and to convince myself that I've still got some fight left — and also still trying to keep my true state of mind from the team, although Hess and Roman have been aware throughout. I've tried to give the impression to the team that the Cairns thing wasn't hard work or consuming, because it's not something they can help me with, and it's not a constructive problem to bring into the team environment. But it's definitely sucked my energy, and in such a close-knit group, that's been difficult to hide. I think they've sensed what I'm going through, and made sure they haven't whinged or complained or done anything to burden me more.

When we get to Adelaide, a significant part of me, anxious and depressed, is with the jury on the other side of the world. I'm aware that they retired to consider their verdict on the Tuesday, 24 November, then they have Wednesday and Thursday off and get together again on Friday 27th, the first day of the third test.

Given the judge's directions, I'm sure it'll take them no time at all to acquit Cairns — what else can they do? And I'm very aware that if Cairns is found not guilty, there'll be people out there who will regard that as a verdict of guilty for me.

I'm surprised the jury don't get to it on the Tuesday, and when they don't, I expect the news will break — all over me — on the Friday, sometime in the evening our time, perhaps when we're trying to deal with a pink ball under lights.

It doesn't happen. The jury doesn't return a verdict on the Friday and gets the weekend off.

Instead, something really surprising happens that day in the context of this tour. I win a toss.

Unfortunately, it's the one toss that doesn't seem to matter, because no one really knows what effect the pink ball will have. I would have liked it to be a 70/30 toss, if only to help square the ledger, but this pitch is not a batting highway — they're worried about the pink ball cutting up and losing shape, so the pitch and outfield have been left relatively lush.

I look at the green pitch, but can't let slip this opportunity to bat first. Sure enough, it turns out to be a low-scoring game dominated by the bowlers. But it's not really the pitch that holds the secret to winning this test.

Once the test begins, it's so exciting, such an antidote to the previous two and to what's happening in London, that I do get into it and enjoy myself. The Adelaide Oval is full to capacity even on the Friday and the atmosphere is vibrant through the new afternoon and evening sessions — we begin at two in the afternoon, stop for tea and then for dinner. The final session under lights finishes at about 9.30 pm.

The honour of scoring the first run in a pink ball test goes to Guppy. Unfortunately, that's also his last run, when he goes lbw to Josh Hazlewood. Kane seems to begin where he left off and moves smoothly to 19 off 19, but then the Aussie plan to strangle him really takes effect, and the next 39 balls bring three runs and, frustrated, he's lbw to a straight yorker from Starc.

The Aussies are bowling superbly as a unit, but we get to tea at 80 for two and are looking good to consolidate a reasonable start. Tom and Ross are settling in as the lights gradually take over from the setting sun . . .

But by dinner, we're 173 for seven and then all out for 202 in the night session, with debutante Mitchell Santner and BJ the only ones to offer any resistance.

Oz have to face 20 overs under lights and are immediately in trouble as Tim and Trent swing the ball prodigiously. Warner's gone for one off Trent and then Joe Burns survives for 41 balls before chopping on to Doug for 14. Steve Smith and Adam Voges survive to stumps at 9.30.

At two down for 54, you could say it's pretty even, but we could have done with another wicket under lights, because Day 1 seems to indicate that the pink ball is a creature of the night. It swings more and is harder to pick up once the lights are on.

That becomes a crucial element of the test, thanks to my old mate from Brisbane, Nigel Llong — what is it with these Pommie Nigels? — who this time is in what you'd think would be the comparatively harmless position of third umpire, looking at the reviews on the television replay.

By the time Llong intervenes on Day 2, we've taken control of the test, with by far our best session of the tour in the field. Tim and Trent swing the ball at reasonable pace, and Doug is consistent and demanding, while Mark and new boy Mitchell Santner also bowl well.

In that first session, Tim gets Voges for 13 and I run out Shaun Marsh for two and Mitchell Marsh edges Doug and is caught by BJ for four. By drinks Oz are five wickets down for 85 runs, and suddenly our first innings total is looking substantial. Steve Smith is still there on 39 and goes through to 53, but when he walks down the pitch to Mark and gets an edge to BJ, Oz are six down for 109. That rapidly becomes eight for 116, when Siddle and Hazlewood fall cheaply.

The moment that turns the game belongs, unfortunately, not to one of the players doing something extraordinary, but to Nigel Llong.

At eight down for 118, Nathan Lyon top-edges Mitch Santner into slip. When Umpire Ravi gives it not out, I ask for a review.

The replays on the big screen clearly show to a crowd of forty-something thousand and 13 players out in the middle a hot-spot where the ball hits the bat. We all think it's open and shut, but the one person who needs to be convinced is not. Despite, as one commentator writes, 'evidence that would have convinced most courts of law' (not a comparison I would have encouraged) Nigel Llong is not sure what that spot is. 'It could have come from anywhere,' says Nigel.

Lyon by this time is halfway to the dressing room — like us, he's seen the pictures on the big screen and, unlike Llong, knows that what made the hot-spot on the shoulder of his bat as the ball passed that precise spot could not have been some stray insect or a UFO.

And that's the game, essentially. Not only because Lyon goes on with wicketkeeper Nevill to establish the best partnership of the Australian innings — though in the context of a low-scoring game that 70 runs is also really significant — but also because the time they take to get those runs means that instead of our being able to begin our second innings in the light of day, we have to bat at night.

When the Oz first innings closes, they're 22 runs ahead, instead of 70 behind, but even more importantly, we begin our innings in the twilight session, rather than in the afternoon. By stumps we've lost five wickets for 116 under lights.

On Day 3, Mitch Santner plays another good hand, supported by Doug, but it's a rearguard action that gets us through to 208, leaving Oz to get only 187 with all the time in the world.

Even so, it's a close, nervy finish. By dinner, Oz are cruising at 113 for three, with Shaun Marsh and Adam Voges well set. But after dinner, under lights, there's a late flurry of wickets from Trent before Oz get home at 187 for seven.

Oh, for another 50 runs in the bank.

It's difficult to be churlish about losing such a brilliant match, close-fought and so well supported by forty-odd thousand people for each of the three days. And it's easy enough to draw positives for the team out of this game — Mitchell Santner showed test match talent and temperament, Doug Bracewell bowled really well, and Trent came back to something like his best, with five for 60 in that last innings.

But we've lost a test series for the first time since June 2013, and by two tests to nil across a three-test series. That'd indicate a gulf between the teams which I don't think exists. Like even the most successful sides, we needed a bit of luck, the rub of the green, and got none. In fact, any luck about seemed to go the other way fairly consistently — not a quality you usually associate with luck.

Nigel Llong's decision had a major bearing on the outcome of this game, but we still had an opportunity to take the game and couldn't quite do it, whereas Australia could. Just. There's some satisfaction in taking it to the wire, and the whole thing has been a great spectacle and, for me, a diversion from my other preoccupation.

Even so, my mind can't help straying to the other English Nigel, who's also been sitting in judgement. I'm very aware as the test finishes two days early on that Sunday in Adelaide that tomorrow in Southwark the jury must surely deliver a verdict. They couldn't reach a decision on Tuesday or Friday, even after those directions from Sweeney. How come it's taking them so long to reach a conclusion?

30
Why?

> The ICC must move to assure players — whose livelihoods rely on the public's trust in the sport — that reports of illicit approaches will be dealt with in a more watertight fashion that leaves nothing to chance while redoubling its efforts and increasing its resources in the wider fight against corruption.
>
> For while Cairns has been acquitted of perjury by a jury in London, the sport itself has been given anything but a clean bill of health.
>
> — *The Guardian*

The jury can't escape Nigel Sweeney's directions and finds Chris Cairns not guilty of perjury.

So I watch him on television being interviewed outside the Southwark Crown Court, saying, quite rightly, that there are no winners and that it's been hell for everyone involved. He says that 'reputationally, he's completely scorched, burnt'.

But, I'm muttering to the TV, not as badly as you would have been if you'd been found guilty, Cairnsy!

And he's not the only one to have his reputation burned. In a lot of minds, a not guilty verdict doesn't mean that the prosecution didn't prove the case beyond reasonable doubt; it means that he didn't do it. And if he didn't do it, then I must have been lying.

So it's really galling when he's asked, 'What would you say to Brendon?'

Cairnsy looks straight at the camera, the very picture of righteousness and says, 'I'd ask him why.'

Then — where else? — in the *Sunday Star-Times*, under a piece entitled 'Please Explain, Brendon', he's quoted as saying: 'Now, it should be McCullum who has to face up to his part in all of this. I ask you again Brendon, why did you bring all this pain and suffering upon my family?'

Okay, Cairnsy, you know when you asked those questions that as captain of the Black Caps, I couldn't answer them, couldn't engage with you publicly. But now I can. Here's your answer.

Cairnsy,

Two moments stick with me, which will make it difficult to ever forgive and forget. They're both of you standing in the media spotlight, where you've always been comfortable and in control.

The first is posing for that photo in the *New Zealand Herald*, with a file marked BMC and the words McCullum and Schwalger strategically placed so that the cameras would pick them up.

It was the first and most overt of several attempts to dissuade me from giving evidence against you. The phone calls that followed, from 'concerned mutual friends' — were just more of the same, and none of it did you any credit. You tried to pressure me and bully me out of doing the right thing. I can understand that you were desperate, but it showed you for what you are.

The second moment that will always stay with me is you standing outside the Southwark Crown Court in London, after the not guilty verdict. Towards the end of the interview, you're asked what you would say to Brendon McCullum. You look to the sky in what I take to be righteously wounded exasperation, and ask plaintively 'Why?'

Why? Seriously? You were a professional cricketer yourself, one of the most naturally gifted and most honoured New Zealanders to have ever played the game, and you don't know why I gave evidence against you?

Let me spell it out, Cairnsy. Call it a recap.

Under the rules that govern my behaviour as a professional cricketer, I'm obliged to report any approaches regarding match fixing to the ICC.

I'm not a man for the fine print, nor for ratting on mates, and I didn't realise until I was told in an ICC seminar in 2011 that I was equally culpable if I didn't report such an approach. As soon as that rule was pointed out to me, I belatedly did what I was required to do as a professional cricketer. No more, no less.

Who knows what the ICC would have done with that? Maybe there wasn't much they could do. You were retired, beyond their power to investigate or punish. The ICL was defunct. The guy from the ICC who interviewed me said it would probably go to the bottom of the file and be forgotten.

You ensured it wouldn't be by suing Lalit Modi. That's the spark that caught fire and escalated this to the Crown Court in London. That's what eventually burned you, Cairnsy, your own bloody ego.

People tweet all kinds of things, and they're just one person's opinion and most of them disappear into the ether, unless someone draws attention to them. You waved a big flag to the world, saying 'Over here! Look at this!' You made sure that tweet went right round the world and got maximum coverage by suing Modi for defamation.

Maybe in retrospect you wish you'd had the nous to keep your peace and maintain a dignified silence instead of suing a rich Indian businessman for an ill-advised tweet.

I'm not sure how my ICC interview came to the attention of the Crown — I certainly didn't call the London Metropolitan Police. But when evidence like mine and that of Lou Vincent did surface, I imagine the Crown was pretty much obliged to charge you with perjury, lying under oath, for the statements you made in the Modi trial.

Once you were charged, I felt obliged to go through with it, for cricket. There's been nothing in it for me, Cairnsy, or for this nebulous entity your QC called Brand McCollum.

In fact, going to London and giving evidence against you was one of the most stressful things I've done in my life. Being cross-examined and attacked in the witness stand, and by media before and after, all for doing the right thing, has been one of the most unpleasant episodes in my life. And it didn't end when I'd finished giving evidence and tried to go back to being a cricketer.

The shadow of that trial fell across the Black Caps' tour of Australia. A three-test series that should have been one of the highlights of my long career became an endurance test. Your bloody trial, Cairnsy, drained me, and tainted and soured what should have been one of the great cricketing experiences of my life. I hate to admit that to you, because I suspect you will take satisfaction from it.

You might say that you had larger concerns: staying out of gaol. I can appreciate that. Once you were charged with a serious crime and were standing in that dock at Southwark, you had to do what was best for Cairnsy. You have a wife and children who depend on you. I get that. I was, am, pleased that you're not languishing in a British prison, even though the not guilty verdict for you meant in some people's minds a guilty verdict for me, and even though I still stand behind every word I said.

In summary, Cairnsy, I could have forgiven you for the approaches you made to me. We all make mistakes — me more than most. And we all panic a bit at the end of our careers, the end of doing the only thing we've ever known. We might grieve for the spotlight and worry because we're not qualified for gainful employment in anything else. I can understand all that, so I can understand the temptations of an unsanctioned no-account hit 'n' giggle tournament in India. So that's not what I find unforgivable, actually. I forgave you for that long ago.

It's everything you did after that. The attempts to discredit me and my motives for giving evidence against you. Your insinuations, without ever giving any evidence or substance to them, that I was part of 'dark forces' lined against you, some conspiracy that you were never able to detail, but kept repeating.

I can understand you fighting your corner. Cairnsy's always done what's best for Cairnsy. Good luck to you. But we know what we know, you and me.

They say we show our true character under pressure. You've shown me yours. It's not the one I thought I knew, and I've no wish to have any future association with it.

Baz

31

The Last Trophy

> At the top of the order, skipper Brendon McCullum ended his ODI career in a manner that seemed entirely appropriate. He played some breathtakingly good shots as he and Martin Guptill savaged Australia's new-ball bowlers, bar Josh Hazlewood. There were some woolly whiffs too, as he plundered his way to 47 off only 27 balls, with six fours and three sixes. In doing so, McCullum became the first player to record 200 ODI sixes and 100 test sixes.
>
> — Ian Anderson, *Stuff*

On 21 December at Hamilton, we complete the second of two hard-fought tests against the rebuilding Sri Lankans — no Sangakkara or Jayawardene — and manage to extend our winning record in tests at home to 13. Unlucky for some.

The test is also notable for King Kane's match-winning ton, his fifth in 2015, equalling Steve Smith. He's averaged over 90 in tests during the year, the best among all 500-plus run-scorers this year. His aggregate of 1172 runs is the highest by a New Zealand batsman in a year, going past my tally from last year. It's no wonder he's gone to number one-ranking test batsman.

I guess the other notable thing is the impression Wags makes. He's relentless, indefatigable, and certainly asks a question about whether it was right to leave him out of Brisbane and Perth.

And, oh yes. One other thing. At the end of the test, I announce my impending retirement. I'd prefer to do it at the last moment, after my final test at Christchurch against the Aussies on 24 February — I don't want the rest of the summer to become an extended farewell tour, but I don't have any choice: the squad for the World T20 in March has a number of warm-up games planned and I was expected to be a part of it.

So my retirement is out there, set in concrete.

That decision back in Perth felt pretty emotional and spur of the moment, even though it was the product of almost subterranean forces that had been working on me for some time. But I find that the further I get from that decision, the righter it seems to be.

Someone once said that if you're climbing a mountain, all you can see is the mountain. I think he was attempting to explain why so many climbers make seemingly illogical decisions to continue climbing in the face of deteriorating conditions. You're too close; objectivity disappears. Now that I've made the decision to get off my mountain, I have a perspective I didn't have before and with every day that passes, I feel better about going. I feel liberated, to be honest. I know that when I finally walk away, I'll have given my best and be free to pursue a different life, and Lis is as excited about that as I am.

Before the tour to Australia, I had thoughts of doing really well and finishing on a high note, which was a bit of a departure from the attitude I'd arrived at in previous years, the mindset that had worked for me and the team: just go and play cricket — if you have a good day, great, don't get too high, and if you have a bad day, that's okay, don't get too low. But in Australia I'd started thinking about the end, started thinking those dangerous thoughts about leaving a legacy. I'd started to formulate plans around how I wanted to finish rather than staying in the moment.

With the Sri Lankans and then the return Australian series in front of me, I'm determined to get back to enjoying the game for its own sake. I can go duck, duck, duck, and quack all the way to the finish and it doesn't matter. What matters is that I relax and enjoy the last few games where I'll be wearing the black cap. I hesitate to use a word like serene to describe myself, but, yeah, a kind of serenity settles over me.

Unfortunately, my back doesn't buy into this serenity stuff.

We easily take the first of the five ODIs against Sri Lanka on Boxing Day, but in the second at Christchurch I'm chasing a ball to the boundary, cannon into the hoarding, and blow out my back.

That's what it looks like anyway, and it's an opportunity for lots of people to tut-tut about the necessity of chasing so hard. In fact — and this doesn't make them wrong — I'd felt the back go earlier, in the dressing room, just reaching out to pick something up off a bench, like my gloves, the most innocuous action possible. That makes it even more worrying.

I have to leave the field and watch Guppy annihilate the run chase. I also miss the rest of the ODIs and watch Kane captain the side to a loss in the third and a win in the fifth, to take the series 3–1 after the fourth in Nelson is washed out, then win both T20s.

They then win the T20 series against Pakistan, good preparation for the Worlds in India in March, then take the first ODI at the Basin Reserve by 70 runs.

It's interesting being on the sideline, watching the team go through its paces, getting to grips with the idea that very soon watching is as close as I'm going to get.

I watch Kane in particular and wonder if the captaincy is going to be too early for him, whether it's going to burden his batting. The irony is that if ever Ross was going to be ready to be captain, it's now, even if it's only for a season or two, to allow Kane to cement his place as the best batsman in the world. But Ross's name never figures in any of the speculation — maybe he's told New Zealand Cricket he doesn't want to revisit that, and who could blame him?

The biggest revelation from watching the Black Caps in action is that it really is the right time to step aside: they don't actually need me any more.

That changes when Ross, who's suffered a side strain in one of the T20s, rules himself out of the ODIs against Australia.

My aim is to play at least one of the ODIs against Pakistan, so that I'm ready for the Aussies when they arrive in early February. But my back is slow to come right, and I'm still on the painkillers and anti-inflams, so I'm not too disappointed when my comeback match, the first ODI against Pakistan at Napier, is washed out without a ball being bowled.

The second ODI at Eden Park is not much better as a test of whether my back is up to it: I'm out first ball for a duck. Being back in the field is good, though, as Pakistan ratchet up 290, and we manage to get the revised Duckworth–Lewis total of 263 after losing time to rain.

When the Australians arrive, Ross's absence doesn't make a lot of difference, to begin with.

We kill the Aussies in the first ODI at Eden Park. For the first 14 balls it looks like we're struggling: one run. Then I take 20 off four balls from Josh Hazlewood and Guppy really gets going in the next over, hitting Kane Richardson onto the roof. We're 79 off 10 overs when I hole out for 44, and even though Kane Williamson goes shortly after for a rare duck, Guppy motors on to 90, supported by Henry Nicholls with a classy 60-odd, topped off by Mitch Santner.

Oz never look like getting close to 307. Trent and Matt have them six for 41 and they end up all out for 148, a massive 159 runs short.

We also set a reasonable target in Wellington, 281, held together by a 60 from Kane. There's support from quite a few others, but none of us kick on to a big one, and Aussie seem to be having no trouble running it down when Warner and Khawaja get them off to a flyer.

After Mitch Santner catches Khawaja off his own bowling on 122, Trent and Matt come back into their own with a flurry of wickets. Smith, Bailey and Maxwell go cheaply, then Mitch gets Warner and Wade. At six for 197, we're right back in it.

That's the last wicket we take, though, as Mitchell Marsh comes right and puts together the winning partnership with John Hastings. A big part of their win is down to Warner — he scored his almost-ton so quickly that there's never any run-rate pressure on Marsh and Hastings.

The decider at Hamilton is my final ODI as a Black Cap, and despite my best intentions to stay in the moment, I'd dearly love to ride off into the ODI sunset carrying the Chappell–Hadlee Trophy.

It all seems to go to script when I blaze away at the top for a 27-ball 47, joining the 200 six club in the process. That's a pretty exclusive club with only four members: me, Chris Gayle, Sanath Jayasuriya and Shahid Afridi (the only one to do it in fewer innings).

Guppy and Kane carry on to a strong position at 120 after 17 overs. Kane goes soon after, then Guppy, but Grant and Corey set up a good partnership. We're five for 223 with 10 overs left and could reasonably expect to be looking at 280 plus, when Corey goes, followed by Luke. Once Grant is caught on 50, our innings folds quickly, and we can't even bat out the 50.

It's hard to hide the disappointment between innings — 246 is not a par score on this pitch. But I tell the guys, for the last time in this context at least, that we have to rise above that disappointment and at least make it tough for the Aussies to beat us. I tell them it doesn't matter what we get, it's a matter of what they get. If we're capable of losing six wickets for not many, so can they.

That prospect doesn't look promising when Warner and Khawaja get them away to another good start. But Matt gets Warner on 16 and Doug gets Khawaja to nick one to Luke on 44, and they're two for 75 after 11.

The first turning point in the game comes when Ish Sodhi gets Smith lbw on 21, then gets Maxwell caught by me two balls later. Oz are suddenly four down for 94 and we're starting to believe that what we spoke about at halftime is actually possible.

Then Bailey and Marsh threaten to take it away from us with a good partnership. Bailey is bowled by Matt when their total is 153, but Mitch Marsh is looking like he might do to us what he did in Wellington and shepherd the tail home.

Then comes the second turning point: Matt squeezes a ball off Marsh's bat onto his boot and catches the rebound. It all happens so quickly, no one's completely sure of the ball's exact trajectory. But Matt has seen something and makes a half-hearted appeal, turning towards Ian Gould, the umpire. When the big screen indicates that it's likely to be out, I ask the umpires what the hell's going on, point out there's been an appeal, and that the right decision now needs to be made. From the moment they decide to refer it to the third umpire there's no doubt — given the absence of Nigel Llong — that Marsh is going to be out.

The pictures on the big screen show that an appeal was made by Matt. It may have been somewhat half-hearted but he asked the question, and there's no law of the game laying down how vociferously an appeal must be made — if a bowler wants to saunter up to an umpire and whisper 'How'zat?' in his ear, that's still an appeal. So the right decision is made when Marsh is given out, and it's good that, among other queries, Steve Smith acknowledges that after the game.

But I also have to admit that if Marsh had not been given out and had stuck around, marshalling the Aussie lower order, they might have got there. It's only fair to say that: if I'm going to lament the rub of the green when we don't get it, I've also got to acknowledge its importance when we do get it.

After Marsh goes, protesting all the way, there's no further resistance and Oz are all out for 191. We've actually managed to win by 55 runs, which looks quite comfortable, but never was.

I'm stoked to be holding the Chappell–Hadlee Trophy as my last act as captain of the ODI side. It was here at Hamilton in 2007 that we chased down 346 to win it, and I was a big part of that: this time it was all about dour defence, but just as satisfying, particularly when we're able to bring in two guys, Doug and Ish, who haven't been part of the ODI side for a while, and have them perform so well. It was Doug's pressure that helped create Ish's double. When I see that sort of thing happening, and see us winning without our most experienced batsman, I know we've built depth, and that makes it easier to walk away.

The win also means we've beaten the world champions. I've always believed that the final of the World Cup in Melbourne wasn't as one-sided as it seemed, and I've also believed that a series would have shown that there's not too much between the ODI teams. This series has at least proved that.

In fact, I reckon we're so evenly matched that luck in its many and varied forms has been — and will be — crucial. Oz had all the luck go their way at home. I'm hoping that what's happened in Hamilton is portentous and spells a change of fortune for us in the upcoming tests.

32

Close of Play

> He's a guy who can leave the game saying he played it his way, that he enjoyed it. In fact, that was infectious among the group. He showed why playing for your mates and a common cause can bring more enjoyment out of what we do. He taught us to be humble and understand that there's more to life than a win or a loss. He brought back the old-school mentality where, if you happened to win, you invite the opposition into the sheds for a beer, or if you lost, make an effort to go to the opposition dressing room and do the same . . . Something Brendon believed more and more was that runs and wickets were cool, but being a good person throughout was the most important thing. He also felt that if you are doing anything in life for a period of time, why not make a few mates doing so?
>
> — Kane Williamson, ESPN Cricinfo

If the tosses at Brisbane and Perth were 70/30, the tosses at the Basin Reserve and Hagley Oval are 80/20, and I botch both of them. Well, sort of. My daughter Maya brings the coin out to the middle in honour of my 100th consecutive test since debut — the only player to ever do that — and hands it to me. I flip it and Steve Smith calls. Logic says that each flip of the coin is unaffected by the last, and the odds are that over time results will even out. Sentiment would suggest that maybe someone in his 100th consecutive test, with a coin brought out by his own daughter . . . No way. Steve makes the right call.

It's traditional to prepare a greenish pitch at the Basin, and this one is no exception — one commentator describes it as so green it has branches. Steve Smith has no hesitation in asking us to bat first on it.

As I pad up and wait for the call, I wonder how the hell I've managed 100 consecutive tests since debut, given the injuries and emotional upheavals and natural ebb and flow of form across all those years since 2004. What I'm most proud of is the number of times I picked myself off the canvas and fought for my place. I don't have long to reflect. Outside, the wickets are already tumbling.

By halfway through the morning session, our top order's gone, five down for 51 runs, including a seven-ball duck for me, and we only get through to 183 by dint of a rearguard action by Corey and Mark Craig. We're all out at tea, but Trent's 24 at number 11 shows the pitch is fast becoming benign, which means the session between tea and stumps is absolutely critical — we have to make inroads before the pitch completely flattens out.

Tim does his bit, getting Joe Burns for a duck and Warner for five. Two down for five runs is exactly where we need to be. A couple more wickets before close of play and we're really in this match.

One of those wickets slips through our fingers, literally. Mark, normally rock solid at second slip, drops Steve Smith. Smith's on 20 at the time: he goes on to make 70. It's not just the extra 50 runs that hurts us. It's the time. Not removing Smith delays our chances of attacking their middle and lower order earlier, when the ball is still moving.

The real doozy comes in the last over of the day. Doug Bracewell bowls Adam Voges. Umpire Richard Illingworth calls a no-ball. Replays show a large chunk of Doug's heel is behind the crease. ICC regulations mean the no-ball cannot be reversed. Voges is on seven. He goes on to 239.

Again — shades of Adelaide — it's not just the 280-odd runs these two incidents cost us, but the time. Getting rid of Smith and Voges in that session would expose the Aussie lower middle order while the pitch still has a bit of juice in it.

By Day 2, the juice is gone and so are we. In fact, the most uplifting moment of the whole day is when Voges gets his century and someone in the crowd yells out to the umpire, 'Raise your bat, Illingworth!'

Otherwise it's just hard graft on a benign pitch. Khawaja, who's batted brilliantly, gets to 140 before he's lbw to Trent, who then sends Mitchell Marsh back caught and bowled for a duck. But Nevill and then Siddle stop any hint of a rot, and support Voges as he grinds on to the end of the day, reaching 176 by stumps, still there with Siddle.

Day 3 finally sees the end of the Australian innings before lunch, when Voges is caught and bowled by Mark for 239. A magnificent innings, for 232 of it.

Our top order all get starts, and at one for 81 or two for 121 or even three for 157, there's still hope of an Indian summer or a Perth type of resurrection. But one of those out is Kane, for 22, and our other premier batsman isn't on the field.

I'm not overstating the importance of my wicket, but in these circumstances getting out lbw to the last ball of the day is really deflating, for me and the team. At no stage do I feel comfortable out there, and get a wee bit caught betwixt and between defence and attack. Henry Nicholls is batting well on debut, but 178 for four is not where we wanted to be chasing a deficit of 379, with all our experienced top-order batsmen gone.

Any remaining hope expires early on Day 4, when Corey goes for a duck and BJ for 10. There's to be no fairytale, though Henry Nicholls goes on to his 50 and the lower order fights well. Mark gets another not out, and Tim hits out for 48. In any other context, a second innings total of 327 would be a reasonable return, but, again, the game was pretty much over at stumps on Day 1.

The optimist in me can say that with a fairer pitch and without the 280 runs the Aussies were gifted by our misses and misfortunes, we'd have been close to even-stevens at the end of our first innings, and our second innings effort would have given us a target to bowl to.

But there's no denying the scoreboard. My 100th consecutive test from debut records an innings and 52-run thrashing, an ignominious end to our 13-match streak of tests without defeat at home. Now we have to go to Christchurch and win, to preserve our undefeated home series record.

By now there's an inevitability to what happens next in Christchurch. I lose the toss again and, again, it's a disastrous toss to lose. This time, it's my son Riley who brings the coin out, in honour of my last game. But Riley and logic and the odds and sentiment still can't save me.

It takes the Aussie pacemen five or six overs to find the right spot, maybe because the ball is doing so much. But once they find it, they're relentless. Guppy goes in the sixth over, runs become very hard to get and it's a battle for survival. Tom holds on for another eight overs and in that time our score advances by two runs. Even Kane is completely bogged down.

I'm padded up, watching the TV in the changing room, BJ keeping me company, because we both like to sneak off for a quick durry. What's happening on screen is unbelievable. Whether or not he's number one batsman in the world at any given moment, Kane has indisputably the best defence in the game. And this guy can't actually get his blade on the ball. He keeps getting hit on the back thigh. At one stage, he's about three off 50 balls.

That's enough to send BJ and me out the back for another furtive durry. While we're sucking it in, I tell him that, Jesus, if King Kane can't defend out there, what chance have I got? BJ gets that mischievous little grin on his face, because he knows what's coming. Fuck it, I'm going to have a crack.

We get back into the changing room and Henry Nicholls is out. We're three down for 32 as I walk to the wicket on the most beautiful Christchurch day — the sun is shining, I can see the tops of the old oaks round the park over the packed stands, and it's clear that this pitch will dry out in a couple of hours and be the perfect batting pitch. We somehow have to still be there when that happens, but I'm determined not to get caught betwixt and between, as I was in Wellington.

The Aussies give me a guard of honour and clap me to the wicket, which is great. It does cross my mind that it won't look that flash if I'm walking back past them any time soon.

I'll have a look at the first ball, I think. The bloody thing careens past my nose. That confirms it for me: if I get out defending in my last-ever test match, when I've already told myself that I don't have the game to defend on a wicket like this, I won't be able to live with myself. The Aussies have figured out that the perfect spot is just on a good length. So I know that they're going to try to bowl that exact length every single ball, particularly if I give them a bit of encouragement.

I normally bat on middle, but I actually want them to bowl at the stumps, because then I know where they're going to bowl every ball. So I change my guard to outside leg stump, so they can see all three stumps. The stumps don't matter to me because I'm just going to whack it. I want enough room to be able to cut, and I want to be able to swing my arms through the ball. I have a slog at the next ball, get a thick edge over slips and into the fence for four. Lift-off.

Kane stays with me and we make it through to lunch at 74 for three. I have a big let-off immediately after lunch on 39, when I'm caught brilliantly by Marsh at gully. But when they check the replay it shows James Pattinson has failed to get his heel behind the crease.

I reckon I'm due a bit of luck, though I'd rather have won the toss.

Kane's out shortly after lunch for the extraordinary figures of seven runs off 98 balls. That says everything that needs to be said about this pitch.

Corey joins me and supports me brilliantly. The rest, as they say, is history, which is just as well, because it's a bit of a blur. I get to 50 off 34 balls, then hit another 50 off the next 20 balls. It's the fastest test century ever. On 145, I try a slog-sweep on one knee over square leg but get caught on the boundary. I'm pretty much done anyway.

Corey's 72 and BJ's 58, with a quick-fire 21 from Matt, get us through to 370, a total I'd definitely have taken at the beginning of the day.

The record gets enormous coverage, but the most valued message comes from one of the men who held it before me, Viv Richards. Generous and gracious.

Meanwhile, Oz put together a huge total of 505, with 170 from Burns and 138 from Smith, we reply with 335, and they get the 201 they need for the loss of three wickets after lunch on Day 5.

A seven-wicket win to Australia, who go to number one in the test rankings.

A couple of months before we toured Australia, I said that I'd rather have our team than theirs. That was true. Yet if you objectively picked a composite team now, after two series, Kane would be the only Black Cap certain to make that team. What happened?

I managed to lose every critical toss. If I'd won the toss more often, our batsmen wouldn't have been batting in the worst conditions, and our bowlers would have been bowling in more favourable conditions. Psychologically, test after test, to be immediately under the pump like that is always going to be difficult. That might be why, when we did have our chances, we couldn't take them, whereas Oz could.

Both our batting and bowling were at fault there, but if you look at the two series as a whole, most of it comes back to the bowling group who have served us so well for the last few years. Tim and Trent and Mark have achieved extraordinary things for us, both here and abroad in the most unhelpful conditions, yet this summer they were individually down on form and collectively unable to put the Aussie batsmen under the same sort of pressure that the Aussie bowlers exerted on us — even when they were without their two premier fast bowlers of recent times, the Mitchells, Starc and Johnson.

At the end of five test matches, having lost four of them, you have to doff your hat. Bad luck, bad umpiring, whatever: they are the better team.

That doesn't make me any less proud of the evolution of this team and the performances we've put up. A lovely part of the game is about the changing room after tough test wins. Seeing a group of guys achieve something over five days with smiles on their faces, music going on in the background, dirty whites, sweaty black caps and a beer in hand. But I'm most proud of being able to keep going when I've struggled for runs under pressure, or when we've been under the pump as a team and managed to turn it round. The fact that it doesn't always happen just makes it that much sweeter when it does. I know they'll do it again.

33
The Aftermatch

A few weeks later, the first few of my retirement from the Black Caps, I watch my former teammates team play Australia at the T20 Worlds in India.

Kane wins the toss — an immediate improvement over my recent efforts — but our innings of 142 doesn't seem enough against an Aussie line-up which has so recently hammered us I'd intended to go to bed at that stage but stay up until the end, unable to draw my eyes away from Kane and the boys as they successfully defend that total. Kane marshals the team brilliantly, pulling every tactical lever with perfect timing, taking every trick that's offered to him, full of nimble initiative and invention.

Any doubts I had about the captaincy being too early for Kane evaporate. The other thing that gladdens my heart is the sight of Ross applauding every play, rushing up to give Kane help and support at every opportunity.

The Black Caps have been such a big part of my life for so long, but that night, watching them on television, is the perfect reinforcement of my decision to go.

We wanted to personify the traits we identified in New Zealanders — to be humble and hard-working, but also to embrace risk and adventure and the sheer joy of playing the game. We wanted to be respected by our long-suffering fans in New Zealand, but also by our opposition; and before we could demand that we had to learn to respect them. In changing the way we approached the game, and the way we respected the opposition, we wanted to be true to our national identity.

I believe we're there. We won't win every game or be the world's best team consistently, but the Black Caps are now an authentic representation of our culture.

The things that work for us may not work for everyone, but some things are universally true.

Former Middlesex captain Ed Smith, writing for Cricinfo, put it best when he said:

> *Athletes and sports teams waste huge space and energy on external motivators: mission statements about trying to be the best team in the world by 2057; blueprints for global dominance; strategic flow charts about key performance indicators. In fact, if every sportsman simply tried to be the best he could be, and attempted to behave decently along the way, you've pretty much summed up every available optimal strategy in one simple sentence. After all, you can't be better than your best. And nothing matters more than how you feel about the way you've lived your life.*

Ed recognised that sportspeople can spend an awful lot of time deep in analysis — every breath they take is analysed, nothing is left to chance.

We tried to remove a lot of the analysis; we tried to be 'blue collar' in how we went about things, not aloof and superior. We reduced the various theories that had dominated so much of what we did; we planned less, had fewer team meetings and we tried to be the very best we could be. We wanted to be a team that people could be proud of; and if in doubt we wanted to play the game aggressively, not fear failure.

I have been given far too much credit for what we achieved — the approach was taken by every member of the squad. Everyone bought into it and lived and breathed it. I thank all those who bought into the belief and vision of Hess, Roman and myself. There were some hard times, when to keep trusting wasn't easy and lesser men would have yielded, yet they kept giving us their hearts, emotions and even careers. They said bugger all that other stuff, we wanna be a part of something special. I hope they feel they made the right choice.

I came into the team as a 20-year-old kid and leave as, I hope, a much better man than I would have been without being part of that environment, having the experiences I've had, rubbing shoulders with the calibre of some of the men I've had as teammates and as opposition.

For some players it was the runs, the wickets and the catches that helped define them, but for me it was about the guys I played with and against, the friendships and camaraderie. I have been so lucky to have met some great people in this game, and in the end, it's not the statistics that go on your gravestone, but rather, you hope, words like loving father, husband and good friend to many.

My black cap, the one I was given when I was first selected, has never been washed. It stinks. It's rancid. But it's also a part of me and a sign of character. It carries the sweat and memories of the hard work I've done to earn it and keep it, the places it's taken me to, the full gamut of emotions I've felt and had to deal with while I've been wearing it.

What I most value, though, is being able to finish my international career with much the same attitude towards the game that I had when I began playing club cricket as a five-year-old. Because what matters is the game, just the playing of it. The rest is dust. I'm lucky enough to have played long enough to travel full circle, to come back around and recapture that feeling I had when I first started playing, when I used to pull back the curtains in Waterloo Street hoping for sunshine. When playing was enough. For that alone, I can leave the game happy.